Sergei Rachmaninoff

Titles in the series Critical Lives present the work of leading cultural figures of the modern period. Each book explores the life of the artist, writer, philosopher or architect in question and relates it to their major works.

In the same series

Hannah Arendt *Samantha Rose Hill*
Antonin Artaud *David A. Shafer*
Roland Barthes *Andy Stafford*
Georges Bataille *Stuart Kendall*
Charles Baudelaire *Rosemary Lloyd*
Simone de Beauvoir *Ursula Tidd*
Samuel Beckett *Andrew Gibson*
Walter Benjamin *Esther Leslie*
John Berger *Andy Merrifield*
Leonard Bernstein *Paul R. Laird*
Joseph Beuys *Claudia Mesch*
Jorge Luis Borges *Jason Wilson*
Constantin Brancusi *Sanda Miller*
Bertolt Brecht *Philip Glahn*
Charles Bukowski *David Stephen Calonne*
Mikhail Bulgakov *J.A.E. Curtis*
William S. Burroughs *Phil Baker*
John Cage *Rob Haskins*
Albert Camus *Edward J. Hughes*
Fidel Castro *Nick Caistor*
Paul Cézanne *Jon Kear*
Coco Chanel *Linda Simon*
Noam Chomsky *Wolfgang B. Sperlich*
Jean Cocteau *James S. Williams*
Joseph Conrad *Robert Hampson*
Salvador Dalí *Mary Ann Caws*
Charles Darwin *J. David Archibald*
Guy Debord *Andy Merrifield*
Claude Debussy *David J. Code*
Gilles Deleuze *Frida Beckman*
Fyodor Dostoevsky *Robert Bird*
Marcel Duchamp *Caroline Cros*
Sergei Eisenstein *Mike O'Mahony*
William Faulkner *Kirk Curnutt*
Gustave Flaubert *Anne Green*
Michel Foucault *David Macey*
Benjamin Franklin *Kevin J. Hayes*
Sigmund Freud *Matthew ffytche*
Mahatma Gandhi *Douglas Allen*
Jean Genet *Stephen Barber*
Allen Ginsberg *Steve Finbow*
Johann Wolfgang von Goethe *Jeremy Adler*
Günter Grass *Julian Preece*
Ernest Hemingway *Verna Kale*
Langston Hughes *W. Jason Miller*
Victor Hugo *Bradley Stephens*
Aldous Huxley *Jake Poller*
Derek Jarman *Michael Charlesworth*
Alfred Jarry *Jill Fell*
James Joyce *Andrew Gibson*
Carl Jung *Paul Bishop*
Franz Kafka *Sander L. Gilman*
Frida Kahlo *Gannit Ankori*

Søren Kierkegaard *Alastair Hannay*
Yves Klein *Nuit Banai*
Arthur Koestler *Edward Saunders*
Akira Kurosawa *Peter Wild*
Lenin *Lars T. Lih*
Jack London *Kenneth K. Brandt*
Pierre Loti *Richard M. Berrong*
Rosa Luxemburg *Dana Mills*
Jean-François Lyotard *Kiff Bamford*
René Magritte *Patricia Allmer*
Stéphane Mallarmé *Roger Pearson*
Thomas Mann *Herbert Lehnert and Eva Wessell*
Gabriel García Márquez *Stephen M. Hart*
Karl Marx *Paul Thomas*
Henri Matisse *Kathryn Brown*
Guy de Maupassant *Christopher Lloyd*
Herman Melville *Kevin J. Hayes*
Henry Miller *David Stephen Calonne*
Yukio Mishima *Damian Flanagan*
Eadweard Muybridge *Marta Braun*
Vladimir Nabokov *Barbara Wyllie*
Pablo Neruda *Dominic Moran*
Georgia O'Keeffe *Nancy J. Scott*
Octavio Paz *Nick Caistor*
Pablo Picasso *Mary Ann Caws*
Edgar Allan Poe *Kevin J. Hayes*
Ezra Pound *Alec Marsh*
Marcel Proust *Adam Watt*
Sergei Rachmaninoff *Rebecca Mitchell*
Arthur Rimbaud *Seth Whidden*
John Ruskin *Andrew Ballantyne*
Jean-Paul Sartre *Andrew Leak*
Erik Satie *Mary E. Davis*
Arnold Schoenberg *Mark Berry*
Arthur Schopenhauer *Peter B. Lewis*
Dmitry Shostakovich *Pauline Fairclough*
Adam Smith *Jonathan Conlin*
Susan Sontag *Jerome Boyd Maunsell*
Gertrude Stein *Lucy Daniel*
Stendhal *Francesco Manzini*
Igor Stravinsky *Jonathan Cross*
Rabindranath Tagore *Bashabi Fraser*
Pyotr Tchaikovsky *Philip Ross Bullock*
Leo Tolstoy *Andrei Zorin*
Leon Trotsky *Paul Le Blanc*
Mark Twain *Kevin J. Hayes*
Richard Wagner *Raymond Furness*
Alfred Russel Wallace *Patrick Armstrong*
Simone Weil *Palle Yourgrau*
Tennessee Williams *Paul Ibell*
Ludwig Wittgenstein *Edward Kanterian*
Virginia Woolf *Ira Nadel*
Frank Lloyd Wright *Robert McCarter*

Sergei Rachmaninoff

Rebecca Mitchell

REAKTION BOOKS

For Andrew and Archie Ray, my two creative muses

Published by
REAKTION BOOKS LTD
Unit 32, Waterside
44–48 Wharf Road
London N1 7UX, UK
www.reaktionbooks.co.uk

First published 2022
Copyright © Rebecca Mitchell 2022

Printed and bound in Great Britain by TJ Books Ltd, Padstow, Cornwall

A catalogue record for this book is available from the British Library

ISBN 978 1 78914 576 2

Contents

Editorial Note

Prior to February 1918, Russia used the Julian calendar, which was twelve days behind the Gregorian calendar in the nineteenth century, and thirteen days in the early twentieth. For the sake of simplicity, dates are given according to the Julian calendar before Rachmaninoff's departure from Russia in December 1917. Letters from his European sojourns are given with both dates. After December 1917, all dates are given in the Gregorian style.

Most Russian names and all Russian-language sources are transliterated using a modified Library of Congress system; familiar versions such as Rachmaninoff, Tchaikovsky, Medtner, Stravinsky and Prokofiev have been used in the main text where they exist. When the figures themselves employed alternative versions after leaving Russia (Sophie Satin, Serge Koussevitzky) these have been preferred. The maiden names of a number of Rachmaninoff's acquaintances have been used in the main text, though their reminiscences were later published under their married names (Skalon rather than Rostovtsova, Kreutzer rather than Zhukovskaia).

Sergei Rachmaninoff, 1921.

Prelude: In Search of Rachmaninoff

Who was Sergei Vasil'evich Rachmaninoff?

For his contemporaries in the West, he was the eternally nostalgic émigré, irreparably cut off from his homeland, an exile from an earlier age.

Shortly after Rachmaninoff's death in 1943, columnist Leonard Liebling concluded that Rachmaninoff 'never got over the tragedy of the Russia he had known. Inside him was a deep melancholy that showed in his face, and especially in his eyes.' He was a man outside of time, a rare link 'between the soft romantic past and the hard realism of nowadays'.[1]

In 1952, music critic Leonid Sabaneev asserted that '[Rachmaninoff] was entirely a person of the nineteenth century. Somehow he already did not recognize the twentieth century, and all his compositions are, as it were, remnants of music of the nineteenth century.'[2]

Rachmaninoff's personal friend, musicologist Alfred Swan, summed up this view in 1944: 'in spite of a deeply affectionate family, in spite of his great success all over the world, and the devotion of his audiences, Rachmaninoff lived shut up within himself, alone in spirit, and everlastingly homesick for his Russia.'[3]

Fellow composer and compatriot Igor Stravinsky called Rachmaninoff 'a six-and-a-half-foot-tall scowl'.[4] Indeed, a typical photograph of Rachmaninoff's stern countenance shortly after his emigration to the United States conveys a serious and unsmiling image. Impeccably dressed, hat in hand, he is a man in motion, yet somehow outside his own time. In many photographs, his mournful face seems virtually identical. Shortly before his death, Rachmaninoff reflected:

> I feel like a ghost wandering in a world grown alien. I cannot cast out the old way of writing, and I cannot acquire the new. I have made intense effort to feel the musical manner of today, but it will not come to me. Unlike Madame Butterfly with her quick religious conversion, I cannot cast out my musical gods in a moment and bend the knee to new ones. Even with the disaster of living through what has befallen the Russia where I spent my happiest years, yet I always feel that my own music and my reactions to all music, remained spiritually the same, unendingly obedient to trying to create beauty.[5]

The Bolshevik Revolution of 1917 and Rachmaninoff's subsequent self-imposed exile aided in creating an eternalized image of 'before' and 'after' in his biography. His sudden shift from composition to performance after 1917 exiled the majority of his oeuvre into the haze of an eternalized 'Russianness' alien to the reality of Soviet tumult, even as he cemented his status as a leading concert pianist via cutting-edge recording technology.

Rachmaninoff's rich harmonic textures, haunting melodies and passionate emotions seemed to listeners to capture the melancholic, nineteenth-century Russian soul, trapped in a world made foreign by external forces. Indeed, the mystical harmonies of Rachmaninoff's romance op. 8, no. 5, 'Dream', practically foreshadow Rachmaninoff's tragic fate. A translation of Heinrich Heine's poem mourning the loss of homeland ('I Once Had a Lovely Fatherland'), it 'conjures up thoughts of his native land and of past happiness there', before the realization that 'it has all been only in his mind.'[6] The first evocative exclamation 'but it was a dream!'

An impeccably dressed Rachmaninoff pauses, hat in hand, for a photograph.

is followed by a pensive piano solo that unexpectedly shifts from the opening key of E-flat major through C minor into the distant key of G-flat major, expressing longing for a lost world while mourning its unattainability. In actual fact, however, the 1893 work maps onto Rachmaninoff's later biography by sheer chance. The dedicatee, Natalia Skalon, older sister of Rachmaninoff's first love interest, Vera Skalon, might well have heard a very different kind of nostalgia in the work – that of a young man reflecting on his first adolescent crush. Only a few close friends and family penetrated the mask of external reserve that Rachmaninoff, an intensely private person, always presented to the outside world. To them, a very different personality was revealed: a sensitive soul in need of human interaction who loved to tease and play practical jokes.

The popular image of a man out of touch with contemporary reality has not always played in the composer's favour. Critics have often attacked his adherence to a 'traditional' or 'conservative' musical style that has outlived its expressive potential. Such a view was captured by musicologist Eric Blom in 1954: 'As a composer', sniffed Blom derisively, '[Rachmaninoff] can hardly be said to have belonged to his time at all. His music is well constructed and effective, but monotonous in texture, which consists in essence mainly of artificial and gushing tunes accompanied by a variety of figures derived from arpeggios. The enormous popular success some few of Rachmaninoff's works had in his lifetime is not likely to last, and musicians never regarded it with much favor.'[7] Bernard Holland offered a more recent reworking of this perspective in his blistering *New York Times* review of the 1996 Australian movie *Shine.* Holland focused not on the film but on the central place it granted to Rachmaninoff's Third Piano Concerto. 'Treating "Rach 3" with awe,' he scoffed, '"Shine" lowers musical values to fast-food levels.'[8]

Enjoying Rachmaninoff's music has in fact been linked to poor musical taste for over a century. In contrast to contemporary pianist-composer Aleksandr Scriabin, in 1912 Leonid Sabaneev denigrated Rachmaninoff's music as that 'of an intellectual whiner', concluding 'perhaps it has found such universal recognition, has so spontaneously subdued the musical masses, because there are many similar personalities [among them].'[9] The virulence of such attacks, which reduce Rachmaninoff to the status of a well-paid musical hack, whose music is nothing more than 'an evocation of adolescence',[10] has in turn inspired several generations of Rachmaninoff's advocates to uncover 'progressive' aspects in the composer's music, his lifestyle (including his love of fast cars and boats), and his pioneering role in the recording industry.[11] Lurking behind both these approaches is a modernist distrust of popularity – the suspicion that a composer who enjoys broad success must, by default, be 'low-brow'.

The broader classical music audience has seldom questioned Rachmaninoff's greatness, however. In 1941, the editor of the popular American music periodical *The Etude* asserted that Rachmaninoff's compositions 'are likely to become among the most important contributions of our generation to the literature of music'.[12] Rather than a sign of backwardness, Rachmaninoff's stubborn adherence to tonal music was touted in a 1932 press release as a selling point:

> Tall, austere, aristocratic in bearing, dignified, aloof and commanding on the concert platform. You might expect crashing dissonances, modernist music, from under those steely fingers and powerful biceps. Instead come delicacy, great emotional feeling, heart-searching, singing tone. 'Music must reveal the emotions of the heart,' says Rachmaninoff. He makes it do it.[13]

Such marketing was effective. According to *Time* magazine in 1942, Rachmaninoff had earned over $2.5 million over the course of his career in America.[14] The regular appearance of his piano works on concert programmes, within conservatory walls and on recordings demonstrates that his style of emotional, heart-rending music found lasting appeal among audiences. Fans adored how his music echoed their own personal strivings, melancholy and failings amid a rapidly changing world, even as mid-twentieth-century representatives of musical 'modernity' abhorred its lush chromaticism, complex harmonies and sweeping melodies.

In the Soviet Union, Rachmaninoff was similarly immortalized as a nineteenth-century Romantic composer. As musicologist Pauline Fairclough has noted, 'far from staying outcast as a "white émigré", after 1932 Rachmaninoff was effectively considered a "classical" Russian composer and presented as though he were a contemporary of Tchaikovsky (as opposed to being a modern composer who lived a comfortable émigré existence in the United States).'[15] Such an interpretation erased Rachmaninoff's kinship with experimental artistic trends in late imperial Russia in favour of a nineteenth-century image purified of 'mysticism', much as Rachmaninoff's mentor Piotr Tchaikovsky was redefined to suit Soviet values.

This book probes the ready-made image of Rachmaninoff the melancholic and nostalgic émigré to excavate a participant in the currents of Russia's 'Silver Age', an era of experimentation wherein the role of art and music in human existence was heatedly debated.

Despite Rachmaninoff's reluctance to engage in such philosophical discussions, his creative work took shape within them. In a 1919 interview, Rachmaninoff cited German philosopher Arthur Schopenhauer to support his claim that 'melody is the supreme ruler in the world of music. Melody is music – the integral foundation of all music, since a perfectly conceived melody implies and develops its own natural harmonic treatment.'[16] He set numerous texts by Silver Age writers and participated in the revival of Russian Orthodox music. His preserved library at Villa Senar includes Russian translations of key influences in Silver Age thought, including German philosopher Friedrich Nietzsche and Russian religious philosopher Vladimir Soloviev.[17]

To reposition Rachmaninoff in the context of his time, one must also recall that the very term 'modernism' conveys an aesthetic stance intimately connected to the era of which Rachmaninoff was an active participant. Musicologist Richard Taruskin has dubbed the inherent value placed on innovation and experimentation (and simultaneous suspicion of popular appeal) 'the modernist argument'.[18] To frame Rachmaninoff as either 'progressive' or 'conservative' is to adopt the very terms through which musical value was debated during his lifetime. Instead, this book defines Rachmaninoff and his music as fundamentally *modern,* but not necessarily *modernist.* Understanding 'modernism' as 'any attempt by modern men and women to become subjects as well as objects of modernization',[19] cultural historian Marshall Berman famously argued that 'to be modern is to find ourselves in an environment that promises us adventure, power, joy, growth, transformation of ourselves and the world – and, at the same time, that threatens to destroy everything we have, everything we know, everything we are . . . to be modern is to be part of a universe in which, as Marx said, "all that is solid melts into air".'[20]

Tradition and stability *never* defined Rachmaninoff's world. It was constantly 'melting into air'. His creative life with its projections of a former halcyon age were, in Berman's sense, modern. Born to an impoverished noble family in imperial Russia, Rachmaninoff eschewed the state-service career that was the typical path for a young Russian nobleman, instead pursuing a professional career as a musician. He achieved both personal and financial success, symbolized by his family estate Ivanovka, located in the Tambov region of Russia. In contrast to the fate of many noble estates that were sold or mortgaged as their owners struggled to adapt to changing economic realities, Rachmaninoff poured his profits as a professional musician into keeping up Ivanovka. This world was swept away by the 1917 Bolshevik Revolution. Through a brutal concert regimen and participation in the nascent recording industry, Rachmaninoff once again achieved sufficient personal wealth and stability to construct a new family estate near Lucerne, Switzerland: Villa Senar. The gathering clouds of war forced Rachmaninoff to abandon this second home in 1939. His final dwelling in Beverly Hills, California, purchased in 1942 for his retirement, would only serve as his home for the final weeks of his life. Even his body has been the subject of debate by regimes seeking to politicize his final resting place.[21]

Yet Rachmaninoff survived and thrived amid the flux and change of modern life, embracing certain aspects. At the same time, he constructed a sense of self rooted in an imagined Russianness that reverberated with his audiences. In this sense he was a quintessential modern subject, struggling 'to make [himself] at home in a constantly changing world'.[22]

Such a framing of Rachmaninoff as 'modern' is not without precedent. Rachmaninoff himself repeatedly employed the word 'modern' in reference to this experience of living in, and responding to, the contemporary world. 'Is not the music of composers like Sibelius or Glazunov *modern* music, even though it is written in a more traditional manner?' he queried in a 1941 interview.[23] In 1919, *The Etude* touted Rachmaninoff's 'Melodie', op. 3, no. 3, as 'a splendid example of the modern treatment of the singing tone against an elaborate harmonic background', and in 1923 it described his compositions as 'modern, but untainted with futurism and sensationalism'.[24]

Nonetheless, Rachmaninoff became increasingly jaded by a discourse in which his own creativity was written out of the historical development of music. Towards the end of his life he concluded:

The new kind of music seems to come, not from the heart, but from the head. Its composers think rather than feel. They have not the capacity to make their works 'exult' as Hans von Bülow called it. They meditate, protest, analyze, reason, calculate, and brood – but they do not exult. It may be that they compose in the spirit of the times; but it may be, too, that the spirit of the times does not call for expression in music. If that is the case, rather than compile music that is thought but not felt, composers should remain silent and leave contemporary expression to those authors and playwrights who are masters of the factual and literal, and do not concern themselves with soul states. I hope that with these thoughts I have answered your question regarding my opinion of what is called modern music. Why modern in this case? It grows old almost as soon as it is born, for it comes into being contaminated with dry rot.[25]

While Rachmaninoff was a modern man influenced by 'modern' sound and technology, he also opposed what he considered the 'futurist' method of composition, in which he believed intent, planning and innovation trumped natural creative instinct. This book returns Rachmaninoff to the flux and uncertainty of the era in which he lived – a rapidly changing society ripe with multiple approaches to how art should relate to life, a world in which the sense of impending threat was real, but the revolutions of 1917 were not foreseeable. Rachmaninoff's early career creatively engaged with contemporary cultural movements and the upheavals wrought by modernity. After 1917, he was a man twice exiled – both from his country and from the modernist 'futurist' discourse that triumphed in specialist circles. Deeply modern, he eschewed modernist aesthetics, and so embodied the very contradictions of his age.

1

The Making of a Moscow Musician

Reflecting back on his childhood from the distance of emigration in 1931, Rachmaninoff waxed eloquent over the lost world of 'old Russia':

> Do not forget, that everything great, in which the entire
> country can take pride, was born and lived in old Russia.
> Our great writers, famed throughout the world, like Tolstoy,
> Dostoevsky, Turgenev and Chekhov were born and died
> in old Russia. All the famous composers, like Tchaikovsky,
> Mussorgsky, Rimsky-Korsakov, were born and died there too.
> Famous scientists like Mendeleev, Mechnikov, Pavlov, also
> belong to this old Russia. Do not forget, that all the artistic
> treasures of the country, located in the museums of Moscow
> and Petrograd, were collected by people of old Russia.[1]

Rachmaninoff's dislike of the 1917 Revolution that drove him into permanent exile is no mystery. And it is small wonder that later interviews are full of nostalgic glimpses of his youth in an idyllic, unchanging Russia – a land of picturesque noble country estates, resonant church bells, sonorous religious chant and *troika* sleds.

But nostalgia is selective in its evocation, often obscuring as much as it reveals. This halcyon image of Rachmaninoff's childhood masks an economic structure already in precipitous decline. The 1861 emancipation of the serfs followed by grain competition from the New World and state prioritization of industrialization spelled ruin for many gentry families. Between 1877 and 1905, personal land holdings of the gentry diminished from 73 to 52 million desiatins, while mortgaged noble estates increased from 41,000 in 1889 to 97,000 by 1900.[2] Divisions between social estates broke down as peasants moved to cities in search of work. New professional identities emerged that challenged older forms of social cohesion.

Rachmaninoff was born on the family estate of Semenova (Novgorod region) as the fourth of six children in a Russian gentry family threatened by rapid decline. Like most young men of his social estate, the young Sergei Vasil'evich initially seemed destined for a government or military service career. The Rachmaninoff family, which traced its lineage to Moldovan princes, owed its financial success to a great-grandfather who in 1741 supported the daughter of Tsar Peter the Great, Elizabeth Petrovna, when she seized the Russian throne from her infant cousin, Ivan VI. In exchange for this support, he was granted Znamenskoe estate in Tambov region. Rachmaninoff's father, Vasilii Arkad'evich (1841–1916), had volunteered for military service and fought in the Caucasus, where he participated in the defeat of Imam Shamil, who led resistance against imperial Russian expansion in the region for approximately 25 years. Vasilii then served in Warsaw for several years before making an advantageous marriage. Rachmaninoff's mother, Liubov, was the only child of General P. I. Butakov, a family connection that made both Sergei and his elder brother eligible to attend the prestigious Pages Corps in St Petersburg, which would have opened the path for either civil or military service careers.[3] Given this background of family service, how was it that Sergei Rachmaninoff ended up pursuing music, not just as a hobby, but as a profession, and even a sacred duty?

In addition to state service, Rachmaninoff's family also had a history of musical talent. Rachmaninoff's grandfather, Arkadii

Alexandrovich Rachmaninoff (1808–1881), had studied piano with
famed pedagogue John Field, and had retired early from his military
career to his Tambov estate to devote his time to music. Though an
amateur, he was a well-known performer at benefit concerts in the
region, as befitted his noble status. Rachmaninoff's father, Vasilii
Arkad'evich, improvised at the piano freely. By the mid-nineteenth
century, the decline of Russia's rural economy and the emergence
of an urban civil society based on professional training yielded a
mismatch between social caste and professional prospects. When
famed piano virtuoso Anton Rubinstein returned from Europe
to Russia, a deacon in Kazan struggled to determine the young
man's appropriate social 'rank' for his record books ('artist' or
'pianist' were not acceptable titles) before ultimately determining

Liubov Petrovna
Butakova,
Rachmaninoff's
mother, 1870s.

his official social status to be 'the son of a merchant of the second
guild'.[4] Rubinstein's solution to this problem was to found the
Russian Musical Society (1859) and its affiliated conservatory in St
Petersburg (1862). Conservatory graduates received the title of 'Free
Artist' (a term originally introduced for graduates of the Imperial
Art Academy), and the right to freely reside anywhere in the Russian
empire. Rubinstein thus laid the foundation for viewing music as
a profession in Russia – a calling also attractive to impoverished
nobles like Rachmaninoff. By the time Rachmaninoff's family
sold their final estate, music was an acceptable (if not necessarily
prestigious) path for a talented, yet impoverished, young man to
follow, particularly as financial constraints made attendance at the
expensive Pages Corps impossible.

Lev Tolstoy's opening observation in his novel *Anna Karenina*, 'All happy families are similar; every unhappy family is unhappy in its own way,' could well be applied to Rachmaninoff's family.[5] Vasilii Rachmaninoff's poor financial management and free-wheeling lifestyle quickly expended his wife's dowry, and in 1882 the final estate, Oneg, was auctioned off and the family moved to St Petersburg. In order to minimize crowding in the family apartment, Sergei was sent for a time to live with his aunt, Maria Trubnikova. The trauma of his sister Sofiia's death from diphtheria shortly after the move to Petersburg was exacerbated by the permanent separation of his parents.[6] Though divorce was not a viable option under the canon laws of the Russian Orthodox Church, his father would eventually enter into a new common-law partnership, fathering a half-brother. His elder sister Elena, a gifted singer who had introduced her brother to the songs of Tchaikovsky and to whom Rachmaninoff claimed to owe some of his most precious musical childhood memories, passed away suddenly from pernicious anaemia in 1885. Though he retained contact with both parents throughout his life and even provided financial assistance to each of them on numerous occasions (despite his own initially limited resources), Rachmaninoff's relationship with both parents was strained. In 1891, he wrote to his friend Natalia Skalon, 'I didn't go visit my family, though they invited me, because it seems to me that they don't love me (apart from father, who does not live there). Although they invited me, it seems to me that it is only for appearances.'[7] At times, his resentment would spill forth in bitterness, as in an 1893 letter, also to Natalia Skalon:

It is as if all of my family set out to wear me out and drive me into an early grave, not intentionally, but just through the state of things. My close relatives comfort me in the following ways: father is leading a reckless life, my mother is very sick, my elder brother is running up debt, which god knows how he will get

out of (hope for my assistance is poor in the current situation);
my younger brother is terribly lazy, and of course will be held
back a grade again, my grandmother is at death's door.[8]

This broken family life imbued the composer with a deeply felt
need for familial affection and a determination to provide a more
stable home life for his own children.

As a youth, however, Sergei responded to the lack of parental
supervision as many children have – he skipped school, spent time
skating rather than attending classes at the conservatory (where
he had received a scholarship based on his musical promise) and
falsified his grades. He later recounted to his friend Alfred Swan
that he would get 10 kopecks a day for expenses and fare to the
conservatory from his grandmother, but 'I would go straight to
the skating pond and spend the whole morning there.'[9] Indeed,
idyllic summers spent with his doting maternal grandmother Sofiia
Butakova both softened the pain of his broken family and cemented
a fondness for the countryside. In 1883 she purchased a small estate,
Borisova, located 6.5 kilometres (4 mi.) north of Novgorod on the
Volkhov river as a place where her favourite grandson could escape
from the stench and heat of Petersburg summers. Here the sound of
church bells resounded over the river. Equally vivid in his memory
was the Orthodox chant that he recalled from visits to Novgorod
and Petersburg churches with his grandmother. His long-standing
interest in both church bells and chant found expression in later
compositions. Throughout his life, Rachmaninoff maintained
warm memories of these childhood days on his grandmother's
estate in the Novgorod countryside, and he later recalled shedding
tears when he departed Borisova for Moscow.[10]

Two years of lacklustre performance at the St Petersburg
Conservatory ended with news that young Sergei had failed every
subject and was in danger of losing his scholarship. Sergei's mother
turned to her estranged husband's young first cousin, Aleksandr

Sergei Vasil'evich Rachmaninoff, aged ten.

Siloti, for assistance. An 1881 graduate of the piano division of the Moscow Conservatory, by 1885 Siloti had established a European-wide reputation as a favourite student of famed piano virtuoso Franz Liszt, with whom he studied from 1883 to 1886. During a brief trip back to Russia, Rachmaninoff's mother prevailed upon Siloti to listen to his twelve-year-old cousin perform and offer advice. After hearing Sergei play, he dismissed the opinion of the Petersburg Conservatory director (that Rachmaninoff was a 'great rogue' without particular talent) and concluded that his gifted cousin needed to learn discipline as well as music – a skill best learned under his own first teacher, Moscow piano pedagogue Nikolai Zverev.[11]

Sofiia Aleksandrovna Butakova, Rachmaninoff's maternal grandmother, 1870s.

This was just the first of many times when Siloti's influence would play a major role in his younger cousin's life. Two years later, Rachmaninoff was one of Siloti's few students during the latter's short-lived teaching career at the Moscow Conservatory.[12] This pupil–student relationship was sufficiently successful to mark Rachmaninoff as a supporter of Siloti in later conflicts at the conservatory with the school's director, Vasilii Safonov; when Siloti was summarily dismissed from the faculty in the spring of 1891 after a disagreement with Safonov, Rachmaninoff petitioned to finish his piano studies early rather than transfer to another teacher. The animosity between Siloti and Safonov had a lasting effect on Rachmaninoff's career – with few exceptions (one being the premiere of the first movement of his piano concerto in March 1892 at the Moscow Conservatory), Rachmaninoff refused to collaborate with Safonov in future concerts. This stubbornness closed off multiple possibilities to the young man (Safonov was one of the most respected conductors of the day), but demonstrates Rachmaninoff's loyalty and unflagging devotion to friends and family. The dedicatee of Rachmaninoff's First Piano Concerto, Siloti also conducted the premiere of Rachmaninoff's Second Piano Concerto in Moscow in 1901, with Rachmaninoff as soloist. Siloti's championing of his cousin's famed Prelude in C-sharp minor during his European tours made Rachmaninoff a household name before the latter's first concert appearances abroad. Their roles reversed in later life in America, where Siloti, a teacher at Juilliard from 1925 to 1942, was little known as a concert artist.

Reflecting back on his creative life in 1930, Rachmaninoff noted that the most foundational impressions 'are confined to a period of the artist's life before he attains success. In that first period the artist meets people destined to influence his later career.'[13] For Rachmaninoff, these figures belonged primarily to Moscow cultural circles, which he joined in 1885 as Nikolai Zverev's protégé. In contrast to the courtly life, state bureaucrats and gentry that dominated St Petersburg society, late nineteenth-century Moscow was home to a wealthy merchant elite who supported a vision of Russia that combined pride in Russia's unique folk heritage with the self-assertiveness of successful entrepreneurs. Inspired by their European-style education, the younger generation of Moscow entrepreneurs turned their financial resources to supporting art, theatre and music, and encouraged the development of an explicitly Russian (yet socially modern) style in painting, architecture and music. They gathered with culturally engaged nobility, liberal intelligentsia and artistic elites in private societies and circles to discuss music, philosophy, art and the problems confronting a rapidly modernizing Russia. Rachmaninoff's cousin Siloti emblemized this new social constellation in 1887 when he married Vera Tret'iakova, eldest daughter of wealthy merchant Pavel Tret'iakov. Tret'iakov was an avid art collector and the founder of the Tret'iakov Gallery, which he gifted to the city of Moscow in 1892.[14]

Nikolai Zverev knew that personal connections were key for a successful musical career, and he sought to advantageously position his three protégés – Matvei Presman, Leonid Maksimov and Sergei Rachmaninoff – within Moscow's cultural and intellectual elite. To this end, Zverev hosted regular Sunday dinners during which his 'cubs' – as they called themselves in joking reference to Zverev's name, which means 'beast' – performed for leading members of Moscow society. Zverev hosted university professors, famous lawyers, artists, actors and musicians.[15] As one attendee at these evenings, Nikolai Averiano later recalled, 'Who *wasn't* there! Rubinstein, Tchaikovsky, Arensky, Taneev, Pabst – figures from Moscow society – wealthy men seeking protégés – everyone!'[16] Indeed, with his move to Moscow, Rachmaninoff was brought into the orbit of composers Piotr Tchaikovsky and Sergei Taneev, whose greater dedication to Western European (specifically German) musical tradition distanced them from the musical style of Nikolai Rimsky-Korsakov and the other members of the Kuchka (Borodin, Cui, Balakirev, Mussorgsky) which dominated in St Petersburg. Though Moscow was still considered less culturally developed than St Petersburg when Rachmaninoff arrived in 1885, over the course of his pre-revolutionary career, musical life blossomed there, ultimately coming to rival that of the imperial capital.

Zverev filled the dual role of loving father and strict taskmaster who enforced his displeasure with physical violence. He instilled

Nikolai Zverev and his 'cubs': Leonid Maksimov, Sergei Rachmaninoff (second from the left) and Matvei Presman, 1885–6.

Rachmaninoff and his fellow boarders with a strong work
ethic (the three boys alternated rising at 6 a.m. each morning
for mandatory practice) combined with intimate knowledge
of the classical music repertoire and a strong basic training
in piano technique that stood them in good stead throughout
their professional lives. Indeed, Rachmaninoff's own legendary
fastidiousness and regular work schedule undoubtedly owed
much to the discipline instilled in Zverev's house. The most
important aspects learned from Zverev were hand placement
and an enduring love of music: 'To play without rhythm, without
grammar, without punctuation signs was never permitted by
Zverev,' Presman later recounted, 'and in this is the entire musical
foundation on which it is already not difficult to build the largest
artistic building.'[17] Rachmaninoff similarly later emphasized
the importance of always teaching 'an interpretation as well as a
technic' when a student was still young.[18]

Zverev insisted upon a broad education in both music and
culture for his protégés. They regularly attended operas, concerts
and theatre productions. Zverev also maintained a large library
whose tomes were accessible to the young men, and he showed a
keen interest in their success in their general studies.[19] The boys
studied French and German alongside other academic subjects
and were expected to excel. A pianist came in once a week to
play through arrangements of symphonic works of Haydn,
Mozart, Beethoven and Mendelssohn in two-piano/four-hand
arrangements with the boys. Indeed, together with another student
of Zverev, his 'cubs' amazed Taneev by performing, from memory,
an eight-hand transcription of Beethoven's Fifth Symphony as well
as the scherzo from the Sixth Symphony.[20]

Of the many concerts Rachmaninoff attended under
Zverev's watchful eye, one cycle left an indelible memory: Anton
Rubinstein's 'Historical Concerts'. In a series of seven lecture-
concerts offered across Europe from autumn 1885 to spring 1886,

Rubinstein presented the history of European piano music, beginning with the English virginalists and ending with contemporary Russian composers, with particular emphasis given to Beethoven and Chopin. A musical phenomenon across Europe, Rubinstein performed each concert twice in both St Petersburg and Moscow, offering the second performance free to music professors and students (Zverev ensured that his protégés attended each concert twice). This massive undertaking was met with particular warmth in Moscow, where the concerts were accompanied by festive dinners attended by Moscow's leading musical stars. Rubinstein adapted the concerts in 1888–9 into a series of 32 lectures that showcased a massive 1,302 separate works.[21] Rachmaninoff was inspired both by the original historic concerts and by the lectures that grew out of them.[22] Though he had only studied with Zverev for a few months at the time of Rubinstein's concerts, Zverev arranged for his young pupil to perform Bach's English Suite no. 2 in A minor for the virtuoso. Rachmaninoff was also tasked with guiding Rubinstein to his place of honour at the dinner table one night.[23]

Rubinstein provided an ideal towards which his younger admirers could strive: an artist who combined European and Russian fame, mastery of the entire range of historic piano repertoire, and an individual performance style. Presman later recalled, '[Rubinstein] amazed us with his graceful, grandiose performance, with his stormy, fiery temperament, his warmth and tenderness. His *crescendo* did not have limits on its increase, his *diminuendo* reached an unbelievable *pianissimo,* sounding in the most distant corners of the massive hall. Playing, Rubinstein created, and created inimitably, brilliantly.'[24] Recalling Rubinstein's playing, Rachmaninoff mused: 'Rubinstein was a pianistic marvel born to master the instrument, to glorify it, to devour it, as it were. Rubinstein had something more than technic.'[25] Similarly, in another interview, Rachmaninoff emphasized the 'vital spark' that

was necessary 'to make each interpretation of a masterpiece –
a living thing'. He continued:

> Rubinstein was technically marvelous, and yet he admitted
> making mistakes. Nevertheless, for every possible
> mistake he may have made, he gave, in return, ideas and
> musical tone pictures that would have made up for a
> million mistakes. When Rubinstein was over-exact his
> playing lost something of its wonderful charm.[26]

Rubinstein remained an emblem of the height of artistic
achievement for Rachmaninoff throughout his life: a true artist,
not just a technical virtuoso.[27] As Barrie Martyn has noted, the
enduring influence of Rubinstein on Rachmaninoff's playing still
echoed years later. Rachmaninoff's choice of performance repertoire
followed that of Rubinstein remarkably closely. Moreover, 'even
[Rachmaninoff's] much remarked-upon fortissimo interpretation
of the reprise of the funeral march in Chopin's B-flat minor Sonata
was in fact a Rubinstein innovation that Rachmaninoff adopted.'[28]
Indeed, Rubinstein held such sway in Rachmaninoff's imagination
that, amid the depression that followed the failure of his First
Symphony, when he was unable to work, it was Anton Rubinstein
whom Rachmaninoff saw in a dream, reproaching him with the
words 'Why don't you work, why don't you play?'[29]

   While Rubinstein served as a pianistic model, Piotr
Tchaikovsky served as Rachmaninoff's compositional idol.
Though never formally Tchaikovsky's student, his impact on
Rachmaninoff's musical formation was significant. Their
acquaintance began at Zverev's, and Rachmaninoff soon attracted
Tchaikovsky's notice. As a surprise birthday gift for Zverev one
year, each of his 'cubs' performed a selection from Tchaikovsky's
piano cycle *The Seasons.* Moved by their ingenuity, Zverev arranged
for Tchaikovsky to hear their performance. Rachmaninoff's

selected piece from the cycle, 'Troika', entered into his regular concert repertoire in emigration, and he recorded it twice, in 1920 and 1928.[30] Tchaikovsky was impressed by Rachmaninoff's 1886 arrangement of his *Manfred* symphony for piano duet, and when he served on the examination board for Rachmaninoff's May 1889 exam (which required a four-part harmonization of a Haydn melody as well as the composition of a prelude that contained an organ point on the tonic and dominant), the resultant 'Song Without Words' received 5+, 'to which Tchaikovsky added 3 more crosses, surrounding the 5 on all sides with crosses'.[31] Despite a rocky moment over Rachmaninoff's less successful four-hand arrangement of *Sleeping Beauty* (a commission Rachmaninoff received through Siloti's influence in 1890–91), Tchaikovsky publicly displayed his support for the young man on numerous occasions. By 1891, Rachmaninoff was sending compositions to the older composer, noting in a letter to Natalia Skalon that 'I implicitly believe him in everything.'[32] Tchaikovsky made a point of applauding loudly at the premiere of Rachmaninoff's first opera *Aleko*, and invited the young man to pair his new opera with Tchaikovsky's own short opera *Iolanta*, to be performed at the Bolshoi the next year. In an 1892 interview, Tchaikovsky listed Rachmaninoff as one of the leading young composers in Russia.[33] Tchaikovsky was similarly impressed by Rachmaninoff's orchestral work *The Crag*, op. 7, and promised to include it in a January 1894 concert he was to conduct. Both these performance opportunities (*Aleko* and *The Crag*) failed to materialize, however, due to Tchaikovsky's sudden death in October 1893.

Tchaikovsky served as a model for Rachmaninoff's own developing compositional style. In January 1892, Rachmaninoff completed his first trio, a one-movement work in G minor. Though not published until 1947, the older man's influence is clear in the title ('Elegaic Trio'), which was borrowed from Tchaikovsky's *Trio elegiac*, dedicated to piano virtuoso Nikolai Rubinstein (Anton's younger brother and founder of the Moscow Conservatory) after his sudden death in Paris. In 1893, Rachmaninoff returned to the same title with his 'Elegiac Trio in D Minor, op. 9', dedicated to Tchaikovsky's memory. Describing his work on the Trio in a letter to Natalia Skalon, he wrote 'as it says in one of my romances ['No, do not leave!' (op. 4, no. 1)], I was in torment the whole time and sick in my soul,' and noted that 'during [the composition] all my thoughts, feelings and strengths belonged to it, to that song.'[34] Indeed, in addition to referencing the last work Rachmaninoff ever showed Tchaikovsky (his symphonic poem *The Crag*),[35] the Trio melody shows a kinship to the song's mournful atmosphere. Rachmaninoff's continuing sense of indebtedness to Tchaikovsky is captured in an early photograph, where the young man sits in front of a black veiled painting of Tchaikovsky, gazing into space. Even in death, the older composer here appears to govern his young admirer's future musical path.

It was also at Zverev's Sunday dinners that Rachmaninoff first became acquainted with composer Sergei Taneev. A specialist in strict counterpoint with whom Rachmaninoff began courses in the autumn of 1888, it has been suggested that Taneev may well have influenced Rachmaninoff's development of horizontal melody and counterpoint, though the composer subsequently regretted his lazy indifference in Taneev's class.[36] In fact, Rachmaninoff continued to show his compositions to Taneev and rely on his advice well after having established his own career.[37] Rachmaninoff also insisted on Taneev's deep influence on his character, arguing that the scholar had taught him 'how to live, how to think, how to work, even how to speak, for he spoke in a particularly Taneev way: concisely, clearly and to the point'.[38] Years later, when preparing to publish Leonid Sabaneev's *Reminiscences of Taneev*, he requested that Sabaneev 'correct his examples of Taneev's wit', finding those offered by Sabaneev to be 'not clever but rude', unbefitting his own memory of the man.[39]

Despite Zverev's central role in advancing Rachmaninoff's musical career, according to Rachmaninoff's sister-in-law Sophie Satin, the 'third great rupture in the life of the sixteen-year-old youth' was the breaking of their relationship in the autumn of 1889.[40] Multiple accounts of Rachmaninoff's dispute with Zverev have been proffered. According to both his fellow boarder Presman and friend E. Somoff, Rachmaninoff's need for an uninterrupted

Rachmaninoff with his dog Levko and an image of Tchaikovsky in the background.

workspace came into conflict with the limited space at Zverev's home (there was only one music room shared by all three young men). His request for a separate work room escalated into a perceived challenge to Zverev's authority,

> and Zverev, losing control of himself, suddenly raised his hand against his pupil. Rachmaninoff was already a young man of sixteen, and would not tolerate such a gesture. He firmly declared to Zverev, 'You don't dare hit me!' whereupon Zverev's fury grew unmanageable, and the interview ended in a total break of relations.[41]

In his biography of the composer, Oskar von Riesemann saw this break as the natural desire of the young man to assert himself as an adult.[42] Music critic Leonid Sabaneev later sensationally claimed (citing a second-hand source) that Zverev's homosexuality was at the root of the conflict, a story picked up by Rachmaninoff's early biographer Seroff.[43] However, it was the outcome rather than the cause of conflict that was of greatest import. Rachmaninoff found himself expelled from Zverev's home and affections, a rift that would continue until the successful premiere of Rachmaninoff's opera *Aleko*.

Though not entirely cut off from his family, visits had been rare during Rachmaninoff's four years as a boarder at Zverev's. After the rift, Zverev arranged a meeting with Rachmaninoff's aunt Varvara Satina (sister of Rachmaninoff's father), who lived in Moscow with her husband, Aleksandr Satin, and their four children. During her conversation with Zverev, Rachmaninoff's aunt Varvara left her two young daughters, Natasha and Sophie, to keep the distressed young man company, instructing them to be 'kind and gentle with him, because he was very unfortunate'.[44] Little could Varvara Satina have suspected how seriously her two young daughters would take this charge. Both Natasha and Sophie would ultimately devote much of their lives to protecting and loving the cousin so unceremoniously thrust into their hands – one as his devoted supporter and unofficial biographer, and the other as his lifelong companion and wife.

2

Ivanovka

Though Zverev played a key role in Rachmaninoff's musical and intellectual development, the composer's 1931 reminiscences omitted reference to his years as a boarder:

> Until I was 16, I lived on the estates that belonged to my mother, but from the age of 16 my parents lost their fortune, the estates were lost, and in the summer I went to the estate of my relative Satin. From this age, almost to the moment when I left Russia (forever?), for a whole 28 years, I lived there.[1]

The factual lapses in this account expose the centrality that the estate Ivanovka came to hold in Rachmaninoff's memory of life before 1917. Every Russian felt an inherent connection to the land, Rachmaninoff claimed in 1931, which was associated with 'some sort of striving for peace, for quiet, for love of nature, amongst which he lives, and in part a desire for isolation, for solitude'.[2] Whether or not this was true in a general sense, Ivanovka unquestionably played such a role for Rachmaninoff.

Situated on the open steppe of Tambov region, about 500 kilometres (310 mi.) southeast of Moscow, Ivanovka was an overnight train journey from the dirt, urban sprawl and cultural vibrancy of the city. It was here that Rachmaninoff would experience the first pangs of adolescent love in 1890, where some of his best-known works would take shape and where he would retreat with his family from the strains of a busy professional life. It was to Ivanovka that he 'always sought to go, either for rest and complete quiet, or, on the other hand, for focused work, which the surrounding quiet helped'.[3] Ultimately unsustainable without the injection of cash from Rachmaninoff's professional success, Ivanovka stood proudly as an emblem of constancy against the waves of noble estates sold to speculators and new merchant elites, or broken up and parcelled out to wealthier peasants.

Though Ivanovka came to symbolize Russia in Rachmaninoff's memories, this relationship developed gradually. After the disintegration of relations with Zverev, Rachmaninoff moved to the Satin family home in Moscow. While his departure deprived him of participation in Zverev's regular gatherings of Moscow cultural intelligentsia, the Satin family offered instead, as his younger cousin Sophie recalled, 'a peaceful family life, attention and caring concern for him, that is, everything that he had lost so early on and which he so needed'.[4] Rachmaninoff took with him the strict discipline as well as the highly placed contacts in Moscow musical life to which Zverev had introduced him. But with the Satins he finally found himself within a loving family circle.

In 1889, the Satin family lived in an old-style two-storey Moscow house on Malyi Levshinskii alley. Sergei's room, where a piano was installed, was located on the mezzanine. His younger cousin Natasha loved music passionately (she later graduated from the Moscow Conservatory as a pianist) and would often run upstairs to listen to her older cousin play. Together Natasha, sister Sophie and brothers Aleksandr (Sasha) – who died of tuberculosis in 1896 – and Vladimir surrounded their reserved cousin with affection.

But it was the Satins' estate Ivanovka that stole Rachmaninoff's heart. His first summer there in 1890 was an idyll of music, creativity and budding romance. The Skalon family, related to the Satins through the marriage of Aleksandr Satin's sister, joined the Satins at Ivanovka, together with 27-year-old Siloti, his family

Rachmaninoff with the Satin siblings in 1902 (from left to right): Sophie, Rachmaninoff, Natasha and Vladimir.

and assorted family servants. In the evening, the young people, particularly Sergei, Natasha Satina and the three Skalon sisters (Natalia, Vera and Liudmila), often gathered on the large bench in front of the house to converse. As Liudmila Skalon later recalled:

Ivanovka was a typical estate of medium size. It was located amongst the steppe with small copses, but in the estate there was a large park, and in the steppe nearby a pond approximately three kilometers in diameter. In the middle of the park there was a two-story house where the owners, the Satins, lived, and Rachmaninoff and Siloti lived together with them. Our family was in the separate outbuilding . . . In front of the house was a large yard with a stable. To the right from the yard – a fruit garden called 'Upper Garden'. Next to it was a gazebo covered with wild grapes. To the side and behind the house was an old park with alleys, and at the end of it began a young park with grass glades.[5]

At Ivanovka, Rachmaninoff developed a love for nature, often strolling pensively in the 'red alley' (named after the red bricks that provided the foundation). His love of lilacs later in life stemmed from memories of the lilac bushes that 'surrounded the house, surrounded the deciduous trees in the young park, grew between trees in the birch alley'.[6]

All the young people were musicians, creating an atmosphere at once inspiring and hectic for Rachmaninoff's compositional development. Of the two pianos in the main house, the downstairs piano was reserved for the renowned pianist Siloti, who was preparing for his upcoming concert season. Sergei, Natasha, Sonia, Vera and Liudmila had to divide time practising upstairs.[7] As Vera Skalon described the summer in her diary, 'from 8 to 5, one musician switches with another and the poor piano is not quiet for a minute.'[8] As the constant practising in the main house bothered him, Rachmaninoff retreated to the smaller house where the Skalons resided to work on composition. After two hours of work, 'Sergei Vasil'evich sits at the piano and for the next two hours plays the same etude of Shletser over and over.'[9]

Outbuilding at Ivanovka, where Rachmaninoff composed many of his works.

Rachmaninoff had few intimate friends. Among these few, however, his shy and somewhat stern demeanour gave way to a fondness for jokes and teasing. All three sisters were dedicatees of Rachmaninoff's early songs, and they inspired several compositions for six hands. Rachmaninoff's love of teasing found expression in some of his nicknames for Vera, including 'brykushka' (Little Kicker) and 'psikhopatka' (Psychopath). Some months after their initial meeting, the Skalon sisters inspired a transformation in his physical appearance: in response to their teasing regarding his unruly hair, he adopted a close-cropped appearance that would become his trademark.[10] Youthful romance blossomed between seventeen-year-old Sergei and fifteen-year-old Vera. Though her parents opposed the relationship and forbade the two from corresponding, Rachmaninoff subsequently maintained a lively correspondence with her older sisters. These extant letters to Natalia and Liudmila give the image of a sensitive youth and provide much of the surviving detail about the genesis of his early compositions. Vera's surviving diary from that summer allows a glimpse into the naive, self-absorbed world of adolescent love. An echo of this youthful infatuation seems to emanate from Rachmaninoff's setting of Afanasy Fet's poem 'In the Silence of the Night', op. 4, no. 3, a romance written that summer and dedicated to Vera.[11] The song bears similarities to Tchaikovsky's 'None but the Lonely Heart', which Rachmaninoff had learned when accompanying his sister Elena on the piano years earlier.[12]

Several close friends from Rachmaninoff's conservatory years would remain intimates of the composer throughout his life, including the singer M. Slonov, music theorist N. S. Morozov, pianists A. B. Gol'denveizer, V. R. Vilshau, A. F. Gedike, cellist A. A. Brandukov, music critic Iu. Sakhnovskii and violinist N. K. Averiano.[13] He was unceasingly loyal to those he considered his friends, and sought to balance honesty with faithfulness. In his studies, the young musician was known for his 'brilliant pianistic

Rachmaninoff prior to adopting what would become his characteristic short haircut.

gifts'[14] and 'sight reading ability, incredible ear and miraculous [musical] memory'.[15] These musical gifts were combined with a reserved, almost taciturn aura. One fellow student later described the young Rachmaninoff as 'tall, thin, with shoulders somehow raised, which gave him a quadrangular look'.[16] Of particular note was his 'very expressive' face, which 'resembled a Roman'.[17] Rachmaninoff's severe demeanour extended to his reserved stage presence. His devotion to music as an art, cultivated in Zverev's house, meant that he took every performance seriously, pointedly avoiding unnecessary gestures or dramatic movements. Already in his conservatory years, he personified his later declaration that he was '85% musician and just 15% human'.[18]

As Siloti prepared for his upcoming concert season in the summer of 1890, Ivanovka resounded with Edvard Grieg's A-minor Piano Concerto. An echo of this work's dramatic opening with an octave flourish is apparent in Rachmaninoff's First Piano Concerto in F-sharp minor, op. 1, begun that summer. Parallels between the Grieg piano concerto and Rachmaninoff's first concerto are even stronger in early sketches than in the published score. The sketch's opening tempo marking *Allegro moderato* mirrors the opening tempo of the Grieg concerto (Rachmaninoff's first movement was marked *Vivace* in the finished score).[19] Though perhaps natural given his own skills and training, the decision to designate a piano concerto as op. 1 put Rachmaninoff at odds with typical genres embraced by the St Petersburg-based Kuchka. Russian classical repertoire could boast many talented pianists and composers, but few piano concertos apart from those by Rubinstein and Tchaikovsky.[20]

Though begun at Ivanovka, Rachmaninoff worked sporadically on the concerto over subsequent months. The summer of 1891 once again found Rachmaninoff and Siloti at Ivanovka, this time without the distracting presence of the Skalon sisters, and the entire concerto was finished that June.[21] Dedicated to Siloti, the first movement was premiered by Rachmaninoff with Safonov conducting at the Moscow Conservatory in March 1892. Critics warmly received the first concerto's 'taste, truth, melody, honesty and unquestionable skill' though noting that perhaps it was 'still not independent'.[22] The work is known today almost exclusively in its 1917 revision (dated 10 November, just days after the Bolshevik Revolution swept away the Provisional Government). While such revision anticipated a pattern common in his later works (to the point that analysis of his various revisions and cuts makes up a not insubstantial part of the scholarly literature), it is generally agreed in this case that revisions effectively restructured and improved the work.[23] The orchestration was reworked based on Rachmaninoff's intervening years of experience as a conductor. He thinned the piano texture while simultaneously incorporating a chromatic style in keeping with his later piano works, an adaptation clearly demonstrated in the opening of the lyrical second movement. While the original version offered a simple arpeggiated chord at the entrance of the piano, the revision showcases the piano entering with a rich chromatic musing layered atop a melody initially introduced by the orchestra, an excellent encapsulation of the path Rachmaninoff's style was to follow in the intervening years.

The haunting opening theme of the First Concerto's lyrical second movement also hints at a possible new romantic interest Rachmaninoff had developed in 1891. It features a direct quotation from Rachmaninoff's song 'Oh No, I Beg You, Do Not Leave' (op. 4, no. 1), written in 1891 to a text by Dmitrii Merezhkovsky and dedicated to Anna Lodizhenskaia, a married young woman of Roma descent to whom he was introduced by his friend Iurii Sakhnovskii.[24] Rachmaninoff's new friendship was noted with disapproval by both the Satin and Skalon girls. Liudmila Skalon recalled:

Almost every evening Serezha visited his acquaintances the Lodyzhenskiis. Anna Aleksandrovna Lodyzhenskaia was his passionate platonic love. One cannot say that she had a good influence on him. She somehow got him entangled in her own petty, drab interests. Her husband was a dissolute reveller, and she often asked Serezha to go looking for him. My sisters and I and Natasha [Satina] did not like the appearance of Anna Aleksandrovna. Her eyes alone were pretty: large gypsy eyes; an unbeautiful mouth, with large lips.[25]

'Platonic love' or not, Rachmaninoff remained a devoted friend to his 'Rodnaia' ('Dear One') throughout her short life. In addition to dedicating his first symphony to her, he provided moral and financial support to her during her lifetime and, after her death, to her husband, Piotr Lodizhenskii.[26] Possibly inspired by Anna's sister, the 'famous gypsy singer N. A. Aleksandrova', 'Oh No, I Beg You' expresses sentiments similar to an urban (or 'cruel') romance. Indeed, another of N. A. Aleksandrova's songs, according to Liudmila Skalon, provided the basis for Rachmaninoff's Gypsy Capriccio (op. 12).[27]

The popularity of 'cruel romances' and other 'gypsy songs' was part of a 'gypsy mania' that swept urban Russian society at the time. Performed by both Roma and Russian singers, the expression of raw emotion, melancholy (*toska*), individuality and melodramatic performance style found particular appeal among urban audiences, and Rachmaninoff himself later frequented the restaurants Iar and Strelna in Moscow's Petrovsky Park on the outskirts of the city, where he would sit until late at night, listening to the singing of 'gypsies'. His friend Fedor Chaliapin's recording of 'Dark Eyes' – possibly the most famous 'cruel romance' – still moved the composer to tears in emigration.[28]

This popular gypsy motif had previously found voice in Pushkin's 1827 poem *The Gypsies*, which was the basis for Rachmaninoff's final composition assignment at the Moscow Conservatory in the spring of 1892. The plot, with certain parallels to Bizet's *Carmen*, centres on the contrast between the freedom of the gypsy lifestyle and the murderous jealousy of Aleko, a Russian man who discovers his young gypsy lover Zemfira has been unfaithful. Though the opera libretto has been critiqued for its hotchpotch character, the topic inspired Rachmaninoff's compositional gifts: of the three students given the final assignment, he was the only one to turn in a complete opera at the end of the allotted time – just under four weeks. The work was premiered in the Moscow Conservatory on 27 April 1892, and was warmly received both by Tchaikovsky and Zverev, who belatedly recognized his former student's compositional gifts, awarding Rachmaninoff his gold pocket watch as a gesture of peace. *Aleko* marked Rachmaninoff's successful completion of his conservatory training, and he was awarded the Great Gold medal, reserved for those who completed their musical studies in two disciplines.

Rachmaninoff with his composition teacher, Anton Arensky (seated, middle), and fellow students Lev Conus (far left) and Nikita Morozov (standing), 1892.

The recent conservatory graduate and Free Artist struggled to achieve financial independence and stability after he moved out of the Satin household in the autumn of 1892. He took on a variety of teaching and performance opportunities, but found teaching 'sheer torment'.[29] In 1895, he abandoned his first paid position as an accompanist for the Italian violinist Terezina Tua in the middle of her tour. His heart remained in composition. Domestic music-making was an important aspect of educated Russian society, and such pieces were generally more profitable than operatic or orchestral scores. It is thus not surprising that Rachmaninoff turned his attention to romances and character pieces for piano. Over the coming years, he moved in and out of the Satin home as he sought to balance his emerging career with insufficient finances. His letters at this time show a young man searching for his place in life, experimenting briefly with alcohol, and dreaming of future success.[30]

Perhaps fitting for a man who was enamoured with modern technology throughout his life, Rachmaninoff's first public performance occurred at the Electrical Exhibition in Moscow on 26 September 1892. Alongside the first movement of Anton Rubinstein's Fourth Piano Concerto and works by Chopin and Liszt, he premiered a recently composed piece that was to define his compositional style for audiences more than any other – a Prelude in C-sharp minor. That autumn he completed four other piano pieces and in 1893 the publisher Gutheil (who had purchased *Aleko* after the opera's premiere) published the five works, dedicated to Rachmaninoff's former composition teacher Anton Arensky, as his op. 3, *Morceaux de Fantaisie*.[31]

As a set, the *Morceaux de Fantaisie* situate Rachmaninoff as an inheritor of the nineteenth-century Romantic character piece popularized by Schumann and Chopin – a short composition, generally in ternary (ABA) form, intended to evoke a particular mood or image, often given an evocative title. The piano writing

Moscow Electrical Exhibition, where Rachmaninoff held his first public performance and premiered his famous Prelude in C-sharp minor, op. 3, no. 2.

already demonstrates Rachmaninoff's thick chordal textures, singable, stepwise melodies, and a marked preference for harmonic movement by thirds, a typical (though not unique) aspect of Rachmaninoff's harmonic style. The opening piece, *Elegie*, bears a similarity to a Chopin nocturne in its lyrical melody over an arpeggiated accompaniment, though already here a thicker chordal texture indicative of Rachmaninoff's style prevails. The third piece, *Melodie*, opens with a simple melody presented in the left hand; a gradually thickening texture builds intensity yet never overpowers the melody. The title of the fourth piece, *Polichinelle*, was suggested by Rachmaninoff's friend Slonov, and drawn from the character in *commedia dell'arte*. This work strikes a humorous tone that is perhaps a lesser-known aspect of Rachmaninoff's oeuvre and captures the composer's love of teasing that his close friends often commented upon. The fifth piece, *Serenade*, has been noted for its 'Spanish' or 'gypsy' flavour, created by the use of an augmented second scale. These pieces held a special place in Rachmaninoff's heart. He performed all five throughout his career, issued recordings of all of them, and later revised two of the pieces (*Melodie* and *Serenade*).

However, it is the second piece, the Prelude in C-sharp minor, that, as Geoffrey Norris points out, 'became for millions the epitome of what they considered Rachmaninoff's style to be, couched as it is in oppressively melancholic terms with a more impassioned central section and a grandiose climax'.[32] Thickly textured thunderous chords that span the range of the keyboard create an ominous opening and finale, while an impassioned middle section features a lyrical melody above a restless triplet accompaniment that builds to cascading diminished sevenths highlighting tonic and dominant chords before returning to the solemn opening, now marked FFF.

Rachmaninoff consistently resisted attempts to link the Prelude to a particular extra-musical inspiration, claiming in 1910 that 'my only inspiration, aside from the pressing necessity to make some money, was the desire to create something beautiful and artistic.'[33] Perhaps in part because of the composer's own reticence when it came to specifying a programme, commentators have ascribed a plethora of interpretations to the Prelude's evocative sounds; among the many imaginative titles assigned to the piece are 'The Bells of Moscow' and 'Crime and Punishment'. Of the countless arrangements, perhaps the most eclectic calls for banjo and male chorus. In a letter to the composer, one young American admirer heard the cry 'We want bread!' and saw the emaciated faces of Russian peasants emanating from the powerful chords, while another young lady asked the composer 'if the C-sharp minor Prelude meant to describe the agonies of a man having been nailed down in a coffin while still alive?'[34]

Legends also surrounded the Prelude's rumoured lucrative proceeds. As Russia had not signed the Berne Convention of 1886, the op. 3 set was not protected by international copyright, a factor that aided its ubiquitous performance.[35] While Rachmaninoff stated that he only ever received a one-time payment of 40 rubles for the piece, one rumour claimed that Rachmaninoff's publisher Gutheil bought an entire house for 500,000 rubles on the profits made from this one composition.[36] Premiered by Siloti in the UK (1895) and the United States (1898), the Prelude in C-sharp minor made Rachmaninoff an international figure before he had ever performed abroad; by the time of Rachmaninoff's first performance in London in 1899, audiences waited breathlessly to hear the author's rendition of a work that had already become, in the description of *The Musical Standard*, 'hackneyed'. Critics looked forward to Rachmaninoff's performance settling the 'vexed question of its proper reading: for as a rule the Prelude is almost unrecognisable, so differently is it played by amateur and professional pianists'.[37] At this inaugural concert, he performed his Prelude twice by audience demand, a foreshadowing of his later career as a virtuoso in America where, though he never programmed the Prelude, it was an expected encore that Rachmaninoff fulfilled with grudging good humour.[38] The performance of the opening of the piece by Mickey Mouse in 1929 in a collage with Liszt's second Hungarian Rhapsody ('The Opry House') captured the Prelude's seamless shift from nineteenth-century Russia to mid-twentieth-century America.[39] By 1951 it received the dubious distinction of being cited by Charles Cooke in *The Etude* magazine as one of the five most overworked piano pieces.[40]

While the op. 3 piano works demonstrate both the essentials of Rachmaninoff's pianistic style and his indebtedness to the Romantic piano repertoire, his op. 4 songs explore a range of Russian styles. Martyn notes that in this opus Rachmaninoff demonstrates that 'far from being a mere epigone of Tchaikovsky, he was heir to a wide range of Russian musical culture, embracing the St Petersburg as well as the Moscow tradition.'[41] The wandering chromatic vocal line of op. 4, no. 4, 'Sing Not to Me, Beautiful Maiden', a setting of a Pushkin text evoking a distant lost love in the mountainous Caucasus territory of Georgia, annexed to the Russian empire between 1801 and 1804, is a nod to the 'orientalist' hallmark of the Kuchka style – indeed, Borodin's *Prince Igor*, an opera that is virtually a poster child of the orientalist idiom, had been premiered just two years earlier.[42] The Kuchka interest in stylized Russian folk music finds expression in the song 'Harvest of Sorrow' (op. 4, no. 5), a setting of a text by Aleksei Tolstoy that imitates the folk practice of a singer directly addressing the natural world. However, as Richard Sylvester argues, 'Tolstoy personalizes it, changing the image of the open field to a man's own field . . . the crop sowed is "thoughts," the intentions and hopes of a life, the soul's dreams, the heart's loves, which have come to naught.'[43] The shifting time signatures, use of double tonic, tempo shifts and melismatic vocal style evoke the folk-style lament of the Russian *protiazhnaia* (drawn-out) song, offering 'a potent reimagining of old formulas and poetic folk language'.[44]

Though Rachmaninoff dedicated his Fantasy for two pianos op. 5 to Tchaikovsky, the evocation of bells in the final movement is most reminiscent of Mussorgsky's *Boris Godunov* or Rimskii-Korsakov's *Easter Overture*. As Liudmila Skalon later recalled, 'this piece was inspired by memories of the Novgorod bells, which in childhood, when he lived with his grandmother, had made an indelible impression on him.'[45] Indeed, the final movement, 'Easter', combines the Russian Orthodox chant 'Christ is Risen' with an imitation of clanging bells.[46]

Resemblance to Kuchka-style compositional techniques notwithstanding, Rachmaninoff sought to establish himself as a well-rounded composer in the mould of Tchaikovsky and Rubinstein. A natural next step in establishing oneself as a serious composer was to tackle a symphony, to which he turned in January 1895. As one of Moscow's most promising young composers, Rachmaninoff's First Symphony was awaited with enthusiasm. He received 500 rubles from Gutheil for the score, unseen and unheard, and he was excited by the possibility of an initial performance in St Petersburg under the auspices of Mitrofan Beliaev's music circle. He seemed at the height of success. Yet Rachmaninoff struggled with his first serious attempt to write in this form, writing to M. Slonov over his concern with the length of the first movement.[47]

Cesar Cui's notorious review of the premiere of Rachmaninoff's First Symphony on 16 March 1897 was all the more devastating to a young man poised on the brink of a brilliant career. Cui concluded viciously:

> If there were a conservatory in Hell, and if one of its talented students were tasked to compose a programme symphony based on the story of the Seven Plagues of Egypt, and if he composed a symphony like Rachmaninoff's, then he would have brilliantly fulfilled his task and enthralled the inhabitants of Hell.[48]

This epic failure, together with Rachmaninoff's subsequent descent into depression and ultimate cure through hypnosis, is one of music history's enduring legends. Indeed, Leonid Sabaneev later argued,

These years (1897–1900) were the most confused and dark time in [Rachmaninoff's] biography. It was said that he decided to give up writing, that he drank, that he fell in love, that he lost his creative gift and was being treated by the hypnotist N. Dahl to get it back. What from this was truth and what was fiction, it is difficult to judge.[49]

Not surprisingly, different theories and interpretations emerged. Both the Skalon and Satina sisters blamed Aleksandr Glazunov's poor conducting for the symphony's failure. Liudmila Skalon recalled: '[Glazunov] wrecked it. Cui shook his head and shrugged his shoulders the whole time.'[50] Natasha Satina later claimed bluntly that Glazunov had been drunk during the performance.[51] In contrast, Rachmaninoff's younger friend, the writer Marietta Shaginian, recalled speaking with 'old men' present at the premiere; in their recollections of the performance, 'not once was the failure explained by the poor conducting of Glazunov.'[52]

Although sources generally concur that, whether through carelessness or some other cause, the performance was lacking, this in itself cannot explain the vitriol Cui poured upon the composition's 'modern' or 'decadent' style, which the famed critic argued

leaves an evil impression with its broken rhythms, obscurity and vagueness of form, meaningless repetition of the same short tricks, the nasal sound of the orchestra, the strained crash of the brass, and above all its sickly perverse harmonization and quasi-melodic outlines, the complete absence of simplicity and naturalness, the complete absence of themes.[53]

For twenty-first-century listeners, it is perhaps difficult to hear what so disturbed Cui and his fellow St Petersburg musicians. But it seems likely that part of the cacophony attacked by Cui was related to Rachmaninoff's exploration of new musical trends – in short, his experiment with 'modernism', 1895-style. By this time, alongside his love of Tchaikovsky, Rachmaninoff had become particularly interested in the music of Liszt and Wagner. Indeed, Liudmila Skalon remembered Rachmaninoff introducing them to Liszt's 'Faust' Symphony and playing the Death of Isolde from 'Tristan and Isolde' in 1895. In 1897, after the failure of his symphony, he played through the entire *Ring of the Nibelung* tetralogue with the Skalon sisters, making them 'identify the appearance of one or another leitmotif', though he would freely skip over what he found to be boring sections of the score.[54] Indeed, the influence of Liszt and Wagner is not difficult to hear in the symphony's tight use of cyclical motifs, as well as the experimental treatment of harmonies and modulations.

While Cui found in Rachmaninoff a 'modernist' who threatened 'real' music with 'decadence', this conflict should also be looked at through the lens of a continued rivalry between Moscow and Petersburg schools. It was through the encouragement of Rachmaninoff's former teacher Taneev that the First Symphony was scheduled for its premiere at Beliaev's Russian Symphony Concerts. A wealthy timber merchant with a love for the Kuchka (as well as Rachmaninoff's Moscow contemporary Scriabin), Beliaev hosted regular concerts in Petersburg ostensibly intended to support new Russian composers generally. In reality, however, the Beliaev circle consisted of students and followers of Rimsky-Korsakov and by 1897 tended to promote its own established style. Though Rachmaninoff's earlier symphonic poem 'The Crag' had received a friendly response at its 20 January 1896 premiere alongside Ippolitov-Ivanov's *Caucasian Sketches* as 'novelties from the young Russian school of Moscow',[55] the premiere of a full symphony was a strong statement of confidence. Rimsky-Korsakov himself set the stage for Cui's virulent attack: after attending the rehearsal, he commented, 'Forgive me, but I do not find this music at all agreeable.'[56]

Rachmaninoff himself acknowledged that 'this Symphony, if it is not decadent, as they write and understand the word, is definitely a bit "new".' Together with Glazunov's poor performance, he wondered if such novelty might explain its failure.[57] In 1915, he complained to Marietta Shaginian that 'everyone, calling himself a musician, who is not ashamed to look for ill-being in music is crowned with the laurels of innovator. He is called advanced, original, and God knows what, but [Rachmaninoff's] innovation was strangled in embryo.'[58] She concluded that 'the sickness came to Rachmaninoff not from the failure of the symphony, not even from personal disappointment in it, but from the sudden loss of his path to the future, that is, from the loss of belief in himself as an innovator.'[59] Might this help to explain Rachmaninoff's later animosity to 'modernist' musical experimentation?

Closer assessment deepens the mysteries surrounding the symphony. The work is dedicated to A. L. (Anna Lodizhenskaia), and the biblical epigraph included in the score 'Vengeance is mine, I will repay' – a reference to Lev Tolstoy's novel *Anna Karenina* – seems to almost beg an interpretation focused on an adulterous relationship, though any attempt along these lines is entirely speculative. The *Dies Irae* chant melody from the Latin requiem mass provides one of the two motivic elements at the opening, from which the cyclic material for the entire composition is derived. This use of the *Dies Irae* marks the first extended exploration of a melody that would repeatedly recur in Rachmaninoff's later works. Indeed, Martyn speculates that 'after the traumatizing catastrophe of the premiere, it is hardly surprising that the symphony's musical motto was to haunt the composer throughout his life, appearing in his work with increasing insistence as he grew older and approached his own day of judgment.'[60] The emphasis on fate that dominates the work, its cyclicality and harmonic relations are reminiscent of Tchaikovsky's late Symphonies. Other characteristics anticipate Rachmaninoff's later music, including a theme based on the augmented second so common in 'gypsy' music and the use of stepwise melodies reminiscent of Russian Orthodox chant.

Accounts also vary as to why, in the aftermath of the failed symphony, Rachmaninoff descended into depression. After the symphony's failure, one acquaintance attested, 'for almost two years [Rachmaninoff] stopped composing.'[61] Further, she claimed, 'The nervous experience painfully expressed itself on the health of Sergei Vasilevich; extreme excitement soon moved to depression; he felt a great weakness, for hours he lay on his bed and could not do anything.'[62] Rachmaninoff later imparted to writer Ivan Bunin and his wife, 'I lost belief in myself, I didn't work, I drank a lot.'[63]

Other evidence contradicts this straightforward account. Rather than complete creative paralysis, Rachmaninoff seemed inclined immediately after the notorious premiere to think critically through ways to revise and improve the work, as a 6 May 1897 letter suggests.[64] Geoffrey Norris argues that 'Rachmaninoff, far from being clinically depressed, was merely (and understandably) low after the First Symphony debacle.'[65] Observing that Rachmaninoff did not immediately descend into depression, Max Harrison suggests some later cause for his depressed state by 1900, an interpretation seconded by Elger Niels.[66] On the advice of a doctor who diagnosed Rachmaninoff with neurasthenia, the composer spent the summer of 1897 at the Skalon family estate of Ignatova (Nizhny Novgorod province), where he was encouraged neither to compose nor to play. Periodic melancholy prompted him to reproach the sisters that 'You love me just because I am a musician. If I were not a musician, you would not pay any attention to me.'[67]

As the months passed, however, Rachmaninoff gradually sank into a darker mood. 'My work goes just as badly,' he wrote to Natalia Skalon in December 1897. 'I am beginning, it seems, to suffer from black melancholy. It's a fact! I surrender to this melancholy no less than an hour per day. Today it swallowed me entirely, and I even howled like a fool.'[68] This was not the first time

Rachmaninoff and the Skalon sisters on the veranda at Ignatova after the failure of his First Symphony in 1897.

that Rachmaninoff had struggled with dark moods. The young man had been prone to anxiety even before the First Symphony fiasco. In 1893, he noted to Natalia Skalon, 'Sometimes I listen to a nightingale, but only occasionally, because in large quantity it affects the nerves, and you know, in our 19th century everyone to a known degree is nervous.'[69] Similarly, Sophie Satin noted that before Rachmaninoff's 1902 marriage he often 'fell into hopeless despair'.[70]

Why, however, if the failure of the symphony was the cause of this intense depression, did it take months for the effects to take hold? Noting that it is at this time that Rachmaninoff's letters to the Skalon sisters break off for almost a year and that his correspondence failed to mention Vera when it resumed, Liudmila Kovaleva-Ogorodnova speculates that Rachmaninoff must have learned of Vera's engagement to Sergei Tolbuzin, whom she married in the autumn of 1899, adding personal disappointment to his sorrow over his failed symphony.[71] Indeed, in his December 1897 letter to Natalia Skalon, Rachmaninoff imagined her weeping over his grave, noting 'on your face there must be tears, in your ears the words of my romance "Dream", dedicated to you, in which, by the way, I dreamed of good people' – very possibly a coded reference to Vera.[72] According to Liudmila Skalon, 'Before the wedding [Vera] burned more than 100 letters from Serezha. She was a faithful wife and tender mother, but she was unable to forget and stop loving Serezha to her very death.'[73] Though sustained by their mutual love of music and culture, Rachmaninoff's letters to the two older sisters, once resumed, lacked the same intensity as before. Be that as it may, a cordial relationship existed between the cousins, and before her own marriage to Rachmaninoff, Natasha Satina dressed for her wedding at Vera's Moscow apartment.

After the First Symphony's failure, Rachmaninoff seems to have become more uncertain of his own judgement. Correspondence with friends (particularly Slonov and Morozov) often shows him asking for advice, and he would later repeatedly revise compositions. Nevertheless, unlike many of his other works, Rachmaninoff never revised his First Symphony. He left the manuscript behind in a locked desk when he left Russia with his family in 1917, and it subsequently disappeared. When Aleksandr Gauk conducted its second performance in the Great Hall of the Moscow Conservatory on 17 October 1945 with the USSR State Symphony Orchestra, he dramatically reclaimed both Rachmaninoff and Russia's late imperial heritage for Soviet audiences. Based upon a score reconstructed from orchestral parts discovered in the Leningrad Conservatory library, the work also featured in the first concert ever televised in the United States. Rachmaninoff's modern voice from 1897 thus pioneered a new technological era of concert experience for audiences eager to award it a respectable place in the performance repertoire.[74]

3

'My Muse Has Not Died'

In an interview with the *Musical Times* in 1930, Rachmaninoff credited his psychological recovery after the First Symphony's failure to timely intervention by the famed writer and moralist Lev Tolstoy:

> In the most difficult and critical period of my life, when I thought all was lost and it was useless to worry any more, I met a man who took the trouble to talk to me for three days. He restored my self-respect, dissipated my doubts, gave me back strength and confidence and revived my ambition. He stimulated me to new work, and, I might almost say, saved my life. This man was Count Tolstoy. I was twenty-four years old when I was introduced to him. 'Young man,' said he to me, 'do you imagine that everything in my life goes smoothly? Do you suppose I have no troubles, never hesitate and lose confidence in myself? Do you really think faith is always equally strong? All of us have difficult moments; but this is life. Hold up your head, and keep on your appointed path.'[1]

The following year, Rachmaninoff gave a similar story to *The Gramophone*: friendship with Tolstoy had helped him overcome 'a very difficult period of my early career'.[2]

In both accounts, Tolstoy embodies the role of a Russian Orthodox religious elder (*starets*): 'an experienced monk who possessed special gifts of spiritual wisdom and acted as a mentor to other monks'.[3] In Rachmaninoff's time, famous elders were seen as holding prophetic powers. While the Church tacitly tolerated pilgrimages by the faithful, Russian literature fans celebrated the elder Father Zosima in Fyodor Dostoevsky's *Brothers Karamazov*: a character likely modelled in part on elder Amvrosii of Optina Pustyn monastery (Kaluga province). Both Dostoevsky and Tolstoy paid multiple visits to Amvrosii as part of their spiritual journeys; though Tolstoy's reaction to these visits has been debated, they seem to have served as a model for his own meetings with members of the common folk and intelligentsia. Thus, it was natural for Rachmaninoff's supporters to encourage a visit to Tolstoy, who, it was hoped, might relieve the young man's moral and spiritual troubles.

In personal conversation, however, Rachmaninoff gave a far less positive account of the meeting. In the same year that he dictated his positive testament to the *Musical Times,* he recounted to Russian émigré writer Ivan Bunin and his wife Vera:

> Shared acquaintances told Tolstoy of my situation and asked him to encourage me. It was evening, I arrived with [the singer] Chaliapin – I always accompanied him then. I forget what he sang first, the second piece was Grieg, and the third was my song on Apukhin's bad lyrics 'Fate', written under the influence of Beethoven's Fifth symphony, which could tempt a musician. Chaliapin sang them incredibly. Fifteen of those present applauded. I noticed immediately that Tolstoy frowned and, looking at him, the others fell silent. I understood of course that he had not liked it, and started to avoid him, hoping to evade a conversation. But he caught me and began to scold, saying that he did not like it, nasty words. He started to reproach me for the repeating leitmotif. I said that it was Beethoven's motif. He attacked Beethoven. And Sofiia Andreevna, seeing that he

spoke heatedly about something, came up behind and said 'It is harmful to Lev Nikolaevich to get excited, don't argue with him.' What kind of argument, when he attacked me! Then, at the end of the evening, he came to me and said: 'Don't be offended with me. I am old, you are a young man.' I answered him rudely, 'Why should I be offended if you don't even recognize Beethoven?' He said to me that he works every day from 7 to 12: 'There is no other way. And don't think that it is always pleasant for me, sometimes it is very distasteful and difficult to write.' I of course never visited him again, though Sofiia Andreevna invited me.[4]

In the account reported by the Swans, similar in many details to Bunin's account, Rachmaninoff concluded bitterly, 'And just think, the first time I went to him, I went to him as to a god.'[5]

What are we to make of these contradictory accounts? Anyone familiar with Tolstoy's intellectual development would scarcely be surprised by this more negative variant. By 1900, Tolstoy had developed his own radical views on contemporary art, which found expression in his short story 'The Kreutzer Sonata', in which a husband is driven mad by jealousy after hearing his wife perform Beethoven's eponymous sonata with a violinist. Similarly, in his 1897 philosophical tract *What Is Art?*, Tolstoy condemned the entire musical tradition of which Rachmaninoff was a representative as a form of societal degeneration. Describing art as an emotional 'infection' that passed from composer to listener via the performer, Tolstoy upheld works that 'infected' an observer with 'Christian' emotions (almost exclusively folk songs he believed embodied the spirit of the peasantry) and excoriated the corrupted taste of high society whose art invariably provoked harmful emotional responses in the audience.

In this light, it was perhaps unavoidable that Chaliapin's rendition of a Russian folk song moved Tolstoy to tears, while Rachmaninoff's lengthy romance 'Fate' prompted scorn. In the poem by Aleksei Apukhtin, as Sylvester summarizes, Fate is personified as a 'malevolent old woman tapping relentlessly with her cane, whose unexpected entrances as an "old friend" bring an end to hopes and happiness'.[6] Apukhtin was inspired by the legend that the opening theme of Beethoven's Fifth Symphony represented Fate knocking on the door, and in his setting, Rachmaninoff used Beethoven's famed opening as the song's dominant leitmotif. Indeed, this emphasis on 'Fate' echoes a dark strand in Rachmaninoff's creative voice further developed in later works, though the *Dies Irae* melody that often accompanied such musical reflections is here absent. In mood, the piece is also reminiscent of Mussorgsky's 'Songs and Dances of Death', which similarly narrates the dramatic contrast between life and death.

While Rachmaninoff's accounts about Tolstoy are mixed, he and his contemporaries were unequivocal in celebrating Nikolai Dahl (1860–1939) for curing his depression.[7] 'For these twenty years almost my only doctors have been the hypnotist Dahl, and my two cousins (one of whom I married ten years ago),' Rachmaninoff commented in 1912. 'All of these people or, better, doctors, have taught me one thing: to take heart and to believe.'[8] In 1928, after receiving a letter from Dahl (who had emigrated after 1917 to Beirut), Rachmaninoff wrote, 'it is a shame that you have given up medicine – otherwise I would immediately travel to you in order to treat my neuralgia, which has tormented me already for ten years.'[9] In 1938 Dahl sent Rachmaninoff his recommended treatment for neuralgia.[10] But perhaps the best evidence of Rachmaninoff's belief in the efficacy of Dahl's care is the dedication of his Second Piano Concerto to the doctor.

Later biographers have nonetheless doubted Dahl's role in Rachmaninoff's recovery from depression. Rather than hypnotherapy, Norris argues, 'it is most likely that Dahl, as a gifted amateur musician and a man of culture, simply conversed with [Rachmaninoff] on subjects of music and art and, together with the friends Rachmaninoff had mixed with on holiday and in Moscow, gradually rebuilt his confidence.'[11] Others minimize the role of hypnotherapy by claiming that Rachmaninoff visited Dahl to see the pretty relative who lived with him.[12] In fact, there was nothing unusual in Rachmaninoff's turning to hypnotherapy in early twentieth-century Russia. Introduced in eighteenth-century Paris by Viennese doctor and occultist Franz Anton Mesmer and discredited by scientists in 1784, the practice gradually resurfaced. In 1842 British surgeon James Braid coined the term 'hypnosis' (from the Greek god for sleep), and sought to ground the practice in physiological rather than occult language. By the late nineteenth century, respectable scientists stressed hypnosis's ability to treat both physical and physiological ailments. In Russia (like much of Europe), as Julia Mannherz has observed, 'hypnosis became a prominent topic in publications of the 1880s and 1890s and reached the peak of its appeal in the first decade of the twentieth century.'[13] Contemporary public debate in Russia focused less on the effectiveness of hypnotherapy *per se*, but rather on controlling its potential powers. Thus, 'in response to doctors' warnings, Russian law was amended in 1890 to require medical doctors to be present during any hypnotic session. In the same year, hypnosis was banned as a form of entertainment, and a second decree restricted its practice to medical doctors only.'[14] While in 1903 a doctor was merely required to be present, by 1910 the use of hypnotic suggestion was once again limited to doctors (a law that was reissued in 1926). These continued rulings point to sustained support for lay hypnotists and belief in their curative power.[15] Dahl himself had studied in France with Jean-Martin Charcot, who had popularized hypnosis for patients suffering from hysteria.

Rachmaninoff's interactions with Tolstoy and Dahl exhibit a late imperial Russian culture seeking new forms of knowledge and understanding in place of traditional authorities, whether positivist science, Orthodox clergy or the autocratic state. Purely scientific answers were insufficient, and the realist aesthetics espoused by Dostoevsky, Turgenev, Tolstoy and 'Wanderer' painters like Ilya Repin shifted to a focus on the internal psyche and the spiritual. Far from a rejection of modernity, this shift was motivated by contemporary concerns that existing institutions had proven unable to address.

Depression notwithstanding, the years after the failure of his First Symphony were formative in Rachmaninoff's creative development as a conductor, performer and composer. In the autumn of 1897, Rachmaninoff began a new position as assistant conductor at the Moscow Private Opera. Founded by a relative of Siloti's wife Vera, Moscow railway magnate Savva Mamontov (1841–1918), the Moscow Private Opera was successfully carving out a niche for itself as the leading performer of Russian operas in Moscow when Rachmaninoff joined the company. Though Rachmaninoff was underwhelmed by the ensemble's relatively low musical performance level and left after a single season, the experience introduced him to some of the most innovative artistic trends of the day. Mamontov himself cared more about artistic sets and staging than musical performance, and Rachmaninoff later fondly recalled the modernist set designs by Mikhail Vrubel and Konstantin Korovin, which drew inspiration from the two-dimensionality of Russian icon painting. Rachmaninoff's debut as a conductor also accustomed him to a desperate pace of studying opera scores in preparation for rehearsals and laid the basis for his later conducting work.

At the Moscow Private Opera, the promising conductor struck up a friendship with the young tenor Fedor Chaliapin (1873–1938), whose boisterous personality presented a sharp contrast to Rachmaninoff's reserved demeanour. Indeed, Chaliapin possessed a unique ability to pull Rachmaninoff out of his typically withdrawn bearing throughout the remainder of his life. N. D. Teleshov later recalled a Moscow evening in 1904:

Fedor Chaliapin and Rachmaninoff, 1900. The two quickly became close friends during their time together at the Moscow Private Opera.

Chaliapin set Rachmaninoff on fire, and Rachmaninoff spurred Chaliapin on. These two giants, encouraging each other, truly created a miracle. It was no longer song nor music in a common sense – it was some sort of attack of inspiration by two of the greatest artists . . . [Rachmaninoff] felt that in his period of friendship and closeness to Chaliapin, he experienced the strongest, deepest and most subtle artistic impressions, which brought him great benefit . . . Rachmaninoff could improvise wonderfully and when Chaliapin rested, he continued his incredible improvising, and when Rachmaninoff rested, Chaliapin sat down at the piano and began to sing Russian folk songs. And then they again came together, and the unusual concert continued long past midnight. There were the most famous arias, opera excerpts that made Chaliapin famous, lyrical romances and musical jokes, and an inspired, engaging 'Marseillaise'.[16]

The son of a peasant, Chaliapin relied on Rachmaninoff's knowledge of musical theory in preparing for many of his early roles, including his famous interpretation of Boris Godunov in Musorgssky's eponymous opera. As Chaliapin later recalled, '[Rachmaninoff] was a first-rate artist, a magnificent musician. He was full of vitality and vivacity, and was excellent company.'[17] When Chaliapin was invited to perform at La Scala in 1900, Rachmaninoff accompanied the singer to Italy to help him study the score of Arrigo Boito's *Mefistofele*. Rachmaninoff's subsequent operas *The Miserly Knight* (1905) and *Francesca da Rimini* (1905) were both conceived with Chaliapin in mind for the leading role, and Chaliapin's refusal to premiere them was a great disappointment.

Nor were these idle years for Rachmaninoff's own concertizing, both inside and outside the borders of Russia. In April 1899, Rachmaninoff made his first international appearance – a performance at Queen Anne's Hall in London, where he conducted

The Crag and performed, among other works, his already famous Prelude in C-sharp minor.[18] In May 1899, his opera *Aleko* was performed with great success (with Chaliapin in the leading role) at the Pushkin festival in St Petersburg.

Given such formative successes, how can one explain Rachmaninoff's own self-narrative of failure in these years? As he wrote retrospectively to his acquaintance Mariia Kerzina:

> From 1896 to 1900 I wrote nothing. This is explained by the impression that the failure of my Symphony in Petersburg had on me. The fact that, after the Symphony I quickly wrote 20 small pieces is explained by my need to pay back a considerably large sum of money that was stolen from me on the train and which did not belong to me. Forgive me for these boring details, but my Symphony is a sore spot for me to this day, and when remembering it I begin to whimper and complain.[19]

Rachmaninoff's dismissal of his op. 14–16 works notwithstanding, his frustration seems to have sprung not from an absolute inability to compose but from his failure to complete a large-scale work. He had promised a new piano concerto for his London premiere, viewing his first concerto as a 'student work' unfit for performance. When it failed to coalesce, he had to substitute the symphonic poem *The Crag*. Though he continued to attempt work on a new concerto, in June 1898 he wrote to his old classmate, pianist Aleksandr Gol'denveizer (who had wanted to perform the promised second concerto in Petersburg) that 'my intensified work on this has so far come to naught.'[20] By summer's end he sent his regrets that the piece would not be ready that season.[21]

Rachmaninoff's friends rallied around him. Siloti provided financial support so that he could focus on composing without the strain of a deadline. In contrast to his later nostalgic memories, Rachmaninoff did not visit Ivanovka from 1897 until the second

half of summer 1900. After spending the summer of 1897 with
the Skalon sisters at Ignatova, in 1898 he spent the summer with
members of the Moscow Private Opera, primarily in the Yaroslav
region at the estate of Tania Liubatovich, a mezzo soprano from
Mamontov's opera. Seeking a quiet space to focus exclusively on
composition that autumn, Rachmaninoff accepted Liubatovich's
offer to return to her estate Putiatino, where he 'lived like a hermit'
in the autumn of 1898 with only Liubatovich's three St Bernard dogs
to keep him company.[22] In the summer of 1899, together with his
dog Levko (a gift from Liubatovich), he again eschewed the intensity
of Ivanovka (which often hosted large groups of people) for the
quiet offered at the Krasnen'skoe estate in the Voronezh region,
where Elena Kreutzer and her family, friends of the Satin family,
resided.[23] At Krasnen'skoe, the strictly disciplined family schedule
helped him to make tentative compositional advances, progress
furthered by a book titled 'On Developing One's Character', given to
him by Vladimir Satin.[24]

Rachmaninoff and
Levko.

Natasha Satina also joined the family circle at Krasnen'skoe, and Kreutzer later recalled that the two of them 'were constantly engaged in finding texts for Sergei Vasil'evich . . . we formed an archive ('*zapisnyi fond*') which Sergei Vasil'evich used when he needed it. All classics, all famous poets were read and reread by us. Then we began to look in thick journals, where sometimes one would find good poems by little-known authors, and sometimes entirely unknown authors.'[25] Among the small-scale works written at Krasnen'skoe was 'Fate', so ingloriously premiered at Tolstoy's house,[26] as well as the humorous song 'Did you hiccup, Natasha?'

> Rachmaninoff came to the library and found us at this work. He sat down, started looking through books, and delved deep into the reading. Suddenly, he let out a cry of triumph: he said he had found a great poem and asked us all to listen to it. He read it out loud with great pathos, changing some of the words, and announced that he would set it immediately.[27]

Though Elena Kreutzer later regretted the song's publication, and it has been dismissed by some critics, it is in fact a keen illustration of Rachmaninoff's sense of humour. It incorporates slightly drunken hiccups into the musical fabric of the piece alongside musical quotes from Tchaikovsky's *Eugene Onegin*, an opera based on Pushkin's masterpiece of unrequited love and noble indolence. Rachmaninoff freely changed the text of the original poem to include Natasha's name, and relocated it to Voronezh. Hidden in the humour of this song is a hint of Rachmaninoff's future: the song dedication reads 'No! My muse has not died, dear Natasha. I dedicate my new romance to you.'[28]

A very different mood is struck in the song 'Night', also initially composed in 1899. A setting of a text by Rathaus, the work can easily be read as an expression of sleepless sorrow reflecting on a lost love, a 'dream of bygone childhood days' as the poem

Natasha Satina, Rachmaninoff's future wife, early 20th century.

reads – perhaps a final reflection on Vera Skalon.[29] Regardless of its inspiration, the work is a serious exploration of insomnia and loss, and though not included in his next song cycle (op. 21), it was approved by the composer for publication in a 1904 anthology.

While any connection between Vera Skalon and 'Night' is purely hypothetical, a direct musical connection exists between the Skalon sisters and the most substantial piece Rachmaninoff worked on at Krasnen'skoe: the Second Piano Concerto. Though the sombre opening chords of the concerto's first movement are among the most famous in the concerto repertoire (possibly an inversion of the equally effective alternating base and middle-range chords that open the Prelude in C-sharp minor),[30] the first movement was actually the final movement composed. It was instead the second, lyrical movement that took shape first. Here, after a brief orchestral introduction in C minor, the piano enters in E major with a mysterious citation of an 1891 six-hand Romance that Rachmaninoff had written for the Skalon sisters. In 1910, Rachmaninoff asked Natalia Skalon to destroy the manuscript of the romance, by which time his one-time flame, Vera, had been dead for almost a year – a request that Natalia could not bring herself to fulfil.[31] Little could the sisters have suspected, when playing through the latest creation of their young composer acquaintance, that they were receiving a foretaste of what would become one of the Romantic piano repertoire's most beloved adagio movements. Here, in contrast to the brief romance, the melody unfolds in seemingly endless lyricism, leading ultimately to a brief cadenza sequence, followed by a return to the tranquillity of the E major melody. The contrasting third movement, a shimmering *allegro scherzando*, showcases Rachmaninoff's mastery of delicate filigree patterns in the piano, and energetic rhythms contrasted with passionate lyricism.

As Gol'denveizer recalled, while the second and third movements came together easily for Rachmaninoff, 'for a long time the first part wouldn't come. He had several variants of it, but he could not decide on one.'[32] For this reason, the concerto's 1900 premiere in Moscow included only the lyrical second and the scherzo-like third movement. Dahl's treatment notwithstanding, Rachmaninoff was seized by nervousness over the upcoming concert, which was also to be Siloti's conducting debut. When Rachmaninoff contracted a cold on the eve of the performance, he was so desperate for the concert to succeed that he seized upon every 'medicine and potion' that his family and friends proffered. As his sister-in-law Sophie Satin later recalled, this nearly ended in disaster when he drank three times the recommended dose of mulled wine and spent a rough night before the concert.[33] Nevertheless, the event was a great success, and Rachmaninoff must have been elated by the comparison drawn by the music critic for the *Russian Musical Newspaper* with the concerts of Rubinstein: 'I have not seen so large a public since the historic concerts of Anton Rubinstein, and long have not heard such a sound, such stormy applause, as on this evening.' The critic described Rachmaninoff's music performed that evening (which also included *Fate*, performed by Chaliapin) as 'a wealth of poetry, beauty, warmth, rich instrumentation, healthy and buoyant spirit of creation. The talent of Mr. Rachmaninoff shines through everywhere and in everything.'[34]

Rachmaninoff's creativity continued to flow in subsequent months in the Second Piano Suite (which has a certain thematic similarity to the concerto) and the Cello Sonata. But it was almost a full year later when the complete Second Concerto was premiered on 27 October 1901, once again with Rachmaninoff as soloist and Siloti conducting.[35] Despite the lag between the completion of the movements, Rachmaninoff maintained a tight thematic unity throughout the composition, with motivic links between the first

Aleksandr Siloti and Rachmaninoff, 1902.

and third movements. Nonetheless, when Rachmaninoff first played through the opening movement of his concerto at a musical gathering at Gol'denveizer's apartment, most of those gathered 'considered the first movement weaker than the 2nd and 3rd'.[36]

The entire concerto demonstrates a certain tonal duality, with each movement opening with a modulation between keys. Despite the concerto's C-minor designation, the first movement opens with dramatic, ponderous chords in F minor, before moving to C minor for the first theme, a stepwise melody with a flat seventh typical of the 'Russian' sound cultivated by the Kuchka. The second movement opens in C minor before shifting to E major with the entrance of the piano. In the third movement, the E major key that opens the piece is soon superseded by C minor, again in the piano. Used here to create a close connection between movements, this duality of key would become increasingly central to Rachmaninoff's compositional style.

In a later review for the Russian émigré press, Leonid Sabaneev celebrated Rachmaninoff's Second Piano Concerto as marking the fully fledged emergence of an exceptional pianist with mighty sound, mastery of rhythm and superhuman hands, like Liszt, 'but with a Russian soul'.[37] Indeed, with the victorious reception of this work, Rachmaninoff entered a new phase in his professional career. As one contemporary later recalled, 'Moscow adored Rachmaninoff . . . The Moscow public greeted Rachmaninoff like no one else. He was their idol. It was clear that his playing penetrated the soul of every person and made those strings sound that no other musician had been able to touch.'[38]

This victorious reception also presaged a fundamental change in Rachmaninoff's personal life. On 29 April 1902, Sergei Rachmaninoff and Natasha Satina were married in a quiet service. This was no easy feat: forbidden by the Orthodox Church, this marriage between first cousins involved both finding a priest willing to perform the service and requesting a personal dispensation from the Tsar. The service was held in a military church, whose priest was subject not to the authority of the Church Synod but to military authority. As Rachmaninoff's cousin A. A. Trubnikova recalled, 'to get to the church, one had to walk through the sleeping quarters of the soldiers, and I remember the curiosity with which they looked at such an unusual event in the barracks.'[39] The witnesses were Aleksandr Siloti and Andrei Brandukov, who had premiered the cello part in Rachmaninoff's *Trio elegiaque* no. 1 in 1892, and who was the dedicatee of Rachmaninoff's Cello Sonata (1901). Though Rachmaninoff had long been on intimate terms with the Satin family, the marriage surprised even some of their closest friends. In contrast to his earlier courtship of Vera Skalon, recalled Elena Kreutzer, the relationship between Rachmaninoff and Natasha had always 'carried a purely friendly, comradely character. He often teased Natasha. In early youth when she was thin and looked much older than her years, he would say in jest:

> Thin like a stick,
> Black like a raven,
> Maiden Natalka,
> I pity you.[40]

Liudmila Skalon later recalled, '[Natasha Satina] loved him from childhood and, one can say, suffered for him. She was smart, musical and very thoughtful. We were happy for Serezha, knowing into what reliable hands he had fallen and were satisfied that beloved Serezha would remain in our family.'[41] Be that as it may, Rachmaninoff's written correspondence with both Natalia and Liudmila Skalon ended abruptly with Rachmaninoff's announcement of his forthcoming marriage, though they continued to see each other at family gatherings and events.

To earn money for his upcoming honeymoon, Rachmaninoff completed his op. 21 songs in April 1902. Whether inspired by Tolstoy, cured by Dahl or pressed by financial necessity, Rachmaninoff's creative spark had returned in full force: ten of the twelve songs were written in just two weeks. Though the mood of several of the pieces (including the final piece, 'Sorrow in Springtime') might seem oddly dark in nature for a young man about to be married, connecting a composer's biography too causally to the mood of music he writes is problematic at best. As Sylvester has observed, the set as a whole contains threads of both the 'problem of Fate' which would come to dominate so much of Rachmaninoff's music ('Fate', 'Fragment from A. Musset'), and the theme of a 'happy or fortunate outcome' ('Lilacs', 'How Fair the Spot'). It is worth noting that these last two works are among Rachmaninoff's most successful and commonly performed songs, and that 'How Fair the Spot' is dedicated to Natasha.[42]

Rachmaninoff's marriage provided him with a stable and loving family life. Natasha dedicated her life to Sergei and his creative muse, allowing Rachmaninoff to focus on music. As Kreutzer recalled, 'the most important thing in [Rachmaninoff's] life was creation, and in order to be fruitful, he needed an atmosphere of friendship, love and concern from the people close to him. To live in a family, which he had been deprived of in his childhood, was for him a vital demand.'[43] Liudmila Skalon noted that Natasha was able to organize Rachmaninoff's life so that the melancholy that had previously weighed him down now passed with relative ease, while his sister-in-law Sophie Satin divided Rachmaninoff's life into 'before 30 and after 30', or before and after marriage.[44] From this stable family basis, Rachmaninoff would launch a successful international career.

4

In Russia's Silver Age

In 1949, Russian émigré philosopher Nikolai Berdiaev ruminated
on the turbulent yet exhilarating culture of early twentieth-century
Russia:

> it was an epoch of the awakening of independent philosophical
> thought, the blossoming of poetry, the sharpening of aesthetic
> sensuality, of religious anxiety and searching, of interest in
> mysticism and the occult. New souls appeared, new sources
> of creative life were discovered, new dawns were seen,
> feelings of decline and death were united with a feeling of
> awakening and with hope for the transformation of life.[1]

Commenting on the emergence of these new artistic tendencies
in 1899, Lev Tolstoy struck a more negative tone. 'It is wrong to
pay so little attention to decadents,' noted Tolstoy in his diary,
'it is the sickness of the time, and it deserves serious attention.'[2]
Though their attitudes clashed, both Berdiaev and Tolstoy noted a
broader cultural shift against the realist utilitarian aesthetics once
preached by revolutionary radicals like Nikolai Chernyshevskii
and parodied by Fyodor Dostoevsky in his novel *The Devils*. A new
generation of Russian artists and thinkers sought alternative forms
of knowledge and expression, a trend that inspired Russian émigré
Nikolai Otsup to name this era the 'Silver Age' in 1933. Intended to
highlight the mystical literary explorations of the early twentieth

century, this term has come to refer to the broader cultural trends of the time.[3]

On one hand, these new artistic tendencies were part of a larger European response to modernity, as artists responded to a rapidly changing world. As Erich Lippman has summarized,

> as the nineteenth century came to a close, both scientific and cultural factors caused Europeans to question the crude materialism as well as the revolutionary socialism to which much of the intelligentsia subscribed. The impacts of Neo-Kantianism and Nietzsche on philosophy, Freud on psychology, energeticism, atomic theory on physics, and other fin de siècle currents amounted to a broad 'revolt against positivism'.[4]

In Russia, the extreme divide between modernizing society and a moribund autocracy propelled cultural life against the narrowness of materialism to seek deeper, metaphysical truths, whether in art, music, politics or philosophy.

Supporters of the independent value of art in human life found voice in the activities of the St Petersburg-based World of Art group (1898–1904), spearheaded by the young impresario Sergei Diaghilev, and artists like Alexandre Benois and Dmitrii Filosofov, who sought to bring European artistic tendencies into conversation with the renewed interest in Russian folk art fostered at Savva Mamontov's Abramtsevo estate workshop and among Moscow's merchant class. At the same time, a renewed interest in revitalizing spirituality found expression in the 'new religious consciousness', a term coined by poet Dmitrii Merezhkovsky, and promoted in two years of meetings in which members of Russia's cultural elite and the Orthodox Church debated questions of theology, aesthetics and the human spirit with unprecedented openness. Though the Church ended its participation in 1903, Religious-Philosophical meetings sprang up in other Russian cities, including Moscow, where cultured society disputed questions of philosophy, spirituality, history and aesthetics.[5]

Perhaps the most influential Russian thinker underpinning this movement was philosopher Vladimir Soloviev, whose idea of artistic theurgy drew on Christian conceptions of both incarnation and transfiguration to claim that human artistic creativity not only transformed, but also spiritualized the material world through the incarnation of Beauty. Soloviev further claimed that music was the most 'direct or magical' expression of Beauty, the artistic form in which 'the deepest internal state connects us with the true essence of things and with the other world (or, if you like, with the "being in itself" of all that exists)'.[6] Assessments of music's unique, mystical power appeared frequently in Russian literary, philosophical and artistic journals. Building on Soloviev's ideas, Moscow musician Konstantin Eiges argued that 'music's central task was the transformation of the audience's relation to reality through the experience of Beauty.'[7] For Soloviev's followers in early twentieth-century Russia, the artist in general – and the composer in particular – was envisioned as a theurgist whose art should spiritualize the physical world.

Mikhail Vrubel, *The Demon Seated* (1890), an early example of Russian Symbolism in art.

The complex, questing nature of these intellectual and artistic tendencies found early expression in Mikhail Vrubel's 1890 Symbolist painting *Demon Seated*, painted at the home of Savva Mamontov. Inspired by Mikhail Lermontov's poem 'Demon', it depicts a demon whose kiss caused the death of his beloved sitting motionless and pensive on a mountaintop as sun suffuses the landscape in shades of red and rose, his emotional suffering leading to the transfiguration of the world around him. Describing the painting, Vrubel claimed 'the demon is not an evil spirit so much as a suffering and humiliated one. At the same time [the demon] is a mighty, great spirit.'[8] Hope, love and despair are ambiguously intertwined.

Perhaps because of his well-known unwillingness to engage in philosophical discussions around music in this hyper-philosophical era, Rachmaninoff's Russian career has typically been framed outside these contemporary cultural trends. Nevertheless, his openness to suggestions for his compositions (including his willingness to let others select poems) brought him, consciously or unconsciously, into contact with contemporary aesthetic visions. Moreover, reception of his music was invariably influenced by these larger trends. To rethink Rachmaninoff thus requires reinscribing him into the Silver Age in which most of his compositions were created and premiered, with its emphasis on artistic Beauty as a way of accessing higher spiritual truths or transfiguring reality itself.

Rachmaninoff emerged from the 1902–6 period as one of Silver Age Russia's greatest musicians, strongly influenced by both contemporary European trends and Russian traditions. Together with the Prelude in C-sharp minor, Rachmaninoff's ten op. 23 Preludes (dedicated, like the First Piano Concerto, to Siloti), with their singing lyricism, thick chords and lush harmonies, played a significant role in further defining the sound of the 'Russian piano school'. Indeed, Soviet music critic Boris Asafiev later stressed a

Russian national narrative for the preludes. Asafiev recounted how, after he performed the preludes for painter Ilya Repin, music critic Vladimir Stasov and writer Maxim Gorkii (three towering cultural figures for Soviet audiences), all three men were struck by the 'entirely Russian sources of [Rachmaninoff's] creativity'. While Gorkii declared simply 'How well [Rachmaninoff] listens to silence,' Stasov was reported to have heard in Rachmaninoff 'a very fresh, bright and supple talent, with a particular new-Moscow stamp' whose 'new bells' sounded 'from a new bell-tower'.[9] Repin heard in the D Major Prelude, op. 23, no. 4, 'a lake in spring overflow, a Russian flood'.[10] Asafiev's insistence on the '*entirely* Russian sources of [Rachmaninoff's] creativity' was overstated, however.[11] For contemporary critics, it was not the distinctive 'Russian' element of the preludes that attracted notice. Written 'with buoyant feeling, lively, interesting, with a shading of light sorrow, impeccable in their technical aspect',[12] they were most notable for their inherently pianistic writing, part of a European tradition.[13]

Indeed, the op. 23 preludes – like Rachmaninoff's op. 22 variations on a theme of Chopin – show the composer in an ongoing musical dialogue both with Chopin and with his illustrious forebear, J. S. Bach. Both these earlier composers had bequeathed a wealth of musical impressions to the world with their sets of keyboard preludes in all 24 keys. Rachmaninoff would ultimately follow suit, though the completion of his cycle of preludes over a large span of years suggests that they were not originally conceived as a complete cycle. Also unlike Bach and Chopin, Rachmaninoff did not arrange his preludes by a clear tonal schema, but rather according to alternating musical mood. As with both Bach and Chopin, however, Rachmaninoff eschewed descriptive titles for these works, favouring a more absolute form of musical expression. Chopin's influence is discernible in the nocturne-like style of no. 4 in D major, and the étude-like challenges presented by the ninth Prelude in E-flat minor, a 'technically cruel study in right-hand double fingerings' with distinct similarities to Chopin's study for double thirds in G-sharp minor, Étude, op. 25, no. 6.[14] Some of the preludes, like op. 23 no. 3, offer a self-conscious calque of tradition and modernity: here, as contemporary critic Grigorii Prokof'ev noted, 'the harmonic freedom of new music' was 'connected together with the dancing, dry rhythm of the [older style] menuet'.[15] Others, like the famous op. 23 no. 5 in G minor, demonstrate Rachmaninoff's vigorous use of rhythm and dramatic pianistic technique. Overall, the preludes offer more complicated harmonies and countermelodies than his earlier Prelude in C-sharp minor (op. 3, no. 2). Indeed, Prokof'ev noted that 'almost all the preludes are polyphonic, because the motifs or melodies contrapuntally connecting to the main melody, are too developed, too insistently presented,'[16] and later commentators have drawn a link between the various contrapuntal passages and Sergei Taneev's continued influence over his former protégé. Rachmaninoff considered op. 23 more musically successful than his Prelude in C-sharp minor, though 'the public has shown no disposition to share my belief.'[17]

Upon first hearing the restrained, reflective joy of the E-flat major Prelude, op. 23, no. 6, Rachmaninoff's former classmate Elena Gnesina commented to the composer that he must have been in a good mood when he wrote it. Rachmaninoff responded that it was inspired by the birth of his daughter, Irina, in May 1903.[18] Indeed, Liudmila Skalon recalled that when Rachmaninoff became a father, he remembered 'how few caresses and care he received from his parents, and promised himself that his children would always be surrounded by passionate love and attention'.[19] After his daughter was born, 'her every cry made him worry. He walked around her with an anxious appearance, not knowing how to help, scared to touch her, as if she were such a fragile object that a touch from his large hands might smash her to pieces.'[20]

His new family status made financial stability even more important, and in March 1904 he accepted an offer from Vladimir

Telyakovsky, Director of Imperial Theatres, of a conductorship at the Bolshoi Theatre in Moscow the following season.[21] For the next two seasons, Rachmaninoff was in charge of Russian repertoire at the Bolshoi, and conducted 89 performances of eleven different operas, including Tchaikovsky's *Eugene Onegin*, *Queen of Spades* and *Oprichnik*; Glinka's *Life for the Tsar*; Mussorgsky's *Boris Godunov*; Borodin's *Prince Igor*; Rubinstein's *Demon*; and a new performance of Rimskii-Korsakov's *Pan Voevoda*. During his tenure, Rachmaninoff improved the quality of orchestral performance, insisting on devotion to the score, bringing greater discipline to the orchestra, moving the conducting podium to make it more visible for the orchestra, and individually coaching singers in their parts.[22]

In 1902, Siloti had given Rachmaninoff and Natasha tickets to the Bayreuth Festival as a wedding gift, where they experienced the entire *Ring* cycle. While at Bayreuth, Rachmaninoff visited Franz Liszt's grave and met Cosima Wagner, Liszt's daughter and Wagner's widow.[23] Rachmaninoff's two operas, *Miserly Knight* (after Pushkin) and *Francesca da Rimini* (after Dante, with a text by Modeste Tchaikovsky, brother of the composer), written during his tenure at the Bolshoi, show the influence of Wagner's music dramas. They premiered on a single bill at the Bolshoi Theatre on 11 January 1906 under Rachmaninoff's baton. Commenting on the premiere, a Moscow critic noted that although *Miserly Knight* fulfilled the principles of musical drama, 'including the specific correspondence of music to words, which demands not a little thoughtful work from the composer', the music was ultimately not memorable. *Francesca*, argued the critic, while perhaps less effective in expressing the text, offered the listener more beautiful, memorable music, though here as well Rachmaninoff 'sometimes uses Wagnerian turns of harmony'.[24] Another contemporary critic tellingly observed in regard to *Miserly Knight* that the 'center of attention of the opera lies in the *orchestra*; here one must seek the aural embodiment of Pushkin's tragedy and here it is truly found,' and concluded that, without Isolde's death (a nod to Wagner's *Tristan und Isolde*), *Francesca* simply could not exist.[25] Rachmaninoff himself acknowledged that, unlike *Aleko*, which was 'written on the old-fashioned Italian model', *Francesca* was written 'in the style of the modern music drama'.[26]

Though Rachmaninoff tailored the parts of both the Baron (*Miserly Knight*) and Lanciotto Malatesta (*Francesca*) for Chaliapin's unique vocal and dramatic abilities, the singer refused to perform either of the works, which led for a time to a rift between the two friends. Though the reason for Chaliapin's refusal is unclear, it is possible that Rachmaninoff's Wagnerian-hued compositional approach did not appeal to the singer. *Miserly Knight* was the last of Pushkin's four 'little tragedies' to be set to music, after *Stone Guest* (set by Dargomyzhskii in 1866–9), *Mozart and Salieri* (set by Rimsky-Korsakov in 1890) and *Feast in a Time of Plague* (set by Cui in 1900). After a performance of *Miserly Knight* at Rimsky-Korsakov's apartment in St Petersburg, Chaliapin complained of the absence of an 'organic, unbreakable connection between the words and vocal melodies' such as that which existed in the operas of Dargomyzhskii and Mussorgskii. Rimsky-Korsakov similarly noted that 'the orchestra swallows almost all the artistic interest, and the vocal part, deprived of the orchestra, is unpersuasive; the ear misses melody.'[27] Such critiques highlight a continued tension between contemporary European trends and Kuchka traditions well represented in the other three Pushkin settings.

'Having once reached this important position [conductor of the Imperial Opera],' Rachmaninoff later reflected, 'the rest came easy.'[28] Indeed, limited operatic success notwithstanding, Rachmaninoff was generally recognized as one of Russia's young musical stars. The *Circle for Lovers of Russian Music* (1896–1912), organized by prominent Moscow lawyer Arkadii Kerzin (1856–1914) and his wife, amateur pianist Mariia Kerzina (1864–1926), to propagandize Russian chamber music, first featured Rachmaninoff's vocal and chamber music in 1903. After hearing him conduct Glinka's *Ivan Susanin* at the Bolshoi in 1904, the Kerzins engaged him to conduct their new series of symphonic concerts in January 1905.[29] Siloti's supportive presence in St Petersburg after his 1903 move to the capital also furthered Rachmaninoff's reputation, as Siloti regularly featured his cousin, both as composer and as pianist, in Petersburg concerts.[30] Recognition of Rachmaninoff as a leading contemporary Russian composer came from broader St Petersburg circles with the 1904 awarding of the Glinka prize, established by Beliaev, for his Second Piano Concerto – the first of five Glinka prizes Rachmaninoff received before 1917. Once divided into hostile 'national' (associated with St Petersburg) and 'Conservatory' (associated with Moscow) camps, by 1912 Petersburg-based music critic V. Karatygin asserted that formerly sharp divisions were disappearing; both Rimsky-Korsakov and Tchaikovsky's styles offered acceptable compositional models for a broadly conceived Russian music fully conversant with European musical life.[31]

Professional tension now came from within: Rachmaninoff struggled with the competing demands of being a successful conductor, composer and pianist. As Sophie Satin noted, 'when he is in the post of conductor, he denies his every talent to play or compose and quits playing for years at a time. When he plays piano, then he relates negatively to his conducting and throws off writing for a long time.'[32] In contrast, after a large amount of concertizing, Rachmaninoff would have the desire to sit and write. A January 1905 feature article in the *Russian Musical Newspaper* placed Rachmaninoff's 'broad multifaceted nature, his outstanding talent as a pianist, composer and conductor' firmly in the European tradition of earlier musicians Hans von Bulow, Franz Liszt and Anton Rubinstein.[33]

One week after this journalistic celebration of Rachmaninoff's success, the Bloody Sunday massacre in St Petersburg pushed the teetering autocratic regime into chaos. Strikes and protests spread across Russia, with peasant unrest and rebellion following in the wake of urban disorder. Educated society, students and workers came together to demand fundamental changes to Russia's political structure. At least on paper, the 1905 Revolution spelled an end to the autocratic power of the tsar, and introduced the beginnings of representative government and freedom of conscience. As Russia's cultural elites and intellectuals witnessed the effects of revolutionary violence, many spoke out for the need of a unifying identity that could reforge the country. For liberal philosopher Piotr Struve, this was not just the need for a new state structure, but the need 'to create absolute values among the people. This must be the task of a resurrected intelligentsia: to create ideal values for the nation and consequently infuse the state with life.'[34] The upheavals of 1905 did not mark a fundamental break with earlier cultural developments but created an even stronger sense of the task facing artists, musicians included.

Deeply aware of these dramatic social and political changes, Rachmaninoff's name featured alongside other leading Moscow musicians in a 3 February 1905 resolution:

'Only free art is true to life, the only free creation is joyful.' We musicians wholeheartedly affirm these wonderful words of our comrade-artists. If art wants to be truly mighty, truly holy, truly able to answer the deepest needs of the human spirit, nothing in the world apart from the internal self-definition of the artist and the basic demands of social life may limit its freedom. But when life is bound hand and foot, art cannot be free either, because feeling is only one part of life. When there is neither freedom of thought nor conscience in a country, neither freedom of word nor press, when every exciting artistic undertaking of the people is obstructed, then artistic creation also wastes away. Then the title of Free Artist sounds like a bitter joke. We are not Free Artists, but victims of the modern unnatural social legal conditions without rights, like all Russian citizens, and it is our conviction that there is only one escape from these conditions: Russia must, finally, embark on the path of fundamental reforms.[35]

Unrest spread through the Moscow and Petersburg conservatories also. In Petersburg, striking conservatory students demanded their classes be suspended until September 1905 (as had already happened in other institutions of higher education). When he sided with the students, Rimsky-Korsakov was unceremoniously fired by the leadership of the Russian Musical Society, an act condemned by leading representatives of the Russian musical world, including Rachmaninoff. In Moscow, Sergei Taneev resigned from his position at the Moscow Conservatory. Rubinstein's Russian Musical Society, once the means through which musicians hoped to gain social status, was critiqued for mirroring the form of the Russian autocracy – a style of governance increasingly viewed as outdated.[36] General discontent forced Vasilii Safonov's resignation from directorship of the Moscow Conservatory; by January 1906 rumours swirled after Ippolitov-Ivanov initially refused the post that it would be offered to Rachmaninoff.[37] Meanwhile, while the October 1905 Manifesto issued by the Tsar created some shared governance principles, this was insufficient for the more radical opponents of the regime. Moscow was paralysed by an uprising in December 1905 that left over 1,000 people dead.[38]

The combination of social unrest and professional obligations was detrimental to Rachmaninoff's compositional work. The director of Imperial Theatres Telyakovsky noted, '[Rachmaninoff] wants fame, but a different fame, that of a composer and a concert artist; he wants freedom and independence.'[39] In March 1906, Rachmaninoff and his family departed from Moscow for Italy. When Moscow music publisher Jurgenson wrote to him that 'the concert question this season is up in the air,' Rachmaninoff resigned from his position at the two girls' schools where he taught music, and withdrew from his concert commitments for the upcoming season.[40] His last task before departing was to compose a set of songs dedicated to the Kerzins, perhaps as partial compensation for withdrawing as conductor for their next season of concerts. These were simultaneously an exploration of new compositional directions and a practical solution to financial need. As he wrote to Morozov after he withdrew from the Kerzin Circle concerts, 'I'll have nothing left, either for soul or for pocket, and nothing in my pocket. Absolutely poor. There is only one way out of such a situation: to write.'[41] Written in little more than a month in the summer of 1906, a number of the poems set in op. 26 offer a 'philosophical force unusual in the earlier songs', and a compositional style often more declamatory than lyrical.[42] With Natasha preoccupied with her young family, Rachmaninoff turned to Mariia Kerzina for textual suggestions, and the shift in philosophical hue might be a reflection of her taste.[43]

It is possible, nonetheless, that the choice to set 'We Will Rest' (op. 26, no. 3), the closing monologue from Anton Chekhov's play *Uncle Vanya*, which promises peace after a life of labour and disappointment, was Rachmaninoff's own selection. Rachmaninoff had long admired Chekhov. His 1893 symphonic poem *The Crag* was inspired by Chekhov's short story 'Along the Way', though the link between Rachmaninoff's score and Chekhov's story was oblique, hinted at through a shared epigraph from a Lermontov poem rather than a direct dedication to Chekhov.[44] Rachmaninoff met Chekhov after a September 1898 concert held by singers from the Moscow Private Opera in Yalta, in which Rachmaninoff served as accompanist. Chekhov told Rachmaninoff after the concert: 'I looked at you the entire time, young man, you have a wonderful face – you will be a great person.'[45] This initial acquaintance blossomed into friendship, and when Rachmaninoff returned to Yalta in 1900, he again visited Chekhov. Even years later, shortly before his own death, Rachmaninoff declared Chekhov his favourite author, and his library at Villa Senar included Chekhov's complete works.[46]

In 1900, Konstantin Stanislavskii's Moscow Art Theatre (MAT), which had a close working relationship with Chekhov, was also visiting Yalta, and 'every day at a set time, all the actors and writers were at Chekhov's dacha, who offered the guests breakfast.'[47] The collaboration between Chekhov and Stanislavskii pioneered a new path in modern theatre. In his early career at the MAT, Stanislavskii developed a naturalistic performance model, which paid special attention to the psychological underpinnings and motivations of characters. In 1898, Stanislavskii's MAT had given the Moscow premiere of Chekhov's play *The Seagull*. In contrast to its limited success two years earlier in St Petersburg, Stanislavskii's innovative commitment to representing everyday life and psychological realism found a perfect pairing with Chekhov's understated text, and the production received universal acclaim. Chekhov's final three plays were all inspired and premiered by the MAT (*Uncle Vanya*, 1899; *Three Sisters*, 1901; *Cherry Orchard*, 1904). Rachmaninoff was a devotee, and attended the premiere of *The Cherry Orchard*, which was also a celebration of Chekhov's career.[48] In 1904, following Chekhov's suggestion, Stanislavskii turned his attention to the Belgian Symbolist Maurice Maeterlinck's play *The Bluebird*. This successful adaptation inspired one of Rachmaninoff's most enduring musical jokes – his 'Musical Telegram' from Dresden. Delivered by Chaliapin at an event celebrating the MAT's tenth anniversary, the musical setting combined the Orthodox chant motif of 'Many Years' with a playful polka by Il'ia Sats that was used in the MAT's production of *The Bluebird*. Delivered, or performed, by Chaliapin, it was a popular success; Rachmaninoff often had to perform this letter at future concerts by public demand.[49] The tour of Stanislavkii's theatre to Europe and America in 1922–3 was joyfully greeted by the composer, then in emigration, who hosted the entire company, both at his apartment at 33 Riverside Drive, Manhattan, and at his summer residence at Locust Point in the Bronx.[50]

Rachmaninoff's friendship with Chekhov was cut short by the writer's sudden death in 1904. Though Rachmaninoff later noted in conversation with Ivan and Vera Bunin that Chekhov 'did not understand music', two years after Chekhov's death he turned to the end of *Uncle Vanya* for one of his song texts.[51] It was unusual for Rachmaninoff to set an excerpt from a play rather than a poem, but Chekhov's heroes, trapped between the shadows of an old world crumbling around them and a new world they are unable (or unwilling) to embrace, spoke to moods and experiences familiar to Rachmaninoff. Sonia's final soliloquy, after the arrival and subsequent departure of her father and his new wife from the family estate for the city has thrown her quiet country life in disarray, eloquently mixes faith and resignation: seeing nothing more to hope for in this world but work, she desperately insists on a better existence in the world to come. The song demands a declamatory rather than lyrical delivery, and Rachmaninoff fretted over the need for a particular kind of performance. He was probably inspired in his desired delivery style by the acting of Vera Komissarzhevskaya, whom he met in St Petersburg at his cousin's house, where he was taken with her declamatory performance of Arensky's setting of Turgenev's poem 'How Fresh the Roses Were'.[52] The vocal line of 'We Will Rest' requires a similarly understated expressivity, while the piano eloquently expresses the emotion underlying the text. Indeed, in general the piano regularly serves to comment on deeper emotional moods in Rachmaninoff's songs.

While the turn to psychological depth and natural declamation pioneered in modern theatre found expression in 'We Will Rest', echoes of the 'new religious consciousness' enter obliquely through Rachmaninoff's setting of Dmitrii Merezhkhovskii's 1887 poem 'Christ is Risen!' Bernice Glatzer Rosenthal has argued that the new consciousness called for by Merezhkovskii and his associates 'was not a religion but the search for one'.[53] Though this poem pre-dates Merezhkovskii's involvement in the St Petersburg Religious-Philosophical Meetings, the sense of the unbridgeable divide between existing religion and the realities of a desanctified world are fully captured here. Rachmaninoff employs the same Easter chant that he had previously used in his First Piano Suite, but it appears here in an ironic form, contrasting the joy of the Easter message with the suffering of the world. As one commentator wrote:

> 'Christ is Risen' gives a strong, striking contrast of that which *is,* with that which eternal Love and Mercy has promised to us. A bright, jubilant hymn is sung in church . . . but [in] the world, life is full of tears and blood, everything is humiliated and disgraced, and if Love, Christ himself heard this Easter chant, he would weep before the crowd of worshippers![54]

Sceptical about how these innovations would be received, Rachmaninoff was not surprised by reports of a lacklustre reception at the 12 February 1907 premiere before a large audience, many of whom were drawn by the promise of hearing Rachmaninoff's latest composition.[55] Reception notwithstanding, their 1907 publication by Gutheil provided much-needed funds that helped Rachmaninoff support his family's sojourn in the relative quiet of Dresden, where he would spend the next three winters.[56]

5

Dresden

Just before Rachmaninoff departed for Moscow in April 1909 after
three winters in Dresden, he sat for a sketch by artist Robert Sterl.
The artist focused on the composer's profile, with edges blurring
into an undefined background. Rachmaninoff's serious, reserved
face and short-cropped hair bore little resemblance to the naive
long-haired youth who had once imagined no greater honour than,
like Tchaikovsky, to hear his own music performed in a restaurant.
It is the eyes that draw in the viewer: confident, calm yet deeply
human, they speak of an artist devoted to the quest to express his
eternal muse.

This sketch resulted from a complex skein of personal and
professional relationships developed during Rachmaninoff's years
in Dresden that defined the remainder of his musical career. In
1909, Rachmaninoff and Sterl had been acquainted for over a year;
their relationship would continue to be fostered by Sterl's repeated
trips to Russia.[1] Rachmaninoff was introduced to Sterl by Nikolai
Struve, a young musician the Rachmaninoffs befriended in the
winter of 1907–8. Born to a Russified German family in Moscow,
Struve had studied music composition at Dresden Conservatory
and, as Natasha later recalled, was 'well connected in Dresden
society'.[2] Through Struve, Rachmaninoff gained access to Dresden's
cultural scene. As one of Rachmaninoff's trusted inner circle of
friends, it was Struve who would accompany Rachmaninoff and
his family on his 1917 departure from Russia, helping to secure his

Robert Sterl,
1909 sketch of
Rachmaninoff.

initial living situation abroad. Struve's November 1920 death in an
elevator accident in Paris devastated the composer, who mourned
the loss of his 'true and only friend' deeply.[3]

While Struve facilitated the personal connection between
Sterl and Rachmaninoff, the sketch was commissioned by Sergei
Koussevitzky (1874–1951). Born to a poor Jewish family in Vyshnii
Volochek on the Volga, Koussevitzky's talent and strength
of character took him to Moscow, where, after being denied
admittance to the Moscow Conservatory, he enrolled in the
Moscow Philharmonic School as a stipend student of the Moscow
merchant millionaire K. Ushkov. This relationship also proved
definitive for Koussevitzky's later career as an impresario: after
divorcing his first wife, he married Ushkov's daughter Natalia

in 1905. He was a double-bass player in the orchestra during Rachmaninoff's tenure at the Bolshoi Theatre, and left Russia in 1905 to study conducting with the famed Arthur Nikisch in Berlin.

Koussevitzky conducted Rachmaninoff's Second Concerto (with Rachmaninoff as soloist) in Berlin and London in 1908. Most significant for the development of Russian music, however, were the conversations between the two men that, starting in 1906, envisioned a Moscow publishing house that could free composers from the exploitation of merchant publishers. Keenly aware of the financial struggle of ordinary orchestral musicians, Koussevitzky had published a scathing attack in the Russian press, accusing the Imperial Theatres of paying orchestral musicians too little to live on. Rachmaninoff meanwhile had won little financial gain from the worldwide fame of his Prelude in C-sharp minor due to lack of international copyright. Together they planned a new publishing house that would generously pay contemporary Russian composers for new works and protect the copyright status of Russian music in Europe. Boasting a board consisting of active composers and offering higher honorariums than other publishers, the Russian Music Publishers was registered in Berlin in 1909, thereby securing author and publishing rights in all of Western Europe and America. Administrative, financial and organizational aspects were handled by Koussevitzky and his wife, while artistic and ideological aspects were in the control of the board of which Rachmaninoff was the de facto head.[4] Born in Germany, Koussevitzky's idea for a new kind of publishing house would transform Moscow musical life.

Nikolai Struve was hired as the secretary for the new publishing house in Berlin, taking on the administrative, artistic and financial oversight. As part of these responsibilities, he travelled frequently between Moscow, Petersburg, Berlin and Leipzig.[5] As a way to increase publicity both for the new enterprise and for contemporary Russian music more broadly, Sterl was commissioned to create a number of sketches of leading figures in

Russian musical life; the 1909 sketch of Rachmaninoff was one of many postcards published by the Russian Music Publishers.

Perhaps most importantly, however, Sterl's sketch reflects the pan-European cultural milieu of the early twentieth century. As historian Philipp Ther has noted, 'Time not only seemed to pass ever faster, contemporary observers noted, but the clocks of different countries and cities increasingly ticked synchronously.'[6] Cultural trends circulated rapidly from one European country to the next, carried by 'countless performers [who] traveled from theater to theater and to various parts of the continent. Thanks to improvements in rail travel and shipping, cities all over Europe and overseas could now be reached more safely and in immeasurably greater comfort . . . It became common for composers and conductors to accept short- or long-term temporary engagements, even on the other side of the Atlantic.'[7] Rachmaninoff, along with compatriots Aleksandr Scriabin and Igor Stravinsky, participated in a general 'Europeanization' of culture that coexisted alongside nationalist tendencies that emphasized distinct national schools of music.

Over the course of three winters in Dresden (1906–9), Rachmaninoff rented a villa at Sidonienstrasse 6 near the main train station for his growing family (his younger daughter, Tatiana, was born on 21 July 1907 at Ivanovka, where they still spent their summers). The house, which stood in the middle of a garden, offered a retreat from both the professional responsibilities and social upheaval that had distracted him from compositional activity in Moscow.[8] As he wrote to his friend M. Slonov in November 1906, 'We live here like true hermits: we see no one, know no one, and don't go anywhere. I work a lot and feel very good.'[9] Such claims of isolation notwithstanding, Rachmaninoff's engagement with the European cultural scene in these years sparked considerable creative development. Thanks to the broad-ranging musical palette of Dresden Semper Opera conductor Ernst von Schuch (1846–1914), Italian, Czech, Polish and Russian operas featured alongside

Rachmaninoff and his wife, Natasha, in Dresden, Germany.

requisite (and stunning) productions of Wagner's operas on the Dresden stage. In 1906 Rachmaninoff thanked Schuch for the 'deep impression' left by a performance of *Der Meistersinger*.[10] Schuch also championed Germany's leading post-Wagnerian opera composer, Richard Strauss, and premiered his modernist operas, from *Salome* to *Elektra* to *Der Rosenkavalier*, in Dresden. In contrast to his eternalized reputation as an arch-conservative, Rachmaninoff relished the brilliant production of Strauss's chromatic, modernist *Salome* when he heard it in 1906. As he wrote to Morozov:

> I listened to the opera 'Salome' of R. Strauss and was in complete ecstasy. Mostly from the orchestra of course, but I liked much in the music itself, when it did not sound too false. And after all, Strauss is a very talented person. And his instrumentation

is amazing. When I, sitting in the theatre and having listened to all of 'Salome', imagined that right now, here they would play, for instance, my opera, then I became uncomfortable and ashamed somehow. I felt as if I had come into public naked.[11]

A certain scepticism towards modernism was nonetheless already apparent in his caveat that he liked the music 'when it did not sound too false', and this scepticism strengthened while in Dresden. Whereas Rachmaninoff gloried in Arthur Nikisch's conducting of Brahms's First Symphony and Tchaikovsky's Sixth Symphony at the Leipzig Gewandhaus, the music of Max Reger left him cold, while his response to Max Klinger's 'Beethoven' statue, first displayed in Vienna's Secession hall in 1902 before being moved to Leipzig, was noncommittal.[12] Any positive tone had vanished when he excoriated Strauss in a 1909 interview with *Musical America*:

Of Strauss [Rachmaninoff] likes only the earlier works, such as 'Don Juan', 'Tod und Verklärung', 'Till Eulenspiegel'. 'The later ones' as he puts it, 'are beneath contempt as music. "Ein Heldenleben" I find intolerable, and the same is true of "Salome". But even these fade into insignificance when compared with the stupendous ugliness of "Elektra" of which I understood not a note. To what end all this polyphonic wilderness when the result is incomprehensible? And when Strauss is not complex he is merely banal. As a young Russian colleague of mine wittily expressed it, "Strauss is a man who walks most of the time on his head, but who, when he walks on his feet, becomes uninteresting and commonplace."'[13]

If Strauss and Reger ultimately left Rachmaninoff cold, the image of Russian music pioneered in Paris by Sergei Diaghilev at this time also failed to resonate. An aspiring impresario and failed composer,

Diaghilev's success with the journal *World of Art* in St Petersburg led him to expand to art exhibitions, first of European art in Russia, and then, in 1906, an exhibition of Russian art in Paris at the Salon d'Automne. This was followed in 1907 by a series of music and dance performances billed as 'Evenings of Russian Music'. The organizing committee included Rimsky-Korsakov, Taneev, Glazunov and Rachmaninoff.

Though Rachmaninoff was on the planning committee and performed both his Second Concerto (as soloist) and his cantata *Spring* (as conductor), he was not particularly enthused about the event. Rachmaninoff's compositions, rooted in European Romanticism, did not fit easily with the modernist and exotic aesthetic that Diaghilev curated for Parisian audiences, and their collaboration did not recur. Diaghilev's artistic star continued to ascend, and the success of these concerts was followed by a performance of Mussorgsky's *Boris Godunov* in 1908. By 1909, Diaghilev had shifted his attention to ballet, culminating in the founding of the Ballets Russes and the legendary scandal surrounding the premiere of Igor Stravinsky's modernist *Rite of Spring* in Paris in 1913.

The Dresden years thus served as a hothouse in which Rachmaninoff devoted himself to furthering his mastery of composition and publicly defining his position vis-à-vis the rapidly developing trends of modernism in music and art. By November 1909, Rachmaninoff had distanced himself both from the modernist trends of Richard Strauss and Max Reger and from the modernist explorations of his Russian compatriots. Instead, he noted his redoubled admiration for Tchaikovsky and Wagner, positioning himself simultaneously as a Russian and European composer free of the excesses of modernist experimentation. He emphasized this in a 1909 interview:

'How infinitely more effective', [Rachmaninoff] exclaimed, 'is the counterpoint at the close of the second act [of *Meistersinger*] than all that of "Salome" and "Elektra", for in this case musical beauty is not recklessly cast to the winds!'[14]

Rachmaninoff thus defined a path for himself that emphasized the 'eternal' laws of music that would ultimately lead to him being labelled a conservative.

If we focus on Rachmaninoff's 'modernity' as a response to contemporary trends rather than on 'modernism' as a particular compositional style, however, each work from his Dresden period demonstrates deep connections to a larger European cultural milieu of which Russia was part. In Dresden, Rachmaninoff began to work on three different large-scale works: his Second Symphony, his First Piano Sonata and the opera *Monna Vanna*. Free of other demands on his time, Rachmaninoff re-evaluated his compositional style, expanding his conception of large-scale musical structures and, as David Cannata has noted, capitalizing 'on the possibilities inherent in late 19th-century, post-Wagnerian syntax', thereby fashioning 'larger and yet more tonally coherent musical constructions'.[15]

Philipp Ther has noted that the psychological drama embodied in Strauss's *Salome* and *Elektra* was part of a larger pan-European trend, both a continuation and rejection of Wagner's musical drama.[16] Though Rachmaninoff's musical language remained within the bounds of tonality, an interest in exploring inner reality, emotional and psychological states, already expressed in *Miserly Knight* and *Francesca,* was further developed in the unfinished *Monna Vanna*. Based on the eponymous play by Maeterlinck, *Monna Vanna* is a Symbolist historical drama set in fifteenth-century Italy that requires deep psychological penetration to uncover the hidden motivations of the heroine Monna Vanna, her husband Guido (military commander of Pisa) and the mysterious enemy Prinzivalle, who offers to lift his siege of Pisa if Monna Vanna will come to his camp dressed in nothing but a mantle. Like Rachmaninoff's earlier operas, Wagner's influence is evident. Its musical language is declamatory rather than lyrical, and this, together with Rachmaninoff's use of 'short leitmotifs to characterize personalities, psychological states and situations', makes it a natural continuation of his developing operatic style.[17] Though Rachmaninoff commented that he 'had rarely worked on anything with such pleasure', only the first act of *Monna Vanna* was completed. The opera's dead end was likely due to copyright: in 1908 Rachmaninoff asked Stanislavskii to approach Maeterlinck to secure German and Russian rights.[18] As it turned out, these had already been granted to composer Henry Février, meaning that *Monna Vanna*, if completed, could be performed in Russia, but not in Germany. Rachmaninoff ultimately abandoned the project, though it continued to hold a special place in his heart. He showed the work along with *The Bells* to fellow Russian musician Aleksandr Gedike in 1913, carried the manuscript with him out of Russia in 1917 and later brought it to Villa Senar.[19]

It is scarcely surprising that after the disaster of the First Symphony, Rachmaninoff was hesitant to return to the symphonic genre. While he discussed other compositions at some length with friends in Russia, work on his Second Symphony progressed in relative silence. Only when rumours flew in the Russian press in early 1907 that he had completed a second symphony did Rachmaninoff admit to both Morozov and Slonov that he had in fact finished a symphony in rough form.[20] He remained uncertain about the value of the composition, however, writing in April 1907, 'Symphonies! I cannot and more importantly, I don't want to write them. My second work is a somewhat better Symphony, but I still doubt its values.'[21] The work was premiered in January 1908 by Siloti in St Petersburg and at a concert of the Philharmonic Society in Moscow.[22] Its dedication to his former counterpoint instructor,

Sergei Taneev, may have been inspired by the fugue that appears in the second movement.[23]

Rachmaninoff returned to several compositional devices employed in the First Symphony, including a motto theme to connect the different sections of the symphony together (a compositional device used to great effect by Tchaikovsky in his late symphonies), and the *Dies Irae* chant that he had previously employed in the First Symphony. Indeed, though seldom featured in works between the First and Second Symphonies, the *Dies Irae* would increasingly dominate Rachmaninoff's compositional output in future years. Though subtly underpinning much of the Second Symphony, it appears most conspicuously in the scherzo-like second movement.[24]

While celebrating Rachmaninoff's talent, Moscow critic Grigorii Prokof'ev mourned what he considered the untimeliness of Rachmaninoff's recent turn towards large-scale works:

> The feverish speed of life, the rapid change of social moods, more or less influencing the spiritual life of the composer, contradict the broad ideas and forms of Rachmaninoff's recent works . . . Our time has lost the ability to create large forms in all realms of art. If someone writes a symphony today, it is only a student or scholarly task in the form of a classical or romantic symphony. And even in the best examples (the second symphony of Rachmaninoff), the composer does not have sufficient spiritual strength to pour living spirit into the mighty form of the symphony.[25]

Prokof'ev might well have found it apt that Rachmaninoff would wait almost twenty years before he wrote another symphony.

While the *Dies Irae* figures prominently in the Second Symphony, it completely permeates Rachmaninoff's final Dresden work, the *Isle of the Dead*. Completed in the first quarter of 1909 and dedicated to Nikolai Struve, it was inspired by Swiss artist Arnold Böcklin's painting of the same name. Although several potential islands have been suggested as the model for Böcklin's work, the painting seeks to evoke a mood rather than depict a specific physical location. For though Rachmaninoff noted in 1909 that 'a poem, a picture, something of a concrete nature at any rate, helps me immensely,'[26] he added in 1927:

> Real inspiration must come from within. If there is nothing within, nothing from outside can help. The best of poetry, the greatest of painting, the sublimest of nature cannot produce any worthwhile result if the divine spark of creative faculty is lacking within the artist.[27]

Böcklin completed at least five different versions of the painting between 1880 and 1886, with subtle differences between each. It is not known which version Rachmaninoff first saw, but it was merely a black-and-white reproduction of the painting. As the composer recounted in 1927:

> I first saw only a copy of the famous painting of Boeklin at Dresden. The massive architecture and mystic message of the painting made a marked impression on me, and the tone poem was the outcome. Later I saw the original painting in Berlin. I was not much moved by the coloring in the painting. If I had seen the original first, I might not have composed my Island of the Dead. I like the picture best in black and white.[28]

In fact, different accounts place Rachmaninoff's initial viewing of this reproduction in a number of cities – Dresden, Paris, Leipzig – an ambiguity that further emphasizes the popularity of Böcklin's painting. As Russian émigré novelist Vladimir Nabokov commented in his 1936 novel *Despair,* prints of it were 'found in

Arnold Böcklin, *Isle of the Dead*, 1880, oil on wood.

every Berlin home'.[29] Musical depictions were also common; in addition to Rachmaninoff's work, tone poems were written by Heinrich Schulz-Beuthen (1890), Andreas Hallén (1898), Dezso d'Antalffy (1907), Felix Woyrsch (1910), Fritz Lubrich (1913) and Max Reger (1913).

The *Dies Irae* motif provides the basis for the rocking accompaniment in 5/8 time, reminiscent of a boat being rowed across the water towards the island. Composed in ABA form, the middle section – symbolic of life in contrast to death – shifts to E-flat major, a world away from the A minor of the first section. In the midst of congratulating Leopold Stokowski in 1925 for his recent performance of the work, Rachmaninoff insisted that the E-flat major section must offer a distinct mood: 'It must be a great contrast to the rest; it must be performed more quickly, more nervously and emotionally: because that part is not connected with the image "picture", it is truly its own sort of addition to it and for this reason contrast is extremely necessary. First – death, then – life.'[30] The sharp transition recurs when this moment of 'life' is shattered by the return of the *Dies Irae* chant, this time in a straightforward citation by the clarinets echoed in other instruments: a reminder of the fleeting nature of human existence. The work ends as it begins, with the rocking 5/8 metre. An echo of the life motif, now transposed into minor, ends the piece on a dour note. Unlike Beethoven's greatest works, which end with an affirmation of the human spirit, a contemporary critic noted, Rachmaninoff's emphasis was on the darker reality underpinning human existence. Death, not life, was the end fate of all.[31]

As Sterl sketched Rachmaninoff's portrait in April 1909, Rachmaninoff regretted the forthcoming loss of solitude and devotion to composition he had found in Dresden. But both professional and personal commitments drew him back to Moscow. As he wrote to Taneev in March 1909:

> How wonderful it is here in Dresden, Sergei Ivanovich! If only you knew how sad I am that I am living here for the last winter! If you were to ask me why I don't stay here longer, I would answer that, first, the obligations of the Musical Society (as a member of the directorship) and Musical Society concerts call me to Moscow. Second, in relation to Dresden I have a contract – this time not with my agent, but with my wife, on the strength of which I promised to live abroad no more than three years. And these years have already passed.[32]

Dresden was a key moment in making connections, both personal and artistic, from which Rachmaninoff sought to build his mature style, inflected by broader European cultural influences. Personal and professional commitments drew him back to Moscow, where he would become a spokesman for the 'eternal' in music against the destructive impulses he perceived in unrestrained modernism.

6

The Twilight of Old Russia

An invisible photographer seems to have caught the composer
unaware. In his garden at Ivanovka, Rachmaninoff was fully
absorbed with his proofs for the Third Concerto when this postcard
image was captured in the summer of 1910 for music shops across
the empire. The peaceful scene is worlds removed from the
revolutionary flames that had swept through Russia in 1905. When
Rachmaninoff moved back to Moscow in 1909, dramatic social and
political changes were underway. Greater civil liberties, including
freedom of conscience, freedom of speech and inviolability of the
person, were granted by the October 1905 Manifesto. Nevertheless,
the Tsar had preserved extensive power, continued to be defined
as an 'autocrat', and had the ability to dissolve the newly formed
parliament (Duma) at his pleasure. Cultural life blossomed against
the backdrop of a troubled political system caught between
autocracy and democracy.

The photograph also excludes Rachmaninoff's anxiety before
his first trip to America and premiere of his Third Concerto. Lured
by America's lucrative concert scene, Rachmaninoff began work
on a new piano concerto immediately after the premiere of the *Isle
of the Dead*. Finished just one week before his departure for New
York, the composer practised the piano part on a dummy keyboard
on the boat to America in preparation for its 28 November 1909
premiere with the New York Symphony under the baton of Walter
Damrosch. He performed the concerto again on 16 January 1910

Сергѣй Рахманиновъ.
Sergei Rachmaninoff.

Rachmaninoff at Ivanovka, working on the proofs for his Third Symphony. Postcard published by Koussevitzky's Russian Music Publishers, *c.* 1910.

at Carnegie Hall with the New York Philharmonic conducted by Gustav Mahler. Bristling with technical challenges, the Third Concerto pushed the lush Romantic features familiar from his Second Concerto 'to the very limits of expressive and virtuoso possibility'.[1]

The Third Concerto evokes a Romantic, Russian-sounding character with its opening stepwise meandering melody reminiscent of Orthodox chant.[2] This apparent 'Russianness' together with its tight thematic unity and technical brilliance, written to showcase Rachmaninoff's own keyboard prowess, seems geared to appeal to an American audience already familiar with the Second Concerto. Though critics in America ranked the work's musical characteristics more highly than the Second Concerto, it did not receive the same immediate audience recognition. The work's dedicatee, fellow Russian piano virtuoso Josef Hoffman, never performed the work, and indeed, the thick chordal textures and stretches demanded of the performer seem better suited to Rachmaninoff's legendary hand span than Hoffman's small hands. Hoffman also critiqued the concerto's lack of form, which he likened derisively to a fantasia.[3] The weighty third movement is indeed unusual for a concerto, though Richard Taruskin notes that 'the formal eccentricities are what give the concerto its wonderfully special character.'[4] However, it was Vladimir Horowitz's 1928 championing of the work that brought it into the standard concert repertoire. As Rachmaninoff exclaimed upon hearing Horowitz's rendition, 'He swallowed it whole!'[5]

Nonetheless, the American tour was a professional and financial success. Rachmaninoff's varied skills as pianist, conductor and composer were equally on display as he criss-crossed the country between such cultural centres as Philadelphia, New York, Baltimore, Boston, Chicago and Cincinnati in a gruelling schedule of 26 performances (nineteen as soloist and seven as conductor) from 4 November 1909 to 31 January 1910.[6] His playing left an

indelible impression on audiences. Indeed, Rachmaninoff's eight
solo piano recitals included in this tour marked the first time he
had appeared alone on a concert programme. While not overly
enthralled by musical life in America, Rachmaninoff was struck
by the financial possibilities it offered, though he could scarcely
have imagined when he turned down conductorship of the Boston
Symphony that a revolution would bring him back to American
shores.

When Rachmaninoff premiered the Third Concerto in Russia,
responses were divided along ideological lines. St Petersburg critic
Viacheslav Karatygin sniffed derisively that the work was that of a
'traditionalist who lost touch with life, an epigon of Tchaikovsky,
who was too sentimental for the new age'.[7] In Moscow, Grigorii
Krein echoed this assessment, noting the 'monotonous wandering
of pianistic passages, based on unoriginal harmonies'.[8] Even a more
positive response from Grigorii Prokof'ev noted the composition's
relative harmonic conservatism, concluding, 'it has a freshness
of inspiration that doesn't aspire to the discovery of new paths.'[9]
Such critical responses reflected stylistic shifts in Russian musical
life. The 1908 death of Rimsky-Korsakov had marked the end of an
era. By 1910, Moscow music critic Iulii Engel asserted that Russian
music had undergone its own 'revolution'. While Rimsky-Korsakov's
generation had cultivated a distinctly national sound based on
their imagining of folk music, new composers such as Stravinsky,
Scriabin and Rachmaninoff offered a form of music equally
Russian and European.[10] Once decried by Cui as a 'decadent',
Rachmaninoff's style now seemed traditional when compared to
the modernist experimentations of Stravinsky and Scriabin.

Moscow cultural life consisted of small, interwoven circles
centred around concert halls, private societies (which often hosted
salons in the glittering mansions of Moscow's new elite), and
aesthetic and philosophical journals that pondered the place of art
in modern life alongside questions of Russia's place in the modern

world. 'Decadent' circles like the World of Art and the emerging Symbolist movement had previously rejected the utilitarian vision of art in favour of celebrating art both for its own sake and as a mystical path through which to gain insight into higher reality. In the aftermath of 1905, music's unique power to unite individuals seemed to suggest a path through which the social divisions that had torn apart the empire might be mended. The composer who would create this new music was envisioned as a contemporary Russian 'Orpheus', whose music could offer a path to a better future. The status granted to music in late imperial Russian discourse reached ever new heights, even as contemporaries disagreed over what this new music should sound like.[11] As Rachmaninoff's admirer Marietta Shaginian recalled:

> for 'cultured' society of the day, music was a part of daily life, not just as a form of entertainment, but as a problem of culture, which we discussed philosophically, not in its separate appearances (one or another composer, one or another work), but in its essence, in connection with its epoch, with world view, with fundamental questions of life and death . . . the state of music in a society was a measure of the relative health or sickness of society itself.[12]

Upon his return, Rachmaninoff found himself inadvertently swept up in this metaphysical discourse alongside former Zverev pupil and conservatory classmate Aleksandr Scriabin.

With their opposing aesthetic, philosophical and personal paths, Rachmaninoff and Scriabin symbolized opposing musical – and, by extension, philosophical – responses to modernity. Like Rachmaninoff, Scriabin's musical trajectory began with the piano; his early works evince a particular fondness for the music of Chopin, and Scriabin claimed that, in his youth, he had slept with a copy of Chopin's music under his pillow. By 1909, however,

Scriabin's compositional and philosophical development had veered into the realm of extreme harmonic experimentation and radical mysticism. Scriabin envisioned himself as a latter-day messiah whose creative genius was destined to bring about the end of the world through the composition of his *Mystery*, a final transcendent 'act' that would unify all humanity in a moment of universal ecstasy and usher in the apocalypse. Scriabin's supporters, while circumspect about his extreme philosophical claims, embraced his innovative harmonies and argued that a fundamentally new type of music was needed to express the experiences of modernity. Scriabin, who rejected tradition and embraced a dramatic utopian leap to the future – as the breathtaking speed of development of his compositional language demonstrated – modelled the emergence of a fundamentally *modern* Russian culture.[13]

For others, Rachmaninoff's tonal music offered a counterbalance to Scriabin's perceived excesses. Moscow Conservatory director Ippolitov-Ivanov lamented the decay of Russian music since Tchaikovsky and Rimsky-Korsakov's deaths. He attacked Scriabin and his imitators for 'decadence', arguing that, while they 'dream of opening new laws of harmony', their musical concoctions were 'not comprehensible' to ordinary ears. He hoped that Russian art would be saved by Rachmaninoff and other 'real Russians' who 'must and will shield their native art from all decadence and superficiality'.[14] At the same time, the dark harmonies and brooding nature of much of Rachmaninoff's music could be heard as echoing a widespread sense of melancholy, uprootedness and 'sickness' that seemed to define contemporary urban existence. A spate of 1910 suicides in Moscow were blamed on the effects of urban poverty and social upheaval.[15] Rachmaninoff's critics similarly lamented the dark 'public mood' affecting Russian society and Rachmaninoff's music alike: recurring descriptors included 'gloominess', 'melancholy' and 'pessimism'.[16]

Aleksandr Scriabin, Rachmaninoff's former classmate and fellow composer. Postcard published by Koussevitzky's Russian Music Publishers, c. 1910.

With his return to Moscow, Rachmaninoff took on a leading role in national musical life. He served as vice-president of the Imperial Russian Music Society until resigning in 1912 in protest over the antisemitic actions of a regional body against Matvei Presman, with whom Rachmaninoff had remained in friendly contact since their days together as Zverev's boarders.[17] A member of the editorial board of Koussevitzky's newly founded Russian Music Publishers, Rachmaninoff exerted aesthetic influence over the press's music publications. Within the board, a sharp aesthetic divide existed between the modernist-oriented Scriabin and

Koussevitzky on one hand, and Nikolai Medtner and Rachmaninoff on the other, who both shared a deep aversion to modernist experimentation. Scriabin's participation was short-lived due to a quarrel with Koussevitzky, but Rachmaninoff and Medtner 'led a sharp line of battle against modernism and decadence', and when conflicts arose over a particular composition, Rachmaninoff's opinion generally held sway.[18] Indeed, the board only approved publication of Stravinsky's *Petrushka* after Koussevitzky threatened to resign if the score was rejected. When a conflict of opinion arose over the question of publishing Sergei Prokofiev's *Scythian Suite,* Koussevitzky ultimately published the score not with the Russian Music Publishers, but under the auspices of the Gutheil firm, which he had purchased in 1915 and which functioned as an independent entity.[19]

Rachmaninoff with his daughters at Ivanovka.

In his personal life, Rachmaninoff enjoyed the stability brought by a successful professional career. In the spring of 1910, he was now co-owner of Ivanovka after his father-in-law Aleksandr Satin's retirement. He co-managed the estate with his brother-in-law Vladimir Satin: Satin oversaw the field harvest, while Rachmaninoff (who had a particular love of horses) oversaw the livestock.[20] In addition to offsetting both long-standing and recent financial losses out of his professional activities, Rachmaninoff invested in Ivanovka's maintenance and improvement. He indulged his love of modern technology, purchasing a massive tractor from an American catalogue that captured his imagination. That it was large enough to work not just his own small estate but half the district was irrelevant to the composer.[21]

The financial success of Rachmaninoff's American trip also allowed him to purchase his first automobile in 1912, a four-seat German sports car 'Lorelei':

Cars in Russia were relatively rare then. With the exception of Moscow, Petersburg and other large cities, there were very few in Russia. Bringing his new car to Ivanovka, Rachmaninoff made long trips with it, visiting neighbours in the region and family living 200–300 versts away. These trips were the best relaxation for Rachmaninoff, who so seldom rested in life generally. He always returned excited, happy and in good spirits. And the very process of driving in the 'big' roads of steppe fields of Russia with its spaciousness and breadth, and the joy with which his hospitable hosts welcomed him, the jokes and mutual teasing in relation to one or another new innovation or improvement in agriculture that he sometimes found in other [estates] – all this was the best distraction for Rachmaninoff from concerts, stage, compositional work.[22]

Rachmaninoff driving his car Lorelei with his cousin A. Trubnikova (right) and N. N. Lanting in the rear seat.

Soon discontent with the Lorelei's 'slow and poor acceleration',[23] by 1913 Rachmaninoff had replaced it with his first Mercedes.[24]

Nonetheless, by the time of his American tour, Rachmaninoff's personal life had been marred by recent loss. In 1909, both his grandmother Sofiia Butakova and his former romantic flame Vera Skalon died. In February 1910, actress Vera Komissarzhevskaia died suddenly of smallpox in Samarkand. Komissarzhevskaia had made her mark as an interpreter of contemporary heroines on the Petersburg stage, including Monna Vanna in Maeterlinck's eponymous play, Nora in Ibsen's *Doll's House*, Nina in Chekhov's *Seagull* and Sonia in *Uncle Vanya*. Rachmaninoff, both a personal acquaintance and a great admirer of her artistry, wrote the mournful song 'It Cannot Be!' to a poem by Apollon Maikov (written on the death of the poet's eleven-year-old daughter), which would later appear as op. 34, no. 7. A masterpiece of tone painting, both voice and piano move through the phases of grief, 'from agitated shock to tender lyricism to final reflection'.[25]

When not pondering improvements to Ivanovka or spending time with his young family, Rachmaninoff continued his deepening exploration of tonality in a series of short piano compositions. Both his op. 32 preludes (1910) and op. 33 *Études-Tableaux* (1911), while still ultimately dwelling within a tonal realm, demonstrate a new level of harmonic complexity and experimentation. Comparisons with Scriabin and Stravinsky have overshadowed Rachmaninoff's developmental trajectory, giving rise to the false impression that Rachmaninoff composed in an unchanging late Romantic style throughout his entire career. In fact, from about 1910, Rachmaninoff's compositional style grew increasingly concise, while simultaneously employing a more daring harmonic and chromatic language – the latter often used to set off moments of increased dramatic tension.[26] Indeed, while one might expect that Rachmaninoff's op. 32, which completes a cycle of preludes in each of the 24 major-minor keys, would be a triumphant reassertion of tonality, a number of the pieces are instead notable for extensively postponing a clearly defined tonic. This pushing against the boundaries of tonality is established in op. 32, no. 1, whose chromatic opening contains 'more altered and embellishing chords than any piece in op. 23', continues in nos 2, 3, 6 and 11, and became a common feature of his later piano music.[27]

Like op. 32, several of the op. 33 *Études-Tableaux* actively obscure tonality while remaining within an overarching tonal system. Op. 33, no. 2 in C major opens with a tonic chord omitting the third and meanders between major and minor for most of the piece; only in the closing bars is a perfect cadence offered, though even here it includes an A-flat out of place in the C major tonality. Rachmaninoff's increased emphasis on harmonic colour, chord quality and voice leading, together with his relative disregard for 'directional' harmonic movement, makes the set vaguely reminiscent of Debussy's *Preludes*, composed at approximately the same time.[28]

Indeed, both European and Russian influences are apparent in these piano works. The finale of op. 33, no. 8 seems to reference Chopin's G minor Ballade with its flourish of a G-minor scale, while Liszt's pianistic virtuosity hovers over both the op. 32 and op. 33 sets. An homage to Mussorgsky's piano cycle *Pictures at an Exhibition* can be discerned in op. 32: no. 2 cites 'The Old Castle', while the 'Promenade' theme is hinted at fleetingly in op. 32, no. 3. Rachmaninoff described op. 33, no. 6 (7) in E-flat major as 'a scene at a fair', and it does bear a similarity to the 'Hopak' from Mussorgsky's *Sorochintsky Market*, which Rachmaninoff later transcribed for piano solo in emigration.

In belatedly conceiving his op. 32 preludes as a unified cycle, Rachmaninoff consciously attempted both to create thematic unity within the cycle and to connect this set with his earlier preludes. The rhythmic motif of op. 32, no. 2 serves as a thematic basis for the entire piece and also recurs in all thirteen preludes, while a descending chromatic line similarly links a number of the preludes thematically.[29] But Rachmaninoff's most striking attempt to create cyclical unity across all his preludes is found in op. 32, no. 13 in D-flat major. The enharmonic parallel major of C-sharp minor, it incorporates several quotations from the original 1892 Prelude, as well as citations from several other op. 32 preludes, ultimately serving as a retrospective for all 24 preludes.[30]

Brevity notwithstanding, Rachmaninoff struggled with these works. He complained to Morozov in 1910, 'worst of all is the work on small piano pieces. I don't like this work and they are difficult for me. Neither beauty nor joy.'[31] Near the end of his life, he noted the particular difficulties that small-scale piano forms presented:

When I write a small piece for the piano, I am at the mercy of my thematic idea which must be presented concisely and without digression. In my concertos and symphonies, there are frequent times when I can write fluently. But every small piece I have produced is the result of great care and hard work. For, after all, to say what you have to say, and to say it briefly, lucidly, and without any circumlocution, is still the most difficult problem facing the creative artist. The artist learns, after long experience, that it is more difficult to be simple than to be complicated.[32]

Despite a reluctance to put his aesthetic values into philosophical language, Rachmaninoff's compositional style was governed by a sense of Apollonian balance. While recognizing the importance of contrast and dissonance in building tension, he argued that 'there must be light and shade. Discord emphasizes beauty, but incessant cacophony, carried to pitiless extremes, is never art and never can be.'[33] During his American tour, he pondered the genre of the piano prelude and the work of his illustrious forerunners, particularly Bach and Chopin. Reflections on the famous Prelude in C-sharp minor led to a deeper discussion of composition that echoed the Silver Age fascination with Beauty as a value in its own right. On his inspiration in composing the famed Prelude, he stated:

My only inspiration, aside from the pressing necessity to make some money, was the desire to create something beautiful and artistic. A prelude, in its very nature, is absolute music, and cannot with propriety be twisted into a tone-poem or a piece of musical impressionism . . . absolute music can suggest or induce a mood in the listener; but its primal function is to give intellectual pleasure by the beauty and variety of its form . . . The salient beauty [of Bach's preludes] will be missed if we try to discover in them the mood of the composer.[34]

Such a claim echoed Moscow music philosopher Konstantin Eiges, who argued that 'music is its own form of mystical being, whose goal is itself and whose meaning has no relation to experiences and feelings of people in concrete life.'[35] Indeed, Rachmaninoff was acquainted with Eiges and his mystical philosophy of music, which Eiges had read aloud at the home of their mutual friend, Nikita Morozov, though, in keeping with his typical reticence, Rachmaninoff offered no comment on its accuracy.[36]

Rich aural symbolism situates both op. 32 and 33 comfortably within Silver Age culture. While the title of the preludes evoked a sense of absolute music, the title of op. 33, 'Études-Tableaux', eschewed specific descriptive titles while encouraging the listener to imagine potential pictorial associations. Like the later op. 39 *Études-Tableaux*, these pieces are 'essentially a collection of character pieces which are designed to express particular moods or programmatic ideas'.[37] According to his acquaintance, pianist Benno Moiseiwitsch, the B minor Prelude (op. 32, no. 10) was inspired by Arnold Böcklin's painting *The Return* (1887).[38] Aspects of what were by now Rachmaninoff's typical style suggest extramusical associations: metrical unevenness reminiscent of chant melodies, imitation of bell-like sounds. The *Dies Irae*, a virtual trademark of the composer after the *Isle of the Dead*, can also be discerned in several of these pieces. Rather than direct references to physical reality or specific experiences, such recurring intertextual compositional devices are best understood within the definition of a 'symbol' offered in the first issue of the Moscow artistic-literary journal *The Golden Fleece* in 1906: 'Art is symbolic, for it carries in itself a symbol – the reflection of the Eternal in the temporal.'[39]

Together with his compositional activity, Rachmaninoff's concertizing activities both as conductor and performer continued in full force after his return to Moscow. Rachmaninoff's supporters crowded into concert halls and vestibules to catch a glimpse of their 'idol'.[40] At his house, the phone would often ring, and a hesitant female voice would ask to speak to Rachmaninoff. Like the Bechstein pianos upon which Rachmaninoff performed almost exclusively in Russia, his admirers followed him from city to city. His concerts were invariably 'accompanied by tremendous ovations', and after a performance 'the public often waited for him at the exit until late at night, not allowing him to leave, and the administration sometimes had to extract fanatical admirers who had managed to climb inside the large black rented carriage that usually carried Rachmaninoff home.'[41] One admirer, Thekla Russo, was awakened from a deep depression after the death of her husband by attending a Rachmaninoff concert. To express her thanks, she subsequently sent a bouquet of white lilacs to every concert, regardless of the time of year or the concert's location – an act of generosity that earned her the nickname 'White Lilac'.[42] Though she remained in Russia after 1917, she still managed to send lilacs to Rachmaninoff's performances in Paris. In another instance, as his relative recalled:

> Once at a concert of Serezha's one of his fans sat in the first rows. When he emerged and began to play, she came up to the floodlights and began to say something. It was impossible to continue the concert because the woman spoke at the top of her voice, addressing Serezha. Someone from the administration suggested she leave the hall, to which she declared that she would not leave the hall because she was Sergei Vasil'evich's bride. Thinking on his feet, he said that Sergei Vasil'evich was calling her and waiting for her in the green room. She quickly and decisively rushed out of the hall.[43]

Rachmaninoff's popularity was due in part to his particular blend of lyrical melody and rich harmonies, an emotional outpouring in which the audience sought an affirmation of their own personal experiences amid the flux of modernity. Similar to the gypsy songs, operettas and other forms of 'popular' entertainment derided by cultural elites, Rachmaninoff's music held immediate emotional appeal. For these audiences, the 'pessimism', 'melancholy' and 'darkness' of his music spoke to a shared sense of living through uncertain times. As M. L. Chelishcheva later recalled, Rachmaninoff's playing 'entered the soul of every person and in response caused those strings to sound which no other musician was able to touch'.[44]

Despite this acclaim, as the singer Antonina Nezhdanova later recalled, 'in those years of his full recognition [Rachmaninoff] was sick with self-doubt.'[45] In February 1912, he received a glowing letter from an anonymous admirer during a trip to Petersburg to conduct Tchaikovsky's *Queen of Spades*. It was fifteen years since the failure of his First Symphony, an anniversary of which he was undoubtedly keenly aware, suggested the young author who signed the letter simply as 'Re' – a reference to the musical note D.[46] Her letter struck a chord with the composer and sparked a productive intellectual exchange that continued until Rachmaninoff's 1917 departure from Russia. In the small cultural circles of late imperial Moscow, it was not long before Re's identity was revealed as Marietta Shaginian, a young poet of Armenian heritage. In keeping with the metaphysical discourse of the age, Shaginian heard in Rachmaninoff 'a creator needed by the people' who would 'oppose the discord and confusion in music, mysticism and theosophy' embodied in modernist music.[47] In Rachmaninoff's music, she believed, lay the spiritual salvation of Russia.

Rachmaninoff confided his hopes and fears to Shaginian: the traumas of his childhood (lack of familial love and beatings from Zverev), his fear of death and even greater fear of immortality, and his psychological sufferings after the failure of his First Symphony. There was at times a tongue-in-cheek quality to Rachmaninoff's letters to Shaginian:

I am afraid of everything: mice, rats, beetles, bulls, robbers, afraid when a strong wind blows and whistles in the chimney, when raindrops hit the window, I am afraid of the dark and so on. I don't love old attics and am even prepared to allow that house spirits are to be found (you are interested in all this!), otherwise it is difficult to understand why I am afraid even in the daytime, when I am alone at home.[48]

Shaginian sought to instil Rachmaninoff with a sense of purpose and mission. Horrified by the philosophical conclusions she drew from the modernist abandonment of tonality, she heard in Rachmaninoff's music a defence of the realm of the individual against modernity's dehumanizing force. In a lengthy philosophical article, she argued that Rachmaninoff's music offered 'not musical symbols, but the uncovering in music of symbols',[49] a reference to the widespread Silver Age vision of music (and art more

Marietta Shaginian, Rachmaninoff's admirer, friend and muse, 1920s.

broadly) as a path to transcendent knowledge. Shaginian heard in Rachmaninoff's music 'not just music that struggles to preserve its own art, but the human self that struggled to preserve its true nature'.[50] She argued that Rachmaninoff's devotion to clear rhythm showed the importance of his music to the contemporary age, drawing a direct parallel between the loss of rhythm 'not only in art (this is particularly notable in painting and in music), but in society and in daily life'.[51] Her analysis – turgid, idealistic and naive – appeared in the Symbolist journal *Works and Days*, edited by music critic, Nietzsche aficionado and Symbolist theorist Emilii Medtner, composer Nikolai Medtner's older brother.

Indeed, the Medtner family represented their own aesthetic faction within the hothouse culture of late imperial Moscow. Rachmaninoff and Nikolai Medtner had become friends in 1906 or 1908.[52] Nikolai Medtner was

unusually attractive as a personality: unboundedly modest, quiet, delicate, shy, like a young woman with a sensitive, elevated soul, he was truly 'a person not of this world', never capable in the practicalities of life. The simplest things seemed complex to him and he entered into their philosophical basis. Rachmaninoff loved Medtner and ranked him extraordinarily high as a composer although he played his works little and seldom.[53]

Theirs was an unlikely friendship: Nikolai Medtner constantly sought intellectual engagement and philosophical discussion of music, composition and aesthetics, which Rachmaninoff avoided, leading to frustration on both sides. Shaginian recalled an evening hosted by Rachmaninoff at which Medtner anticipated a deep philosophical conversation about musical creation; Rachmaninoff instead waxed eloquent on the correct manner of preparing Italian pasta.[54] Nonetheless, mutual respect and admiration consistently

Николай Метнеръ.
Nikolaus Medtner.

Nikolai Medtner, Rachmaninoff's contemporary, fellow composer and friend. Postcard published by Koussevitzky's Russian Music Publishers, *c.* 1910.

won out over short-term disagreements and differences in character, and Rachmaninoff remained Medtner's staunch ally and supporter throughout the difficult years of emigration.

In contrast, Rachmaninoff's attitude towards Nikolai Medtner's elder brother, Emilii, was fraught. Closely connected to Symbolist writers, an admirer of Goethe, Nietzsche, Wagner and 'Teutonic' culture, Emilii was also fanatically devoted to his younger brother, in whom he saw an embodiment of the true 'music of the future' devoid of decadent modernism. Emilii held a racialized vision of culture, decrying the impact of Jews on contemporary life and calling for a revival of the cultural values of Goethe. His attitude towards Rachmaninoff was tepid. At best, Emilii saw in Rachmaninoff a potential rival to his brother Nikolai's compositional success; at worst, a virtuoso performer who lacked intellectual depth. This distrust was mutual. In 1912, when Emilii Medtner sent Rachmaninoff a copy of his newly published book, *Modernism and Music*, the composer's response was limited to a brief note of thanks. When Shaginian recriminated him for failing to engage with Emilii's ideas, Rachmaninoff's response was unusually harsh. 'I do not like the book. From almost every line the shaved face of [Emilii] Medtner looms over me, as if to say: "Everything there that is said about music are trifles, and that is not the point. Most important is to look at me and be amazed at how 'smart' I am."'[55]

Nonetheless, an inspirational swirl of Symbolist ideas occupied Rachmaninoff in 1912. Shaginian's influence is first noticeable in the op. 34 songs, composed in June 1912, where her literary influence is combined with the sparser, declamatory style Rachmaninoff had explored in his previous song cycle. The first song, op. 34, no. 1, 'The Muse', on a poem by Pushkin, was dedicated to Shaginian. Pushkin's poem is an allegory of a young poet's relationship to his artistic muse. The young artist struggles to master his flute with his 'non-artful fingers'. His devotion is occasionally rewarded by his muse taking the flute in her own hands and performing marvels of which the boy can only dream. When Shaginian showed Rachmaninoff's song to Nikolai Medtner, he critiqued the setting and offered his own version, also dedicated to Shaginian. The two songs take different approaches to the problem of the relationship between music and words (and their underlying symbolism). Rachmaninoff offered a restrained, 'Apollonian' vision, in which Beauty is achieved through restraint, balance and structure. The song ends as it begins, with 'delicate piano figures and arpeggios', referencing the sound of the pipe in Phrygian mode (here E minor).[56] Medtner instead structured the song as a developmental arch, building to a virtuosic Dionysian celebration at the song's conclusion. Despite their differences, however, both settings stand as eternalized tributes to Shaginian, this young poet who believed passionately in music's ability to transform human existence.

In 1900, Symbolist poet Konstantin Balmont had exploded onto the Russian literary stage with his poetry collection *Burning Buildings*, which melded Nietzschean individualism and religious striving, a fame that he built upon with his 1903 collection *Let Us Be Like the Sun*. His formal innovations in poetry served as a model for younger contemporaries. His 1895 poem 'Wayward Wind', whose text sounds the Symbolist depths of 'world-extinguishing night and life-renewing day', appears in Rachmaninoff's op. 34, no. 4, evoking the 'wayward wind caught in flight' with a 'delicate, restrained piano accompaniment'.[57] Though tonally based, the piece moves from A minor to C major, with each key receiving equal emphasis, thereby undermining the concept of a single dominant key.[58] In op. 34, no. 8, Rachmaninoff returned to an old muse: Tchaikovsky. The poem 'Music', by Yakov Polonsky, offers a lyric celebrating the effect that music has on the poet's psyche, and Polonsky dedicated the poem to Tchaikovsky. Rachmaninoff followed suit, dedicating his song to 'P.Tch'. The song employs pared-down, minimalist piano textures and striking, unusual harmonies.[59]

Both Tchaikovsky and Balmont continued to occupy Rachmaninoff's mind through several months of hectic concert engagements. In December 1912, Rachmaninoff and his family left for Switzerland and ultimately Rome. There Rachmaninoff rented the same flat where Tchaikovsky had worked, spending his days writing at the same desk as his deceased mentor. The composition that drew his attention was based upon another Balmont text, suggested by an anonymous admirer in the summer of 1912: Balmont's translation of Edgar Allan Poe's poem 'The Bells'.[60] Whether it was the poetic evocation of bells (which already held a powerful place within the composer's aural imagination), or their symbolic use by Balmont/Poe to signify the different phases of life and ultimately death (the silver sleigh bells of youth, the golden bells of marriage, the bronze bells of fire alarm symbolizing the destruction of individual hopes and aspirations over the course of life, and finally the iron funeral bell), Rachmaninoff found ample inspiration for his op. 35, which he would later describe, together with the *All-Night Vigil*, as one of his favourite pieces.[61] As Rachmaninoff reflected in his unfinished 1931 reminiscences:

> If I have been at all successful in making bells vibrate with human emotion in my works, it is largely due to the fact that most of my life was lived amid vibrations of the bells of Moscow . . . in the drowsy quiet of a Roman afternoon, with Poe's verses before me, I heard the bell voices, and tried to set down on paper their lovely tones that seemed to express the varying shades of human experience. And there was the added stimulus of working in the room where Tchaikovsky had worked, of writing on the table where he had written.[62]

Similar to the moment of 'life' in *Isle of the Dead,* even the seemingly joyful wedding bells of the second movement contain an echo of the *Dies Irae* chant in the orchestral introduction, 'reminding listeners that even in the most joyful chapter, the inevitability of death lingers'.[63] In the fourth movement, which depicts the iron funeral bell, Rachmaninoff inscribed the same initials he used in the dedication of his op. 34, no. 8 song – 'P.Tch' (Piotr Tchaikovsky). Rather than a musical reference, David Cannata has suggested the reference is to Balmont's text, 'And we weep, remembering that we will also close our eyes.'[64] Bell-like cadences and the *Dies Irae* motif also suffused his Second Piano Sonata, similarly begun in Rome, though Rachmaninoff's work was cut short when his daughters fell ill with typhoid fever.

The Bells together with the Second Sonata, was premiered in the autumn of 1913. Konstantin Balmont, with his short stature and long, flowing hair, attended the Petersburg premiere and congratulated the composer after the concert, striking an incongruous image next to the lanky Rachmaninoff.[65] *The Bells* thus served to publicly associate Rachmaninoff with the Symbolist movement.

A presentiment of death struck Rachmaninoff before his departure for a concert tour in England in early 1914. When French pianist Raoul Stephane Pugno died alone in a Moscow hotel 'without friends or help', Rachmaninoff feared 'that some kind of catastrophe would happen to him in England, and he would not return home again'.[66] Though this was not the case, the outbreak of the First World War caused the cancellation of a performance of *The Bells* in Sheffield, England. By the time Rachmaninoff next appeared in London in 1922, he would be an exile from his homeland.

7

'All That Is Solid Melts into Air'

Rachmaninoff was summoned for military review in July 1914. His family wept at his departure from Ivanovka, terrified he would not return. As he later described to Siloti:

> In truth, it was even funny to me at first. What a bad soldier
> I would make! Be that as it may, I got into my car and drove
> to Tambov to enroll . . . When I was going to Tambov, almost
> the whole hundred versts I was overtaking carts full of reserve
> ranks travelling to the military inspection – dead-drunk, with
> some sort of beastly, wild mugs, greeting the passing cars with
> whoops, whistles, and throwing their hats at the car, yelling that
> they were going to get paid and so on. Then I was seized with
> horror, and at the same time there appeared the heavy awareness
> that, regardless of who we fought, we would not be the victors.[1]

Rachmaninoff would not be one of the 18 million Russian subjects mobilized by the autumn of 1917.[2] Nonetheless, the threat of military service hung over him until the summer of 1915, while the reality of wartime conditions threatened the family's financial stability. Concert engagements outside Russia were impossible, while concert activity within Russia was curtailed. Rachmaninoff obsessively read the newspapers, writing to Siloti in September 1914, 'We are all healthy, but our life, like everyone's now, is from paper to paper . . . I do almost nothing. Only sigh. And when, and how will it all end?'[3] Nonetheless, Rachmaninoff felt called to offer his own patriotic sacrifices. In October, together with Koussevitzky and with the support of the Moscow city council, Rachmaninoff organized a series of charity concerts in the provinces and capitals for wounded soldiers.[4] By January 1915, having given five benefit concerts and with one upcoming in Petrograd, he was exhausted.[5]

Wartime disruptions exacerbated social and political divisions. As Leonid Sabaneev later concluded, 'the root of all later events in Russia was in the war.'[6] Rachmaninoff's participation in the inherently pan-European nature of musical life clashed with the exclusionary nationalist sentiment stirred by the war. Works by German composers, once common, were politically suspect. In May 1915, a pogrom against Moscow's German business owners devastated Rachmaninoff's long-time publisher Gutheil, along with the music shops of Zimmerman, Diderichs, Lembert-Lekaine, Besselia, Detlaf, Eberle, Zeivang and Gross. As Vasilii Shirinskii later recalled, 'on the pavement, grand and upright pianos were lying around, smashed to smithereens. In front of the Conservatory building piles of torn-up music scores were lying around.'[7] In the aftermath of this violence, Gutheil sold his business to Koussevitzky and left the country, while Zimmerman, another long-established Moscow music publisher, moved his publishing house to Leipzig.[8]

As at previous moments of personal crisis, Rachmaninoff faced a creative roadblock. Seldom interested in the philosophical discussions of his colleagues before, Rachmaninoff now occasionally met for evening conversations with Anna and Nikolai Medtner, the Hegelian philosopher Ivan Il'in, Marietta Shaginian and Nikolai Struve. At one of these evening gatherings in February 1915, Rachmaninoff argued with Medtner 'over whether an "objective judgement of Beauty exists, that is, whether anything exists in which one can be entirely certain". While "touched to his very depths" by Medtner's belief in objective truth, Rachmaninoff admitted that he had "no such conviction himself",' concluding that all such judgements were subjective in nature.[9] The war had deeply shaken his aesthetic beliefs.

Despite Rachmaninoff's self-criticism, the war years were nonetheless fruitful for his compositional output. In December 1914, he contributed a short song to an interdisciplinary album published to raise money for war victims (other contributors included Symbolist poets Konstantin Balmont and Valerii Briusov, the painter Ilya Repin, artist Leonid Pasternak, writer Ivan Bunin, and composers Aleksandr Glazunov and Aleksandr Scriabin).[10] The brief text was taken from the Gospel of John, 15:13, 'Greater love hath no man than this, that he lay down his [life] for his friends.' This brief work offers 'a moving musical expression of the Church Slavonic text', with extensive chromaticism in the piano part, though its lack of resolution lends the piece an anxious, open-ended feeling.[11]

Far more substantial was Rachmaninoff's *All-Night Vigil* (op. 37). Composed in January 1915, this work has been described as 'crowning the tradition' of the New Russian Choral style pioneered by the late empire's greatest scholar of ancient Russian chant, the Moscow Conservatory teacher Stepan Smolenskii (1848–1909), to whom Rachmaninoff dedicated the work.[12] Already in his youth, Rachmaninoff had revered the stark beauty of Orthodox chant that resounded from churches and monasteries around his grandmother's Borisova estate and in St Petersburg. As an adult, Rachmaninoff would not infrequently wake at 7 a.m. and take a cab to the Andronikov monastery on the outskirts of Moscow where he would stand through an entire liturgy, 'listening to ancient strict singing' that was 'performed by monks in parallel fifths', which never failed to evoke a strong impression in him.[13] However, it was the aesthetic path pioneered by Smolenskii that found clearest expression in the *All-Night Vigil*.

Smolenskii's career carried him from the regional centre of Kazan to the directorship of the Moscow Synodal School of Church Music and simultaneously the position of Professor of Church

Music at the Moscow Conservatory, where he served from 1889 to 1901 before being appointed director of the Imperial Court Capella in St Petersburg (1901–3). A scholar who sought to reconstruct 'pure' Russian chant through his study of ancient manuscripts, Smolenskii in fact propagandized a new approach to church music. He called for the rejection of existing harmonizations by composers like Dmitrii Bortnianskii (1751–1825), whose music he considered to be overly influenced by Western musical style. Instead, Smolenskii encouraged the development of a 'natural' or 'Russian' treatment of ancient chant melodies. Though Smolenskii's actual compositional output was small, his ideas had an outsized effect, leading to the emergence of the 'New Direction' of Russian church music, pioneered by his students. Major stylistic devices used by New Direction composers drew equally from Smolenskii's research in chant and from his questionable assumption of the 'supposed kinship of old Russian chant and Russian folksong', giving rise to a compositional style that featured musical traits considered to be audibly 'Russian', including heptatonic harmonizations, heterophonic textures similar to folk music, and the omission of the leading tone.[14]

Rachmaninoff's interest in Orthodox music and the style forged by the New Direction had found expression in his earlier work the *Liturgy of St John Chrysostom* (1910). While Tchaikovsky's own eponymous composition provided a natural precedent, Rachmaninoff intended his setting to correct what he considered weaknesses in Tchaikovsky's earlier work. A series of letters to Aleksander Kastalsky, leading representative of the New Direction, demonstrates Rachmaninoff's search for an appropriate musical expression for the liturgy. In June 1910, he wrote to Kastalsky, 'I decided to trouble you specifically, because from all my heart I believe in and will strive to follow the path that you follow and to which you alone belong.'[15] Rachmaninoff's letter evinced a limited knowledge of the Orthodox liturgy:

I looked up psalm 102 and it is very long. Does one really have to set the entire thing? At the same time, to entirely not set it (like Tchaikovsky), I also consider undesirable. It seems to me necessary specifically here to place a number that separates the first 'Lord have mercy' from later ones. But can't some other, shorter words be used?[16]

Work on the *Liturgy* proceeded quickly, and it was complete by 31 July 1910. In a note to Morozov, he commented, 'I have thought of and striven a long time for the liturgy. I started work on it unexpectedly and was immediately absorbed, and so I finished very quickly. It is a long time since I have written anything with such pleasure (since "Monna Vanna").'[17] Contemporary reception of the liturgy was mixed, however, with a general sense that Rachmaninoff's compositional style retained a secular aspect not fully suiting a sacred work. Rachmaninoff himself became increasingly dissatisfied with the *Liturgy*, and in 1915 he turned his attention to the *All-Night Vigil*.[18]

The *All-Night Vigil* is a service that incorporates both vespers and matins. In contrast to the *Liturgy*, which was freely composed, Rachmaninoff's *Vigil* utilized both pre-existing chant melodies and newly composed melodies written in 'conscious counterfeit of chant'.[19] Aspects of the New Direction compositional approach (absence of progressive harmony, avoidance of leading notes and functional dissonance, multiple co-existing key structures and stepwise movement of voices) exist in conjunction with voice-leading and harmonies typical of Western common practice. As musicologist Marina Frolova-Walker has noted, Rachmaninoff 'freely uses the characteristic devices of the New Trend, and with equal freedom forsakes them'.[20] Assessing the *Vigil* from the perspective of Western tonality, Ellen Bakulina concludes:

though tonal in many respects, the harmonic language of the *Vigil* is situated on the boundaries of the tonal era on both chronological sides. It is both before and after tonality: before because it employs ancient musical material (the chant) and harmonic idioms proper to Russian church music outside of the so-called common-practice style; after because the work was composed in 1915, at a time when many composers had already begun to abandon the tonal system.[21]

Rachmaninoff's relatively free movement between Western tonal and New Direction styles is apparent in the opening movement. 'Come Let Us Worship' is based on a 'conscious counterfeit of chant'. It lacks 'any clear tonal center for the entire movement', associating it with New Direction practices even as the melody employs greater chromaticism than one would find in Orthodox chant.[22] In the second movement, 'Bless the Lord, O My Soul', Rachmaninoff follows three heptatonic-based harmonizations of the Greek chant melody, which offer an ancient-sounding colour, with a fourth appearance that employs a Western tonal-style setting made more striking through its contrast with the previous sections.[23] Also noteworthy is movement five, based on the Kievan chant 'Now Let Thy Servant Depart'. The only solo number in the *Vigil*, it is a 'singularly beautiful melody over pairs of rocking chords, which evoke a distant echo of *Dies irae*'.[24] The piece demands a tremendously low range for the basses, including a long stepwise descent stretching down an octave (B-flat to B-flat) at the end of the piece. Rachmaninoff associated this sound specifically with the Russian Orthodox chant tradition. When the choir director despaired of finding basses capable of the low notes in the score, the composer asserted that 'I know the voice of my countrymen.' It was this piece that Rachmaninoff wished to have played at his funeral.[25]

Though critics were divided about the work's 'ecclesiality', the *All-Night Vigil* succeeded as an expression of a unified Russian identity within the existential threat of military conflict.[26] Indeed, the 10 March 1915 premiere of the *Vigil* in Moscow was sold out, and an additional four performances in March–April attest to the work's popular success. Though performed without applause, as was expected at concerts of Orthodox liturgical music, the *Vigil* left a palpable impression on the audience.[27] Iurii Sakhnovskii concluded the work showed Rachmaninoff 'broadening his creative flight, seizing new realms of the spirit', and his movement beyond the 'narrow confines of lyrical pessimism that is so characteristic of the state of soul of our intelligentsia of the past decade' through his engagement with 'folk' art.[28] For Kastalsky, Rachmaninoff's 'loving and conscientious attitude towards our church chants' was of particular value.[29]

In April 1915 Rachmaninoff turned his attention to a composition that abandoned text entirely: the 'Vocalise', op. 34, no. 14, a stark setting for piano and voice whose wordless evocation of pure mood and emotion transcends its basis in the vocal exercise tradition. Earlier experimentation with vocalise passages had appeared in Rachmaninoff's songs such as 'Harvest of Sorrow' (op. 4, no. 5), in which a wordless passage laments the cruelty of fate, and 'The Soldier's Wife', (op. 8, no. 4), which evokes the tragic suffering of a soldier's wife whose husband has been selected for lifelong military service.[30] The 'Vocalise', like the *All-Night Vigil*, could be likened to a meditation on the impact of war, not least when the *Dies Irae* appears in rhythmic transformation in the opening melodic line.[31] The dedicatee who premiered the work, Antonina Nezhdanova, inspired Rachmaninoff as he refined the piece's phrasing and key. After the gifted soprano and Koussevitsky premiered the work in Moscow on 24 January 1916, it was initially published separately, then appended to Rachmaninoff's op. 34 songs in their 1922 publication.[32] Immediately successful for its evocative beauty, the 'Vocalise' has undergone countless adaptations, the earliest being Koussevitzky's arrangement for double-bass and piano and Rachmaninoff's own 1918 transcription for orchestra in E minor.

Amid his work on the 'Vocalise', Rachmaninoff was interrupted by news of Scriabin's sudden death from blood poisoning in April 1915. Professional divisions notwithstanding, Rachmaninoff had greatly admired Scriabin as a musician. Just two months later, in June 1915, the death of Sergei Taneev (who had reportedly caught cold at Scriabin's funeral) was a further blow. Rachmaninoff's subsequent decision to perform a series of concerts devoted to Scriabin's music was an important shift in a performance career that had previously highlighted his own compositions. Opponents and supporters alike critiqued Rachmaninoff's interpretation for lacking the ethereal character of Scriabin's performance style. 'After all, Sergei Vasil'evich, you performed well,' the young composer Sergei Prokofiev jabbed after a concert, to which Rachmaninoff replied curtly, 'did you expect anything else?'[33] Rachmaninoff's involvement with the newly formed Scriabin Society lapsed as his emphasis on Scriabin as a great composer conflicted with their more grandiose project to turn him into a prophet of Russia's future. Rachmaninoff never fulfilled an initial request from Scriabin's widow, Tatiana Schloezer, to participate in editing Scriabin's unfinished compositions, and he was excluded from the list of honorary society members.[34]

The weight of death and war frustrated Rachmaninoff's compositional energies. In June 1915, he wrote to Aleksandr Gol'denveizer, 'I will come to life, if my work moves forward. But now I am only half alive.'[35] By 3 August 1915, his wife Natasha noted that 'news from the theatre of war has seriously impacted Sergei Vasil'evich's mood. His work does not come together at all. The last while he even stopped working and only reads newspapers.'[36] Absorbed with fears of death, Rachmaninoff opened up to Shaginian in Rostov-on-Don after a November 1915 concert, asking:

with a very touching and uncertain tone, 'What is your
attitude to death, dear Re? Are you afraid of death?' . . .
'Earlier I was afraid of everything a little bit – thieves, bandits,
epidemics, but at least one could deal with them. But here
it is the uncertainty that is terrifying, if there is something
after life. Better to rot, to vanish, to cease to exist – but
if there is something beyond the grave, that is terrifying.
It is the uncertainty, the unknown that scares me!'[37]

When Shaginian (who would later become a Stalinist activist)
tried to reassure him that Christianity provided an answer to his
concerns, Rachmaninoff disagreed, telling her, 'I never wanted
personal immortality. A person wears out, grows old, becomes
tired of himself in his old age, though I have already become tired
of myself before old age. But there – if there is something – it is very
terrifying.' She then recounts: 'He suddenly grew pale, and even his
face appeared to tremble.'[38]

Though in the summer of 1915 Rachmaninoff began sketching
material he ultimately used in his Fourth Piano Concerto, it
was Symbolist poetry that helped to revive his compositional
productivity.[39] In June 1916, Shaginian met Rachmaninoff in the
spa town of Essentuki, where he had travelled on the advice of his
doctor to receive treatment for the recurring pain in his hands
and temple. She brought a notebook that included 26 poems by
'new' poets, and they analysed the texts together. In particular,
Symbolist Fedor Sologub's poem 'Dream' drew their attention, and
Shaginian envisioned an accompaniment with moving intervals
(from seconds to sixths or octaves) that conveyed a sense of 'wings
of sleep, hovering motionless in an airless space'.[40] Recovering from
this latest bout of uncertainty, Rachmaninoff set to work on the six
songs of op. 38, premiered in October 1916.[41]

Though the songs were published, however, they were dedicated
not to Shaginian but to a talented young singer named Nina

Koshetz.[42] Trained at the Moscow Conservatory, Koshetz's dramatic performance style inspired Koussevitzky to call her 'a Chaliapin in petticoats'.[43] Her musicality, beauty and vibrancy drew the attention of more than one composer. Rachmaninoff's professional collaboration with her began in February 1916 when they performed several of his songs in concert.[44] In June–July 1916, the two saw each other frequently in Kislovodsk, a spa town near Essentuki. Speculations on the romantic nature of their relationship ran rife. Perhaps the composer was seeking distraction from the wartime atmosphere or his own creative uncertainties; regardless, surviving correspondence from Rachmaninoff to Koshetz reveals a playful intimacy different from his serious tone with Shaginian:

> Much respected Nina Pavlovna, or dear Ninochka
> or Ninushka, or cunning Naina,
>
> So, you abandoned the Caucasus and now it has become peaceful and quiet there, undisturbed by your mischief and despair. The sick will begin to recover. I am happy for them! And it is better for you in Moscow. There, at least, there is supervision.[45]

Whatever the case, Rachmaninoff's wife was soon aware of her husband's interest in Koshetz. In a separate letter to the singer, appended to a letter from her husband, she wrote:

> I asked Serezha to tell me every detail about you. I learned that you often sang his songs, that he accompanied you, and that everyone liked your performance very much. This does not surprise me and makes me very happy. I am also interested in your performance in Tchaikovsky's operas. I definitely want to hear you perform in 'Onegin' or some other opera this winter, whichever you find most to your taste.[46]

Nina Koshetz, the dedicatee of Rachmaninoff's op. 38 songs, in 1916.

The op. 38 songs were premiered with Koshetz at a series of five concerts in October 1916–January 1917 in Moscow, Petrograd, Kharkov and Kiev, alongside some of Rachmaninoff's earlier songs. They received a relatively positive reception, with critics noting in them a 'new page in Rachmaninoff's creativity'.[47] Like the op. 39 *Études-Tableaux* that followed, the compositional language is harmonically experimental, possibly reflecting Rachmaninoff's recent immersion into Scriabin's early harmonic world. Nikolai Medtner observed that the playful no. 4, 'The Pied Piper' (poem by

V. Briusov), pensive no. 1, 'Night in my Garden' (poem by A. Blok), and the final piece, no. 6 (poem by K. Balmont), 'stand out for their freshness and remarkably touching beauty'.[48] Even Sergei Prokofiev noted in his diary that '[Rachmaninoff's] latest cycle, to words by new poets, is sheer delight,' and was inspired to compose his own op. 27 songs to poems by Anna Akhmatova.[49]

Any possible romantic interlude between Koshetz and Rachmaninoff had cooled by July 1917. When Prokofiev visited Koshetz in Kislovodsk, the singer informed him, 'of the two suns that bestowed their rays upon her she wished to be warmed not by the old, long-standing one, but the young one. As decoded: Rachmaninoff and Prokofiev.'[50] When the infatuated young Prokofiev escorted her on the train as far as the neighbouring spa town of Mineralnyi Vody during her return to Moscow, she commented to her attentive companion, 'Ah, Mineralnye Vody! It wasn't long ago that I myself was seeing someone off here!' According to Prokofiev, she then

> wrote on the photograph of herself she had given to me: 'Tout passe, tout casse, tout lasse.' [Everything passes, everything breaks, one tires of everything.] When I observed that it was strange to give such a promise on her own portrait, she replied that I had not understood her: a month ago this was where she had said goodbye to Rachmaninoff, but . . . everything passes.[51]

In emigration after the 1917 Revolution, Koshetz premiered the leading role in Prokofiev's *Love for Three Oranges* in Chicago in 1921, but her association with Rachmaninoff never revived. In 1921 she even wrote an irate letter accusing Rachmaninoff of 'destroying' her 'first steps in America' by failing to organize concerts on her behalf. This elicited an icy response from Rachmaninoff.[52]

Rachmaninoff's father died of a sudden heart attack in the summer of 1916, and the op. 39 *Études-Tableaux*, written in December–January 1917 (though not published until 1920), offer a predominantly dark, reflective mood, haunted by the *Dies Irae* chant and the familiar chiming of bells. Though the most obvious appearance of the *Dies Irae* is in op. 39, no. 2, where it serves as the basis for the recurring left-hand accompaniment, it has been discerned in veiled form in all but the final piece of the set.[53] Though Rachmaninoff seldom offered extra-musical associations for his short piano works, in 1930 he provided brief programme descriptions for five of his *Études-Tableaux* to Italian composer Ottorino Respighi, who was commissioned by Koussevitzky, by then conductor of the Boston Symphony Orchestra, to prepare an orchestral transcription. The images evoked included, in Rachmaninoff's own words, 'seagulls and water' (op. 39, no. 2, A minor), 'Little Red Riding Hood and the Wolf' (op. 39, no. 6, A minor), a scene at a Russian market (op. 33, no. 7, E-flat major), and 'an Eastern march' (op. 39, no. 9, D major).[54] Perhaps most telling in reference to the wartime context in which it was written, however, was op. 39, no. 7 (C minor), which Rachmaninoff described in the greatest detail:

> The main theme is a funeral march. The other theme represents choral singing. In the sections beginning with the sixteenth-note movement in C minor and a bit later in E-flat minor, I imagined a fine, incessant and hopeless little rain. The development of this movement reaches its climax in C minor, which is church bells. Finally the finale is the beginning theme or march.[55]

In fact, the piece seems to hint at a specific funeral – that of Scriabin. The *lamentoso* section, marked by a chromatic descending melody, is reminiscent of Scriabin's chromatic descending lines, such as the opening of his no. 9 'Black Mass' sonata.

Rachmaninoff's continued compositional evolution is evident in the op. 39 set. One contemporary reviewer noted that 'the soft lyricist begins to employ a more severe, concentrated, and deepened mode of expression.'[56] Another contemporary, Iulii Engel, wrote, 'A new feeling hangs suspended over the entire opus. In one the shadows are faint (2, A minor), in another, tempests gather force (6, A minor), in another a break can be seen through heavy, heavy clouds (5, E-flat minor), but nowhere do we find happiness, calm, ease.'[57] Intended to showcase Rachmaninoff's own masterful piano technique, op. 39 was composed on a larger scale than the op. 33 *Études-Tableaux*, and poses 'often dauntingly virtuoso technical demands'.[58] Rachmaninoff performed the entire set several times before his departure from Russia in December 1917, part of a gruelling concert schedule of 38 concerts as pianist, soloist (with orchestra) and conductor.[59]

In February 1917, social unrest exploded into revolution, bringing an end to three centuries of Romanov rule. Like many educated Russians, Rachmaninoff welcomed the advent of a new, democratic Russia. But as months passed, Rachmaninoff grew increasingly unnerved by the unravelling of Russian society. Growing peasant unrest and economic concerns predominated in a June 1917 letter to Siloti:

> I have spent almost everything I have earned in my life on my Ivanovka estate. About 120,000 rubles are now invested at Ivanovka. I consider this lost. Moreover, the conditions of life there are such that, after being there 3 weeks, I decided not to go back. I have about 30,000 left. This is of course something, especially if I am going to work and earn.[60]

He complained of his inability to concentrate on his work and hinted at the possibility of going abroad. His next letter was blunter concerning the situation at Ivanovka:

> I lived and suffered there three weeks and decided not to go back. Nothing can be either saved or fixed. I have a small amount

of money minus the bills on Ivanovka, so that if I just gave
Ivanovka to the citizens now, which occurred to me, the bills
would still remain with me. For this reason, I must work.[61]

In his unfinished memoirs dictated some years later, Rachmaninoff
was even more explicit regarding his experiences in those weeks.
Having arrived in early summer in the countryside, 'disorder',
'willful seizing of land' and 'excitement among the peasantry'
were noticeable. The Provisional Government delayed any
solution to the ongoing land crisis, and revolutionary activists
in the countryside agitated among the peasantry to seize land
for themselves. As the war effort faltered, peasant soldiers voted
with their feet, abandoning the military front to return home.
Amid this loss of state control, Rachmaninoff was visited by a
group of about one hundred peasants, including a 'Bolshevik
agitator' instigating the peasants to action. No violence came
out of the confrontation, and the agitator stormed off with a
small number of peasants. Rachmaninoff was then approached
by one of the older peasants he knew well, who suggested that
Rachmaninoff would be best served to abandon Ivanovka.[62] The
reminiscences of both Natasha and Sophie Satin corroborate this
account. After Rachmaninoff's departure, Sophie and her father
Aleksandr remained to oversee the crops. Sophie recalled 'rumour-
mongers' spreading unrest among the peasants, culminating
in several evening visits from older peasants who encouraged
her father to leave for his own safety. Fearing that her father, a
symbol of the gentry class, would be murdered, Sophie prevailed
upon him to leave for Moscow, while she remained to oversee the
harvest. In early September 1917, she also departed for Moscow
and never returned to Ivanovka, though rumours reached her of
the fate of their former home.[63]

There seems to be no direct evidence supporting an oft-repeated
legend of Rachmaninoff and his family fleeing Ivanovka, only to

watch it be burned to the ground by a revolutionary mob while they hid in the forest. Reality is far more tragic. Amid the social upheavals that followed the October 1917 Revolution, famine swept through the region, culminating in armed resistance to prevent state seizure of grain. While the main house at Ivanovka burned down at some point in 1918, the remaining buildings were most likely destroyed amid the Tambov rebellion from 1920 to 1921. Led by Aleksandr Antonov, a former member of the Socialist Revolutionary Party, this was one of the largest peasant uprisings against Soviet power in history, leading to the Bolshevik execution of at least 15,000 peasants and the displacement or imprisonment of many more. Indeed, according to the most definitive analysis of the revolt, the total losses among the population of Tambov region (executed, imprisoned or displaced) was approximately 240,000. By 1921, the region bore little resemblance to what Rachmaninoff would have known.[64]

On 28 July 1917, Marietta Shaginian met Rachmaninoff for the last time after a concert in Kislovodsk at which he accompanied Koshetz and conducted the French 'Marseillaise'. Rachmaninoff, she noted, was depressed with the path the revolution was taking, and feared for his estate, for the fate of his children and of being 'left poor'. He told her he was moving abroad with his entire family 'in expectation of a more peaceful time'. When she told him that leaving Russia now would mean 'to tear oneself away, to lose one's place in the world', Rachmaninoff listened patiently and kindly like always, but Shaginian sensed that he was already too far away for her words to have any resonance.[65] The two would never meet again.

In late August 1917, General Lavr Kornilov's forces staged an attempted military coup in Petrograd that the Provisional Government only suppressed with the aid of the Petrograd Soviet of Workers' and Soldiers' Deputies and its voluntary militia. Rachmaninoff's final Russian concert took place in Yalta on 5 September 1917. After performing the Liszt Concerto in E-flat major, he raced back to Moscow to devote himself to revising his First Piano Concerto.[66] On 25 October, on the eve of the Second Congress of Soviets, Vladimir Lenin's Bolshevik party seized power in Petrograd in the name of the Soviets of Workers', Soldiers' and Peasants' Deputies. Street fighting ensued in Moscow from 25 October to 3 November, leaving approximately 540 dead. Rachmaninoff completed revisions to his concerto amid this uncertainty, permanently cut off from Ivanovka and taking his turn at guard duty in his apartment building on Strastnoi Boulevard.[67]

Just three weeks after the Bolsheviks had seized power in Petrograd, Rachmaninoff accepted a concert tour in Sweden. On 23 December 1917, cheered by a meal of caviar and bread provided by Chaliapin, Rachmaninoff set off for Stockholm with his family and his friend Nikolai Struve. Travelling by train and then sledge

Robert Sterl, *Fireworks over the Kremlin*, with added text in German (bottom right): 'To Mr. Sergei Rachmaninoff, a friendly reminiscence on Easter 1914 in Moscow. Robert Sterl.'

across the Finnish frontier, he carried bare necessities, including only 2,000 rubles, the first act of his never-completed opera *Monna Vanna*, a musical sketchbook and the score to Rimsky-Korsakov's opera *Golden Cockerel*.[68]

Perhaps his most enduring baggage, however, was an already profound nostalgia for the world he remembered before the war. So very recently and yet so long ago, Struve and Rachmaninoff had hosted their mutual friend Robert Sterl for Easter in 1914. Sterl had immortalized their pleasant evening at the Moscow Kremlin in a painting dedicated to the composer. As Rachmaninoff later recounted:

> One of the unforgettable memories of the past days in
> Russia is Easter Night in the Kremlin. Whoever spent
> this Holy Night in Moscow, who went with thousands of
> pious people to the Kremlin, who felt the deep significance
> of the religious ceremonies, who saw the unique sight
> of the city from the Kremlin – he will always remember
> the beauty and mystic emotion of this night.[69]

By the time he received the painting from Sterl in 1922, Rachmaninoff saw in it an embodiment of his lost world: a muse that inspired him to 'think of my homeland with hope'.[70] Hung first in his New York apartment and later in Villa Senar, Sterl's visual representation of Moscow's Easter night captured the nostalgia already crystallizing in the composer's mind as he departed his homeland, never to return.

8

The Virtuoso in Emigration

Writing to Rachmaninoff from self-imposed exile in Paris in
April 1922, Symbolist poet Konstantin Balmont insisted that
they would meet again someday in Russia. Two years under the
new Communist regime had been both physically and spiritually
draining, and Balmont, together with his wife and daughter,
abandoned Soviet Russia in 1920. Life in French emigration was
scarcely easier, but his financial hardship was temporarily eased in
1922 by a gift of 400 francs from Rachmaninoff. Amid his thanks,
the poet mused:

> From my youngest days I loved you as a high artist of musical
> sounds. I remember your first performances in Moscow. I
> remember first the charming performance of your 'Isle [of
> the Dead]', then the many thunderous deafening sounds
> released by your charming fingers, and the cries of 'Bell-
> Players and Bells' [Balmont's title for *The Bells*] and much
> else that passes from soul to soul, from artist to artist.[1]

When three years later Balmont thanked Rachmaninoff for further
financial aid, however, the past had drifted further into memory:
'while I write to you, in spirit I am in Moscow, in an overfilled hall,
and your unerring fingers enchantingly scatter a diamond rain of
crystal harmonies.'[2] No longer did Balmont express hope for an
imminent return.

In the years after Rachmaninoff's departure, at least 1.5 million refugees fled or were expelled from the former Russian empire. Scattered in urban centres from Harbin to New York, with cultural focal points in Paris, Berlin and Prague, 'Russia Abroad' was a society united through bonds of culture. Stripped of their citizenship by Soviet governmental decree in 1921, it was in culture that these refugees sought to preserve 'an essential aspect of their national identity', even as hope for actual physical return dwindled.[3] Written in the final years of imperial grandeur and decline, Rachmaninoff's major compositional achievements took on new meaning for 'Russia Abroad' as an aural space of memory that captured some essence of a once-tangible world forever lost. As David Lowenthal has observed, 'memory transforms the past we have known into what we think it should have been. Selective recall eliminates undesired scenes, highlights favored ones, and makes them tidy and suitable.'[4] The world of 'Old Russia' that Rachmaninoff's music helped to construct for Russian émigrés after 1917 was just this: selective images of a world made timeless. Uncertainties, hopes and fears were glossed over in favour of an eternalized image more halcyon than it had ever been in reality.

A year after his flight from Russia, the *Boston Daily Globe* captured Rachmaninoff's tragic aura: '[Rachmaninoff] returns the same introspective figure, tall, a trifle more stooped, his close-cropped hair a little more gray, still indifferently awkward in walk with a suspicion of a limp, with the air of a man who had suffered, who had seen strange and terrible things, who could not yet escape memory of them.'[5] For the next 25 years, Rachmaninoff was the consummate performer of nostalgia. Svetlana Boym has noted that 'nostalgic manifestations are side effects of the teleology of progress' that are 'dependent on the modern conception of unrepeatable and irreversible time'.[6] As Rachmaninoff successfully negotiated the international musical stages of America and Europe to become one of the most celebrated pianists of his generation, his 'old-fashioned' compositional style projected the inherently modern contradictions of nostalgia to rapt audiences, striving pianists and the emerging recording industry.

Rachmaninoff had left Russia intent on finding a quiet place where he could support his family. When he found it impossible to locate a suitable living place in Stockholm, Struve suggested Copenhagen, where Irina was enrolled in the local school and Natasha had learned how to cook. Returning to Russia was not an option. As he wrote to an old conservatory acquaintance, Modest Altschuler, who had built a music career in the United States:

> Concerning Russia, even under Nicholas II I felt more freedom and breathed easier than now. The word 'freedom' sounds like a joke from present-day Russia. It was not in vain that we fled from there with the whole family to Denmark. In order to fill out the picture I shall add that I lost everything I had earned. My estate, into which I had put all my money right through the last days, has been destroyed. The money and securities I had in Russia were in a steel box that I turned over to my brother for safekeeping, but according to information received, these valuables have also been confiscated. It was impossible to bring them here, it was forbidden. And even if they had allowed it, neither our money nor the securities would be worth anything. Thus, in the material sense, I am a new-born babe. Poor as Job! They say they will return all this someday under a different setup. I don't believe it![7]

Based on a number of offers (including a two-year engagement with the Cincinnati Symphony and conductorship of the Boston Symphony), Rachmaninoff concluded that a virtuosic career in America held the greatest promise for re-establishing his financial security. He practised continually through the summer of 1918, broadening his concert repertoire beyond his own compositions

to feature works by Mozart, Beethoven, Schubert, Chopin and
Tchaikovsky. After fourteen concerts in September–October 1918
to test this new repertoire, he set sail with his family from Oslo to
America on 1 November 1918 without a single contract arranged.[8]
As the *Christian Science Monitor* soon reported, Rachmaninoff 'has
taken up his residence in America until political affairs in his own
country become settled'.[9]

As the family moved into the Sherry-Netherland Hotel on Fifth
Avenue in New York, Rachmaninoff's youngest daughter, Tatiana,
lightened the family's gloomy mood with her declaration 'we can
take comfort in the fact that we all love each other,' a comment her
father often recalled in later years.[10] Though street noise affected
everyone's sleep that first night, fears that revolutionary upheaval
had followed them was quelled the following morning with news
that the war had ended. Meanwhile, the arrival of one of Russia's
most recognized musical figures was warmly welcomed both 'by
the colony of Russian artists now in New York',[11] which included
Sergei Prokofiev and Josef Hofmann, and by the American musical
community. At his first recital on 8 December 1918 in Providence,
Rhode Island, Rachmaninoff played Mozart, Beethoven, Chopin
and Liszt, as well as (by request) his Prelude, op. 3, no. 2.

Though Rachmaninoff had managed his own professional life in
Russia, in America he relied on an agent and a full-time secretary to
navigate the challenges of English-language bureaucracy. He selected
Charles Ellis (who also managed the Boston Symphony Orchestra)
as his agent shortly after his arrival. In the early 1920s, Charles
Foley of Boston took over from Ellis, a business arrangement that
lasted until Foley's retirement in 1932. After this, Rachmaninoff was
represented by NBC. Rachmaninoff's first secretary was Dagmar
Rybner, a Danish-American musician who had corresponded
with the composer before the war. After her 1922 marriage, this
role was taken over by Evgenii Somoff, a Moscow acquaintance
of Rachmaninoff. Somoff had befriended Vladimir Satin when

Rachmaninoff poses for a photographer on 10 December 1918, two days after his first American concert.

both young men had been studying in Moscow University's maths department, he had spent several summer holidays at Ivanovka and Somoff had even served as the chauffeur for Rachmaninoff's wedding. After a career as an electrotechnical engineer in Brussels (brought to an end by the First World War), Somoff arrived in the United States in 1919, where he revived his friendship with Rachmaninoff. He ultimately served as Rachmaninoff's secretary until the Second World War, when he began to work in munitions in Ohio and California. Rachmaninoff then retained Nikolai Mandrovskii as his secretary until the composer's death in 1943.[12]

In America, Rachmaninoff forsook his once-preferred Bechstein piano for a Steinway. In their advertising campaign as the 'Instrument of the Immortals', Steinway listed Rachmaninoff's name alongside Franz Liszt, Anton Rubinstein and contemporaries Josef Hofmann and Arthur Rubinstein. As a perk of being a 'Steinway artist', Rachmaninoff was provided with his own special pianos, which were 'transported across the country at Steinway expense, complete with travelling tuner'.[13] Rachmaninoff's habit of travelling with three Steinways (including a brighter-toned instrument for orchestral concerts and a back-up instrument 'just in case'), as well as with his own tuner, made this no small expenditure.[14] Rachmaninoff's American fame rose alongside the successes of Steinway as a company. He remained loyal to Steinway, even when, due to financial difficulties exacerbated by the 1929 stock market crash, the company transferred the cost of piano and tuner transportation to the artist in the mid-1930s.[15]

In choosing to centre his career in America, Rachmaninoff also made a conscious choice to distance himself from Paris. The centre of the Russian cultural emigration, Paris was also the centre of musical modernism and the focal point for the musical career of fellow émigré Igor Stravinsky. Indeed, Rachmaninoff did not perform in continental Europe again until 1928, when his reputation as one of the greatest living pianists was well established

Rachmaninoff at his Steinway

STEINWAY
THE INSTRUMENT OF THE IMMORTALS

HALF a century ago Anton Rubinstein, like his immortal contemporaries, Wagner and Liszt, pronounced the Steinway "unrivaled" among pianos. Today Sergei Rachmaninoff, the greatest Russian pianist since Rubinstein, has said: "Only upon a Steinway can the works of the masters be played with full artistic justice." Generation after generation the Steinway stands supreme—the chosen piano of the masters—the immortal instrument of the Immortals of Music.

Steinway & Sons and their dealers have made it conveniently possible for music lovers to own a Steinway. Prices: $875 and up, plus freight at points distant from New York.

STEINWAY & SONS, Steinway Hall, 109 E. 14th St., New York

Advertisement for Steinway pianos featuring Rachmaninoff, 1922.

in America. In the American press, Rachmaninoff positioned himself as 'modern' but not 'destructive' in orientation, a savvy move that appealed to American audiences:

> By the word 'modern' I do not refer to the Futurists. I have little regard for those who divorce themselves from Melody and Harmony, for the sake of reveling in a kind of orgy of noise and discord for discord's sake. The Russian Futurists have turned their backs upon the simple songs of the common people of their native land, and it is probably because of this that they are forced, stilted, not natural in their musical expression.[16]

He particularly attacked his former colleague Scriabin, noting that he was 'not at all Russian' and concluded that 'Futurism is a kind of fungus growth, with little solidity, to withstand the test of time.'[17] In the post-1917 context, it is not difficult to see in this rejection of Futurism a rejection of political as well as cultural trends.

Accompanying this interview, which was featured in the October 1919 edition of *Etude* magazine, was a new composition, 'Fragment[s]', described as 'distinctive in style, indisputably Russian in its atmosphere, as modern as the latest works of Debussy or Ravel, and yet as logical in its harmonies as is characteristic of Rachmaninoff'. The melancholic, wandering 'Fragments', written shortly before Rachmaninoff left Russia, dwells in the same experimental realm as his op. 39 *Études-Tableaux*. It tests the bounds of tonality without stepping outside them. The *Etude* commentary concluded, 'all of Rachmaninoff's works, like those of Chopin and Schumann, which seemed so exotic and iconoclastic when they were first heard, have the element of earnestness and sincerity which distinguishes all "permanent" music.'[18] This rejection of 'modernism' became a marketing device for Rachmaninoff's American agents, who framed Rachmaninoff as a Romantic 'genius', a self-made man

Hear Rachmaninoff on the New Edison

NOW you can make a straightforward comparison and find out which is the best phonograph. Rachmaninoff himself, the great Russian pianist, gives you this opportunity.

He has made recordings for one of the standard talking-machines. We are very glad that he has done so. For now you can compare.

Your Edison dealer will gladly play Rachmaninoff's RE-CREATIONS on the New Edison for you. Watch for his announcements in your local newspaper. You *must* hear this most astonishing phonograph comparison,—before you buy your Christmas phonograph.

The photograph, from which this illus-

tration is reproduced, was taken in Mr. Rachmaninoff's home, in New York City. It shows the great Russian pianist playing the Second Hungarian Rhapsodie (*Liszt*), while the New Edison RE-CREATED his previous rendition of the same composition.

The three music experts who listened from behind the screen, were amazed and astounded at the absolute fidelity of the RE-CREATION to the artist's original performance. Once more, the New Edison's perfect Realism triumphed in the test of direct comparison.

Be sure to look for your Edison dealer's announcements. Hear Rachmaninoff on the New Edison. THOMAS A. EDISON, INC., Orange, N. J.

Edison
Rachmaninoff RE-CREATIONS
Now on Sale

No. 82169	Second Hungarian Rhapsodie (*Liszt*) Part 1
No. 82169	Second Hungarian Rhapsodie (*Liszt*) Part 2
No. 82170	Second Hungarian Rhapsodie (*Liszt*) Part 3
	(With Mr. Rachmaninoff's Cadenza)
No. 82170	Pastorale (*Scarlatti-Tausig*)
No. 82187	Prelude in C Sharp Minor, Op. 3 (*Rachmaninoff*)
No. 82187	Polka de W. R. (*Rachmaninoff*)
	(Others to be released later)

The NEW EDISON *"The Phonograph with a Soul"*

Edison advertisement from *The Etude* (December 1920).

and a composer whose music was appealing, 'not modern or dissonant'.[19]

Nostalgic image notwithstanding, Rachmaninoff's recording career demonstrates his fully modern persona. Even before leaving Russia, he had experimented with early recordings for the London pianola company Aeolian.[20] Rachmaninoff signed his first recording contract shortly after arriving in America and made his first Edison recording in April 1919.[21] The limitations of these early recordings were obvious: a piano was placed near a horn through which sound was funnelled to a diaphragm with a needle apparatus. The pianist was typically instructed to play as loudly as possible and to restrict use of the pedal when hands were close together. The maximum length of recording time available was 4.5 minutes, and longer works had to be spread out over a number of sides.[22]

Though a pioneer in the realm of sound recording, Edison was also far from a connoisseur of classical music (indeed, Edison called Rachmaninoff a 'pounder' rather than a pianist).[23] Rachmaninoff's perfectionism quickly came into conflict with Edison's methods. Though Edison made multiple takes of each piece, Rachmaninoff was not permitted to destroy unsatisfactory recordings, as a rare wrong note in his recording of Scarlatti-Tausig's *Pastorale* suggests. Perhaps for this reason, in April 1920 Rachmaninoff signed a five-year contract with the Victor company which included the stipulation that takes he rejected would be destroyed. Rachmaninoff was intrigued by the potential for perfection that recording offered. 'If once, twice or three times I do not play as well as I can,' he noted in 1931, 'it is possible to record and re-record, to destroy and remake until, at last, I am content with the result.'[24] Indeed, it took three years and eleven takes for Rachmaninoff to be satisfied with the first work he attempted to record for Victor – Chopin's Waltz in B minor, op. 69. Though this was perhaps extreme, multiple takes were not unusual: his own Prelude in G minor, op. 23, no. 5, required four takes, while the op. 32, no. 12 in G-sharp minor Prelude required five takes.[25]

The reproducing piano offered a promising alternative for wealthier customers in the early years of recording. First manufactured in Germany in 1904, these instruments were famed for their ability to 'reproduce' nuanced pre-recorded performances by contemporary stars, such as Ignacy Paderewski and Arthur Rubinstein, through 'elaborate pneumatic mechanisms for recreating the colors, phrasing, and pedaling of a recorded performance'.[26] Many pianists, Rachmaninoff included, considered this a good alternative to the lower-quality sound available in contemporary wax recordings. A 1927 advertisement by the American Piano Company (Ampico) touted that their reproducing piano offered listeners

> the actual playing of Rachmaninoff just as if he were personally at the keyboard . . . The same strings are vibrating identically as they vibrated when Rachmaninoff himself controlled them. This is not a copy or an imitation or a reproduction, but the actual playing of Rachmaninoff himself.[27]

Rachmaninoff made piano rolls for Ampico through 1929, when the company suffered financial distress as a result of the stock market crash. Six Ampico rolls contain repertoire never recorded for Edison or Victor: Rachmaninoff's arrangement of 'The Star-Spangled Banner' (which prefaced all American recitals immediately after the First World War); Anton Rubinstein, Barcarolle, op. 93, no. 5; Chopin, Scherzo in B-flat minor, op. 31; Chopin, Nocturne, op. 15, no. 1; Rachmaninoff, *Étude-Tableau* in B minor, op. 39, no. 4; and Rachmaninoff, *Elegie*, op. 3, no. 1.

What do these various early recordings reveal of Rachmaninoff's playing? First, they show that he tended to have a standard interpretation of a work; the repeated Edison takes demonstrate close similitude from one performance to another. This corroborates contemporary accounts of Rachmaninoff's 'analytic', 'stark' and 'literal' performance style. As the *Chicago Daily Tribune* reported, 'Rachmaninoff played as if his purpose were to exhibit to the audience just how each piece was composed; as if bent on holding a dissector's clinic rather than putting through the design.'[28] A reviewer for the *New York Times* agreed:

No performer who confronts the public does so with a
more complete lack of any artifice, either of manner or of
interpretation. The simple, clear, and on occasion gigantic lines
of his interpretations are stripped of every superfluous ornament
or excrescence of any kind. Mr. Rachmaninoff often disdains
soft and romantic colorings and then his playing has analogy to
sculpture rather than to a gorgeous canvas of the romantic era.[29]

Immediately striking for listeners today are what might seem to be
idiosyncratic, ahistorical interpretations. Rachmaninoff's robust
performance of Chopin's op. 42 waltz is surprisingly virtuosic
and fast, while his rendition of Mozart's 'Theme and Variations'
from the Sonata in A, K.331 is Romantic, full of *rubato* and
overemphasized cadences. Particularly striking is the breathtaking,
shimmering rendition of Liszt's *Hungarian Rhapsody*, no. 2, the
longest of the solo works recorded, with a new cadenza composed
by Rachmaninoff that recalls the harmonic world of op. 39 *Études-
Tableaux* more than Liszt.

With the development of superior electronic recording
technology after 1925, Rachmaninoff insisted on rerecording many
of his works: 'Formerly, the artist was haunted by the knowledge
that with him his music also must vanish into the unknown.
Yet today, he can leave behind him a faithful reproduction of
his art, an eloquent and imperishable testimony to his life's
achievement.'[30] Rachmaninoff's recordings allowed his playing to
reach an audience that stretched from San Francisco, California,
to Harbin, China, and even penetrate the airwaves of Moscow,
where his performance of his Second Concerto with Leopold
Stokowski and the Philadelphia Philharmonic was broadcast in
1939.[31] For many Russian émigrés, cut off from their homeland,
Rachmaninoff's recordings helped to create a shared sense of
community across Russia Abroad. Ivan Gumeniuk, former Higher
Secretary in imperial Russia's Foreign Affairs office, wrote from

Harbin to Rachmaninoff mourning the loss of their Russian homeland, particularly the ability to hear 'our outstanding artists, our pride, our glory'. While he and his wife had heard and seen Rachmaninoff perform in Russia, 'our children, who have lived in exile for 10 years, hear you only with the help of the gramophone.' Nonetheless, his older son Boris, aged sixteen, was a pianist who listened to Rachmaninoff's 'unforgettable playing' every day, an act that connected him with a Russian homeland he had never known. Gumeniuk asked the composer to send a signed photograph so that his children could 'see and hear you', a request that Rachmaninoff (or more likely his secretary Somoff) fulfilled.[32] Similarly, N. Dauge wrote from Riga in 1931 that he and his family 'constantly listen[ed]' to Rachmaninoff's recordings, thereby capturing a shared sense of Russian identity in exile.[33]

Rachmaninoff's accessible repertoire and virtuoso performance style also appealed to those for whom Russia had little significance. Personal letters poured in from across the globe attesting to the power of Rachmaninoff's music to speak directly to the individual. A conservatory student from State Park, South Carolina, wrote that the first movement of Rachmaninoff's Third Concerto 'wept for' her, expressing emotions to which she could not give voice.[34] A young Italian boy found in Rachmaninoff's music the only solace for his 'attacks of moral depression'.[35] Sixteen-year-old Ulya Shakir wrote from Istanbul to beg the composer to allow her to come and live with him: 'My parents don't have enough money for me to have my complete education. They want me to be a teacher or a business girl. I am only living for music. I don't want to be a famous person for money, just for music.'[36] Rachmaninoff's admirers craved his music and recordings for their intimate sense of personal connection amid the overwhelming flux of modernity.

Rachmaninoff's savvy self-fashioning was crowned with financial success. As David Cannata has observed: 'As if to whet the appetite of his audience, [Rachmaninoff] would first perform any new work, by which time he would have already initiated its publication. Only then did he set about recording the piece – reckoning that his disc or roll would be issued sometime around the publication of the music.'[37] In 1925, *Time* magazine published the income tax payments of one hundred famous Americans, among whom only two, Rachmaninoff and Paderewski, were musicians. Rachmaninoff paid $8,026 in income tax versus Babe Ruth's $3,432.[38]

This financial success allowed Rachmaninoff to provide aid to fellow Russian émigrés like Balmont as well as family and friends who had remained in the Soviet Union. By November 1922, he had sent at least $4,600 in aid to a range of institutions in Russia; in subsequent years he continued to send financial assistance to a number of 'pensioners', including his old friends Vladimir Vilshau and Nikita Morozov, as well as his mother.[39] Nor did his music vanish from the Soviet stage. Although politically charged organizations like the Russian Association of Proletarian Musicians (RAPM) attacked Rachmaninoff as the product of an outlived, bourgeois era, such critiques gained limited traction in 1920s Soviet life. There was no clearly defined musical style in which the values of the new revolutionary state were best expressed, and former colleagues in Russia expressed continued interest in Rachmaninoff's works. In 1927, Konstantin Eiges dedicated his Impromptu-Étude, op. 25, to Rachmaninoff.

Amid Rachmaninoff's financial success, however, dissatisfaction crept in. The strain of constant performance, exacerbated by Rachmaninoff's own exacting standards, was draining. He mourned to Somoff in 1923, 'Five years ago, when I began to play, I thought that I might achieve satisfaction in fortepiano performance; now I have been convinced that this is unrealizable.'[40] Similarly, in a letter to his friend Vilshau who remained in Moscow, he complained, 'honestly – the more I play, the more I see my own insufficiencies. I will probably never master [piano playing], and if I do, it will probably be on the eve of death.'[41] He was plagued by recurring health problems, particularly pain in his hands and head. Emotionally and physically exhausted from four years of extensive concerts, in 1922 Rachmaninoff began to spend summers in Europe, first in Dresden (where his in-laws the Satins took up residence after leaving Russia in 1921), and later Italy, France and finally Switzerland. These European sojourns provided important moments of rest and recuperation, and the chance to connect with friends and family whom the 1917 Revolution had similarly displaced. During summers in Europe, Rachmaninoff also sought to carve out time for composition.

Rachmaninoff's compositional 'silence' after leaving Russia has often been linked to separation from his homeland. This image was perhaps fed by the queries that poured in from his colleagues in Russia who, together with expressions of thanks for the financial and material support he sent to them, expressed curiosity and concern about his creative life 'in exile'. Rumours of Rachmaninoff's fame in America, homesickness for Russia, creative paralysis and even death swirled. In a 1921 letter, Marietta Shaginian asked him bluntly:

> Most important: You, they say, are now the idol of America. But do you write? Are you content? Has constant satisfaction from external triumphs silenced your holy internal dissatisfaction with yourself? Can you live without Russia? I want to say, your creative potential, can you create in a foreign land? And if so, then how and about what, and with what?[42]

Nor did Rachmaninoff counter this interpretation. Instead, in a 1922 letter to Vilshau detailing his life since leaving Russia, he stressed, 'In all this time I have not composed a single line. I only play piano and give many concerts.'[43]

Just as in earlier moments of apparent creative paralysis, however, the truth is more complex. Rachmaninoff's immediate energies were focused upon the rapid expansion of repertoire and perfection of his pianistic technique. Though he carried a notebook with him on tour, he found scant time to make use of it between performances. It was not until 1926 that his next major compositional work – the Fourth Piano Concerto – was completed. Nonetheless, if one includes the numerous piano transcriptions that Rachmaninoff prepared (in large part for his own performances), rather than silence, an 'unbroken chain of creativity' emerges.[44] The list includes 'The Star-Spangled Banner' (1918), J. S. Bach, Partita in E major (1933), Schubert, 'Wohin?' (1925), Bizet, 'Minuet' (1923), Mussorgsky, 'Hopak' (1923/4). Several of the transcriptions, including Schubert's 'Brooklet', Kreisler's 'Liebesleid' (1921) and 'Liebesfreud' (1925), and the new cadenza written for Liszt's Second Hungarian Rhapsody, are expansive enough to be considered commentaries on the earlier works rather than transcriptions.[45]

In 1924, Rachmaninoff's daughter Irina married Prince Piotr Wolkonsky, a Russian émigré painter with whom she became acquainted during family summers in France.[46] In the spring of 1925 Rachmaninoff sold the house he had purchased on Riverside Drive in New York 'which we all loved very much', probably with the intention of devoting more time to his family circle, which seemed to have shifted, with Irina's marriage, to France. Without a permanent home in America, he continued to rent summer homes in France for subsequent years. Then tragedy struck with Wolkonsky's sudden death on 12 August 1925, rumoured to be suicide, when Irina was more than eight months pregnant. Tragedy was followed by joy with the birth of Rachmaninoff's granddaughter Sophia. Just as he had been a caring father, he was a doting grandfather, writing to Sophie Satin shortly after Sophia's birth: 'I made the sign of the cross over her and kissed her several times because I already love her very much.'[47] In order to provide a means of financial support for Irina in these tragic circumstances,

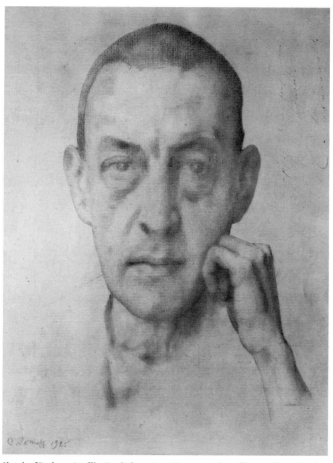

Sketch of Rachmaninoff by Symbolist painter Konstantin Somoff in 1925 (in emigration in Paris).

Rachmaninoff founded the publishing house TAIR in Paris (the name derived from his daughter's names, TAtiana and IRina). His daughters were to manage the company, which published both music scores and Russian-language books. From 1928 through 1933, all of Rachmaninoff's music was published through TAIR.[48]

Among the books published in TAIR's short existence was Nikolai Medtner's scathing attack on musical modernism, *Muse and Fashion* (1935). In this book, Rachmaninoff found a reflection of his own understanding of modernist compositional techniques as reflecting a deep sickness in contemporary society. In December 1934 he wrote to Medtner,

> I read [the first half] in one sitting and want to congratulate you for your accomplishment in a new field. There is so much interesting, witty and deep in it! And timely! Even if this sickness passes somehow which, I admit, I really don't see, the description of it will remain forever.[49]

Rachmaninoff's friendship with the Medtners had been rekindled after their 1921 departure from Russia. In an October 1921 letter, Rachmaninoff wrote to Medtner, 'You have brought me much joy with your new compositions, and I repeat what I told you still in Russia: in my opinion, you are the greatest composer of our time.'[50] Both men increasingly felt themselves to be isolated from contemporary musical trends. In December 1921, Rachmaninoff commiserated with his friend 'in relation to your isolation which you feel, I must say that I feel it here too . . . I see few genuine and honest musicians around! It seems that you alone remain.'[51] Rachmaninoff worked tirelessly to organize a concert tour to America for Medtner, and the two artists regularly saw each other during Rachmaninoff's summers in Europe. Indeed, their friendship reached a sufficient level of intimacy for Medtner to find himself the target of Rachmaninoff's teasing. During one of Medtner's visits to Rachmaninoff's rented summer home in France in 1928:

> One evening, when we were all sitting at the table, Irina stealthily crawled to Medtner's feet and pinned big yellow

bows to his shoes. There was an outburst of laughter when everybody got up and Medtner proceeded to the drawing-room unconscious of his strange footwear. Rachmaninoff laughed in his peculiar, silent way, but inwardly he was rocking with glee, so that he had to wipe the tears from his eyes.[52]

More sophisticated was Rachmaninoff's light-hearted imitation of a modernist musical composition in the style of compatriot Artur Lourie. A composer who had briefly enjoyed great influence in the Bolshevik government, Lourie had regularly harassed Medtner with the need to attend meetings organized by the new regime. When his relationship with the Bolshevik state deteriorated, Lourie made a new life for himself in Parisian emigration as an ardent supporter of Stravinsky and convert to Catholicism. Rachmaninoff knew Medtner's dislike for Lourie and his music, and used this in 1927 as the basis for a joke:

> [Rachmaninoff] appeared with a bundle of music and ceremoniously presented it to Nikolai Karlovich . . . he carefully watched [Medtner]'s facial expression, while he leafed through it. The astonishment of Nikolai Karlovich was great: fistfuls of notes printed without any order, without bar lines and in general without any thought . . . The dedication on the score, titled 'Formes en l'air' in Rachmaninoff's handwriting, read 'A memento to N. K. Medtner, from A. Lourie (?)' Nikolai Karlovich was stunned, but Sergei Vasil'evich was delighted that his joke was successful.[53]

Perhaps the most poignant sign of Rachmaninoff's admiration for Medtner was the dedication of his Fourth Piano Concerto, op. 40, to his younger compatriot. Transcriptions notwithstanding, the completion of a concerto was a dramatic step in Rachmaninoff's return to large-scale composition. Sketches suggest that he began work on the concerto as early as 1914 and continued to work on it in patchwork fashion in the early years in the United States. In January 1926, taking a deserved break from his gruelling concert schedule, he turned to work on it in earnest, finishing it in August. The concerto was premiered on 18 March 1927 by Leopold Stokowski and the Philadelphia Orchestra, with whom Rachmaninoff had developed a close working relationship.

Despite its roots in Russian life, as Martyn emphasizes, the Fourth Concerto 'was written mainly in New York, finished in Western Europe and the composer, as a sensitive and intelligent man, had naturally been affected by the sights and sounds of the country in which he had chiefly lived for several years. The romantic haze had gone forever.'[54] By 1924, Rachmaninoff had gained familiarity with jazz, even attending the premiere of Gershwin's *Rhapsody in Blue*. Stylistically the Fourth Concerto demonstrates Rachmaninoff's continued evolution to a sparser writing style and terser themes.[55]

It was perhaps the very success of Rachmaninoff's image in America as a representative of the lush era of Romanticism (still present in his Second and Third Concertos) that doomed his Fourth Concerto. Critics and audiences alike were generally dissatisfied. *New York Times* critic Olin Downes overlooked Rachmaninoff's shifting style, considering the work 'wholly characteristic in the melancholy and sensuousness of the singing themes, the alternation of vigorous, sometimes savage, rhythms, and the brilliant and exacting part for the piano'. Nonetheless he concluded dismissively, 'it cannot be said that the concerto, aside from the expertness of writing, offers very much that is fresh or distinguished.'[56] The *Washington Post*, while relatively positive, similarly framed the work around existing expectations, calling the first movement 'typically Rachmaninovian' with its 'spacious melodic designs'.[57]

The self-doubt that had nagged at Rachmaninoff since the failure of his First Symphony crept into a September 1926 letter to Medtner:

Before I left Dresden, I was sent the piano arrangement of my new Concerto. Looking at the length of it (110 pages), I was horrified! From cowardice I have not yet measured its time. Probably it will be performed like the *Ring*, several evenings in a row. And then I remembered my ranting to you on the topic of length and the necessity of concision, to cut and not be long-winded. I was shamed! It seems like the entire problem is in the third part. I piled up something there! I have already begun to search for cuts in my thoughts. I found one, but only 8 measures, and that is in the first part, whose length does not frighten me so much. Moreover, I noticed with my eyes that the orchestra is almost never silent, which I consider a great vice. It means it is not a concerto for piano, but a concerto for piano and orchestra. I also noticed that the theme of the second part is the same theme as the first part of Schumann's concerto. Why didn't you tell me this? There is still more that I noticed, but I won't write everything. I will confess before you at the end of October.[58]

While audiences and critics alike turned to Rachmaninoff in expectation of a nostalgic repetition of a former musical style, Medtner recognized the impossibility of this task. In his reply to Rachmaninoff, he wrote:

I personally don't experience the material excellence of our epoch with all our Steinways and automobiles as a spiritual plus. But at the same time, I cannot force myself to play on a Steinway like Mozart, just as, for example, you cannot drive in an automobile at a speed no faster than a post carriage of the good old times.[59]

But while Medtner remained content in his self-defined task to defend what he considered the eternal laws of music, Rachmaninoff's self-doubt caused him to take the critical reception of the Fourth

Concerto to heart, and he withdrew it for revisions before its 1928 publication. Continued critique led to Rachmaninoff issuing a final revision in 1941, which is probably the best-known version of the concerto today. With each revision, Rachmaninoff further thinned down the piano writing. In 2000, the Rachmaninoff estate released the original score so that today three versions of the concerto exist: 1926, 1927 and 1941. Critical reception has gradually turned to favour the original score as best capturing Rachmaninoff's true intent.[60]

Though the Three Russian Songs, op. 41, premiered alongside the Fourth Concerto in 1927, have sometimes been framed as a return to a 'Russian' sound in contrast to the terse angularity of the Fourth Concerto, in actuality both works are suffused with Rachmaninoff's émigré experiences. Each melody in op. 41 is presented in a straightforward choral setting, while the orchestral accompaniment offers 'commentary of an original and even, at moments, an introspective character', suggesting a reflective, nostalgic relationship to the original folk melodies.[61] Though choral, the op. 41 songs were inspired by solo performers.

While the first two songs were part of Fedor Chaliapin's repertoire, the third, 'Powder and Paint', was inspired by the folk performance style of Russian émigré performer Nadezhda Plevitskaia. Plevitskaia, born to a peasant family in the Kursk region of Russia, had been a leading performer of Russian folk song, and had even been nicknamed the 'Kursk Nightingale' by Tsar Nikolai II. Centred in Paris after the 1917 Revolution, she sold folk song nostalgia to Russian émigrés. Rachmaninoff had accompanied Plevitskaia at a Russian benefit concert in New York and insisted on immortalizing their collaboration in a private 1926 recording. Her performance, with its flirtatiousness and folksy sliding between notes, is matched by Rachmaninoff's subtle, playful accompaniment that comments upon, but doesn't overshadow, the voice. Two volumes of Plevitskaia's autobiography, steeped in an idealized image of Russian peasant life, were also printed by Rachmaninoff's press TAIR in the late 1920s. Plevitskaia would later be the subject of a scandalous unmasking in 1937 as a Soviet spy at a public trial in Paris, linked to the spectacular Soviet kidnapping and murder of a former White Army officer and the simultaneous disappearance of Plevitskaia's husband.[62]

Rachmaninoff felt particularly alienated from his homeland by 1930. Though their relationship had been burdened, the 1929 death of his mother in Novgorod severed one of his closest remaining familial ties.[63] Moreover, by 1929 the Soviet Union was gripped by the transformative rigour of Stalin's first Five-Year Plan, and news of the wanton destruction of churches by the Bolshevik regime was lambasted in the Russian émigré press. In a 1930 interview with the *Musical Times,* Rachmaninoff reflected on an unshakeable feeling of isolation from his homeland:

> There is, however, a burden which age perhaps is laying on my shoulders. Heavier than any other, it was unknown to me in my youth. It is that I have no country. I had to leave the land where I was born, where I passed my youth, where I struggled and suffered all the sorrows of the young, and where I finally achieved success. The whole world is open to me, and success awaits me everywhere. Only one place is closed to me, and that is my own country – Russia.[64]

Though always taciturn in discussing his own music and career, it was at this time that Rachmaninoff participated in several short-lived biographical collaborations. A list of dates, factual narrative and photographs compiled by his sister-in-law were sent to two long-time acquaintances who had expressed interest in preparing a biography: Richard Holt and Oskar von Riesemann. The collaboration with Holt never materialized, but Riesemann visited Rachmaninoff at the French estate he rented at Clairefontaine, near

Rambouillet, in the summer of 1930 for further discussion.[65]
A further, unfinished dictation of his memoirs was abandoned,
half-finished, after 1931.[66]

The only published book that emerged from this short-lived
exercise in nostalgia during the composer's lifetime, *Rachmaninoff's
Reminiscences, as told to Oscar Riesemann*, which Rachmaninoff
called 'boring and false in many aspects', appeared in 1934. Though
often cited in discussions of the composer, the book is as much
a reflection of Riesemann's own nostalgia for a lost world as an
account of Rachmaninoff's life. Born in Reval (present-day Tallinn),
Riesemann's acquaintance with Rachmaninoff dated back to
Moscow, where Riesemann had served as the music correspondent
for the *Moscow German Newspaper*.[67] Disturbed by inaccuracies
in the finished proofs, Rachmaninoff paid out of pocket for
numerous corrections. Only generosity to his financially strapped
acquaintance prevented him from demanding a change in the
book's title.

When Rachmaninoff visited Riesemann's home near Lucerne,
Switzerland, in the summer of 1930, however, the beauty of
landscapes the Rachmaninoffs had previously visited during their
honeymoon melded with longing for the lost world of Ivanovka.
On 7 September, Riesemann informed Rachmaninoff that nearby
Villa Carolina in Hertenstein was for sale. Against his wife and
daughters' protests, Rachmaninoff immediately bought the house
and grounds for 205,000 CHF. Drawing from the names SErgei and
NAtasha, he called his new home 'Villa Senar'.[68]

9

Villa Senar

At 8 p.m. on 10 April 1934, Sergei and Natasha Rachmaninoff drove through the gate of Villa Senar. 'Darkness notwithstanding, it made an imposing impression,' he noted in a letter to Somoff the next morning. 'I walk around the house and feel myself to be a millionaire. Yes, and not all millionaires find such a house.'[1] Villa Senar was a dramatic restructuring of the Hertenstein property. Not just the existing buildings, but 5 metres (16 ft) of rocky outcrop into Lake Lucerne were blasted away to create a park. A small gardener's house with integrated garage was completed by August 1931; three years later the large house was finished in modern Bauhaus style by Lucerne architects Alfred Möri and Karl-Friedrich Krebs. Rachmaninoff was deeply involved in planning the layout of both the gardens and the house, which boasted many state-of-the-art features, including three built-in bathrooms and a lift.[2]

Senar was designed with an eye for solitude, family life, nature (with large gardens and stunning views of Lake Lucerne and Mount Pilatus) and work. 'Cypresses, larches, silver firs, birches, maple trees, tulip trees, plum trees, rose hedges, weeping willows' were all carefully planned under Rachmaninoff's oversight, pointing to his continued love of nature awakened at Ivanovka.[3] A boat and bathing house with room for two motorboats allowed Rachmaninoff to indulge in his love of modern, fast motor vehicles. The main house was an austere cubic structure in which 'free, functional floor plans and facades, corner windows, fronts with glazing from floor to ceiling, flat roofs for sunbathers, and the orientation towards the view, the lake and the sun, all adhere to the principles and vocabulary of new objectivity.[4] A note of contrast to this modernist style was provided by historicist furnishings in some of the rooms.

The most spectacular room was Rachmaninoff's study. Three steps lower than the living area, the 3.73-metre (12 ft) ceiling offered spectacular acoustics. A large southwest corner window offered a stunning view of the park, Lake Lucerne and mountains beyond. In contrast, the mostly windowless western, northern and eastern walls provided an ideal workspace, with desk and piano positioned so that natural light would fall on Rachmaninoff's work while he faced inward, away from the distracting view. In honour of the composer's sixtieth birthday, Steinway presented Rachmaninoff with a custom-made instrument, a full metre longer than a regular grand. Music scores, organized alphabetically by composer, offered constant inspiration. Together with technical

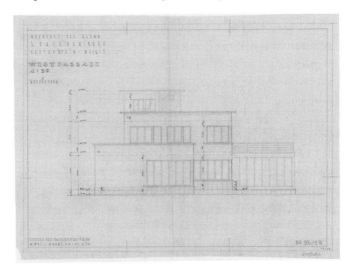

The approved final architectural design of Villa Senar, 1933.

Rachmaninoff at his desk in his study at Villa Senar.

studies by Clementi, Czerny and Moszkowski, keyboard scores
of Bach, Beethoven, Mozart, Chopin, Schumann, Schubert, Liszt
and Debussy testified to Rachmaninoff's preferred performance
repertoire. Other scores, such as Corelli's Violin Sonata, op. 5,
no. 12, and Paganini's 24 Caprices for Violin, point to Rachmaninoff's
compositional activities. More surprising is Dmitrii Shostakovich's
24 Preludes, op. 34 (published in Moscow in 1935), which suggests
Rachmaninoff's continued interest in Soviet musical developments.

The literature collection offers a similar glimpse into the
reading habits of a man deeply committed to Russian history
and culture. Pushkin, Tolstoy, Dostoevsky and Chekhov coexist
with Silver Age philosophers Vladimir Soloviev, Ivan Il'in, poets
Merezhkovsky and Balmont, and historian Kliuchevskii, whose
pre-revolutionary work *History of Russia* Rachmaninoff read on
the train amid American concert tours. Pre-revolutionary Russian
editions of Friedrich Nietzsche share space with émigré authors
such as Ivan Bunin and Soviet authors Ilf and Petrov.[5] Indeed, after
reading Ilf and Petrov's 1937 caricature of life in America (which

included a depiction of Rachmaninoff laughing and telling jokes before a concert, but 'assuming the great sorrow of a Russian exile on his face' when he stepped on stage), Rachmaninoff wrote delightedly to Vilshau:

> read [*One-Story America*] without fail, if you wish to become acquainted with and understand America. There is much interesting in the book. There are several funny lines about me. It is the only place where I found something was untrue![6]

The expenditure required for Villa Senar strained Rachmaninoff's financial reserves just as the 1929 stock market crash limited his recording ventures. From a high of 106 million in 1927, record sales had dropped to a mere 6 million by 1932. Phonograph sales similarly decreased from 987,000 to 40,000 per year. At the same time, 1929–33 was an era of rapid growth for radio, which further undermined record demand. By 1936, nearly 60 per cent of u.s. households owned a radio in comparison to 33 per cent at the end of the 1920s. In 1929, RCA (the Radio Corporation of America) acquired Victor Talking Machine, and after completing his contracted recordings in 1930, Rachmaninoff would not record another work until the popular success of his *Rhapsody on a Theme of Paganini* attracted RCA's interest in 1934.[7] Success of the *Rhapsody* notwithstanding, in 1937 Rachmaninoff had to 'bribe' RCA to record his Third Symphony by promising to record his First Piano Concerto to make up for revenue loss.[8] His suggestion of recording a series of his recital programmes was rejected.[9]

In January 1931, Rachmaninoff, Iwan Ostromislensky and Count Ilya Tolstoy co-signed a letter on behalf of the 'Circle of Russian Culture' that detailed abuses by the OGPU (Stalin's secret police) and condemned Bolshevik misrule. In retaliation, a 1931 article in the Soviet paper *Evening Moscow* attacked a recent Moscow performance of Rachmaninoff's *The Bells* as a surreptitious Orthodox liturgy attended by 'a very strange public' consisting of 'old men in long frocks', 'old women in old-fashioned scarves', and an assortment of 'long stockings' and 'lorgnettes' – all physical symbols of outlived, bourgeois culture that, the author made clear, were out of place in a modern worker's state.[10] Nonetheless, though British and American papers announced a boycott of Rachmaninoff's music by the Moscow and Leningrad Conservatories, such actions were short-lived.[11] While certain works (particularly the *All-Night Vigil* and *The Bells*) were ideologically suspect due to their liturgical and symbolic resonances, Soviet pianists and audiences proved unwilling to remove Rachmaninoff from their repertoire. Indeed, though no major state choir performed the *All-Night Vigil* between 1928 and the 1960s, in 1931 Soviet composer and ideologue Aleksandr Davidenko complained of radio broadcasts of workers' choirs performing the *Vigil*.[12]

Meanwhile, Rachmaninoff feared the prospect of another European conflagration. Writing to Sophie Satin from France in July 1931, Rachmaninoff noted:

> War is even possible, or communism, which is probably worse than war. And thinking about this, the purpose of work becomes unimportant and small. Will we really have to live through that horror again? I would like to die before that. Of course, it doesn't affect my children that way, or Natasha either. They, thank God, are calmer and cheer me. Today's papers were not so hopeless, but it is such a time that you wait for the paper all morning, and when it arrives you throw yourself upon it. It is just the same as in the accursed war time.[13]

Senar was intended as a space where Rachmaninoff could retreat from such concerns. But though the smaller guest house was completed in 1931, family pressures and health problems limited the time Rachmaninoff spent there. His daughters preferred life in Paris, and in 1932, Rachmaninoff's younger daughter, Tatiana, married Boris Conus, son of fellow Russian émigré Iulii Conus. Personal connections between the families were already well established: an accomplished violinist, Iulii had premiered Rachmaninoff's Second Piano Trio, op. 9, with the cellist Anatoly Brandukov in 1894. The Conus family had left Russia shortly after the 1917 Revolution, settling in Paris, where they were active in émigré musical life. Rachmaninoff's grandson, Alexandre, was born in 1933, strengthening Rachmaninoff's familial connections to France. Continued health problems also plagued Rachmaninoff, and he regularly spent time at sanatoriums to treat back pain and the arthritis developing in his hands.

Nonetheless, the purchase of Senar inspired a new burst of compositional energy. In 1931, Rachmaninoff commenced his last major work for piano solo, the op. 42 'Corelli Variations', based on a popular seventeenth-century dance tune, 'La Folia'. Though the melody had been used by Franz Liszt in his *Spanish Rhapsody* (which Rachmaninoff had performed), the reference to Corelli and the work's dedication to Austrian violinist Fritz Kreisler suggest that the composer's immediate inspiration was Corelli's Violin Sonata, op. 5, no. 12, also a set of variations on La Folia, written in 1700. Kreisler's sweet, expressive performance tone and repertoire choice, like Rachmaninoff's, tended towards a Romantic flavour, and Rachmaninoff admired Kreisler as the greatest living violinist. He had previously transcribed two of Kreisler's most popular pieces, 'Liebesleid' (1921) and 'Liebestraum' (1925).[14] Rachmaninoff and Kreisler also performed together frequently, though their recording of the Grieg C minor Sonata for piano and violin caused Kreisler's optimism to clash with Rachmaninoff's perfectionism, as Rachmaninoff insisted on rerecording the Grieg piece at least five times.[15]

Like the Fourth Piano Concerto, the lush Romanticism of Rachmaninoff's earlier period appears only sporadically in the

Rachmaninoff at Villa Senar with his grandchildren, Alexandre Conus and Princess Sophia Wolkonsky, in 1936.

'Corelli Variations'. Instead, the work offers a post-Romantic emphasis on concision, innovative rhythmic elements and a stripped-down expressive style reminiscent of Neoclassicism. Though the theme is strictly diatonic (in D minor), Rachmaninoff freely subjects the melody to transformation over twenty variations that range from lyrical to extremely chromatic. After thirteen variations of varying moods, the formal structure is interrupted by an 'intermezzo' with cadenza-like filigree. In conversation with his friend Alfred Swan, Rachmaninoff noted, 'All this mad running about is necessary in order to efface the theme.'[16] The end result is a shocking move from the original key of D minor to the distant key of D-flat major, presented in Variation xiv in chorale-like textures reminiscent of Bach. A lyrical variation 'in the form of an enchanting Rachmaninoff nocturne' follows in Variation xv, after which the piece shifts suddenly back to D minor in Variation xvi. Most surprising is the ending. Rather than a recapitulation of the theme, the coda offers a retrospective musing, in which the theme is displaced upward on the piano keyboard, offering a mysterious, retrospective closing.

Finished in June 1931, Rachmaninoff premiered the 'Variations' at a concert in Montreal. They received a lukewarm reception from audiences, as Rachmaninoff noted in a December 1931 letter to Medtner:

> I've played the Variations about fifteen times, but of these fifteen performances only one was good. The others were sloppy. I can't play my own compositions! And it's so boring! Not once have I played these in their entirety. I was guided by the coughing of the audience. Whenever the coughing would increase, I would skip the next variation. Whenever there was no coughing, I would play them in proper order. In one concert, I don't remember where – some small town – the coughing was so violent that I played only ten variations (out of twenty). My best record

was set in New York, where I played 18 variations. However,
I hope that *you* will play all of them, and won't 'cough'.[17]

Such comments hint at Rachmaninoff's tendency as a performer to
respond to audience mood.

One review of op. 42, by Iosef Iasser in the Russian-language
New York-based *New Russian Word*, caught Rachmaninoff's
attention. Iasser noted the fleeting presence of the *Dies Irae*, already
a mainstay in Rachmaninoff's earlier works. In a subsequent
meeting, Rachmaninoff informed Iasser of his intense interest in
this 'famous medieval chant' which 'is usually known to musicians
(including himself) only by its 2–3 beginning phrases'. Given his
lifelong interest in the chant, it is striking to note Rachmaninoff's
limited knowledge of the *Dies Irae,* which was limited to its
previous use by Romantic-era composers (Berlioz, Liszt, Saint-
Saens, Tchaikovsky and Mussorgsky) as a symbol of death.
Rachmaninoff's reported conclusion after speaking to Iasser was
even more striking:

> it seemed to [Rachmaninoff] unlikely that a chant used so
> often, and moreover its appearance at one time in the Russian
> Orthodox chant book, could be, as many thought, simply a result
> of an unspoken tradition among composers, who sometimes
> needed a characteristic and easily remembered requiem
> melody. – 'A custom – yes, it is – he noted uncertainly, but . . . it
> seems, that it is not just for that reason!' Having said this, Sergei
> Vasil'evich suddenly fell silent, without clarifying his thoughts.

From their discussion, Iasser concluded:

> first, that the *Dies Irae* melody had a deeply symbolic meaning
> for Rachmaninoff, already long answering some kind of thoughts
> haunting him particularly in his last years; and second, that he

internally felt some kind of extra-musical elements in it, perhaps a certain 'call' from the other world, and even seemed inclined to ascribe this unconscious sensation not to himself alone.[18]

Though Soviet musicologists critiqued Iasser for ascribing a false 'mysticism' to Rachmaninoff's creative impulse, recent scholarship has reconsidered Rachmaninoff's relationship to Symbolism.[19] A. V. Liakhovich has argued that the *Dies Irae* was for Rachmaninoff 'an example of a musical symbol in all the breadth and complexity of that concept', linking Rachmaninoff explicitly with the mystical questing of the Symbolist movement.[20] Indeed, the *Dies Irae* occupies a dominant place in all of Rachmaninoff's remaining works: the *Rhapsody*, Third Symphony and *Symphonic Dances*. The intertextual references between these compositions, as well as with his earlier compositions, suggests a consciousness of the larger symbolic potential of this motif.

Rachmaninoff's work on the *Rhapsody on a Theme of Paganini* (op. 43) coincided with his move into the 'Big House' at Senar at the end of July 1934. Indeed, Rachmaninoff referred to the 'Paginini Variations' as 'some small compensation for the many stupidities I allowed myself in building Senar'.[21] Like the 'Corelli Variations', the compositional style Rachmaninoff employed was not limited to Paganini's era: diverse influences range from Liszt to George Gershwin, whose *Rhapsody in Blue* might have inspired the composition's title. Like the opening theme in the 'Corelli Variations', Paganini's theme from the 24th violin caprice had inspired earlier composers, including Liszt and Brahms. Indeed, Brahms' piano variations on the same Paganini theme featured in Rachmaninoff's repertoire for his 1927/28 season. A further source of inspiration was Liszt's *Totentanz*, a virtuosic set of variations on the *Dies Irae* for piano and orchestra, that Rachmaninoff had conducted several times in Russia (and would perform himself in 1939). He had already begun exploring possibilities in the

Paganini theme sometime between 1923 and 1926, sketching out an inversion of Paganini's theme – literally turning the melody upside-down – that transformed Paganini's playful melody into an unabashedly Romantic melody whose basis in contrapuntal devices would almost certainly have made Sergei Taneev, his one-time instructor of counterpoint, proud. This ingenious manipulation earned worldwide fame in the eighteenth variation, often excerpted as a stand-alone piece.[22] The *Rhapsody* was a great success, and in January 1935, Rachmaninoff wrote to Sophie Satin with unusual satisfaction: 'I begin to get used to this and after each performance confidently await an expression of ecstasy.'[23]

For a composer so inspired by Tchaikovsky and aware of Stravinsky's success with the Ballets Russes, it is perhaps surprising that Rachmaninoff never wrote a ballet. In fact, he had raised the idea of a ballet in the midst of the First World War, approaching first Siloti and later Marietta Shaginian for plot suggestions.[24] Though he sketched some initial drafts for a ballet tentatively called *The Scythians*, any thought of a ballet vanished in the immediate strain after 1917. In 1914 he had expressed interest in collaborating with choreographer Mikhail Fokine, who had worked with Diaghilev's Ballets Russes on multiple works, including Stravinsky's ballets *The Firebird* and *Petrushka*. However, this idea did not bear fruit until 1935. After the 1917 Revolution, Fokine founded a ballet school in New York City (1921) and the American Ballet Company (1924); by the time Rachmaninoff approached him in 1935, Fokine was a choreographer of world renown.[25] Rachmaninoff's initial query inspired interest, but no tangible results. By the time Fokine visited Villa Senar in the summer of 1937, Rachmaninoff probably already had the *Rhapsody* in mind as suitable music for a ballet. Indeed, it was Rachmaninoff who proposed the subject of Paganini to Fokine:

Tonight I dreamed of a subject, and here is what came in my head: I give only the main characteristics, the

details are still in shadow for me. Might one not depict
the legend of Paganini, selling his soul to the Devil for
the perfection of art, and also for a woman?[26]

In its overall scope, the *Rhapsody* is structured around a conflict
between the Paganini melody and the *Dies Irae*. Rachmaninoff
associated the figure of Paganini with his theme, while 'all the
variations with the Dies Irae are the Devil.' After introducing
the playful Paganini melody in the first six variations, the *Dies
Irae* is clearly presented in Variation 7. Rachmaninoff described
Variations 8–10 as 'the development of the Devil [evil strength]'.
The entire middle sections (Variations 11–18) were deemed 'love
episodes', within which the minuet of Variation 12 is 'the first
appearance of the woman' and Variation 13 the first confession of
love between Paganini and the woman, culminating in the famous
18th Variation, whose lush Romantic melody (in D-flat major, like
the lyrical nocturne of the 'Corelli Variations') hearkened back
to Rachmaninoff's earlier compositional language. In Variation
19, Rachmaninoff explores the affinity between the two themes,
with the Paganini theme serving as background counterpoint to
the *Dies Irae*. According to Rachmaninoff, this variation could be
portrayed in the ballet as a 'dialogue with Paganini', and ultimately
the 'victory of Paganini's art, his diabolic *pizzicato*'. In the 23rd
Variation, by contrast, Paganini would be 'defeated', after which
the ballet would close with a final 'celebration of the victor' – the
Devil.[27]

Rachmaninoff's plot sketch notwithstanding, it is open to
question which theme is victorious at the end of the *Rhapsody*.
Though the *Dies Irae* blasts out with a powerful statement near
the end of the piece, the final bars undermine this strength with
an almost whimsical gesture back to the work's opening Paganini
motif. In 1939, Fokine's adaptation of the work into the ballet
Paganini was premiered by the Royal Ballet at the Royal Opera

House in Covent Garden, London. While Rachmaninoff was unable to attend the premiere, he was generally content with the reports he received. Indeed, he demonstratively signed his last letter to Fokine 'from a "ballet composer"' and expressed hope for future collaboration.[28]

Rachmaninoff began work on the Third Symphony, op. 44, in June 1935 at Villa Senar. Poor health necessitated a three-week cure at Baden-Baden, and the third movement was completed in June the following year. The piece has been called his most 'Russian' symphony. After hearing it for the first time, Sophie Satin told Rachmaninoff, 'I have no doubt at all that the symphony is about Russia, about Russia's history; and that it expresses your own devotion to our beloved country.'[29] Alfred Swan similarly emphasized the Russian character of the opening.[30] Indeed, the opening motif is a chant-like, stepwise unison melody, followed by a Kuchka-inspired harmonization reminiscent of the opening of Mussorgsky's *Boris Godunov.*

Paganini is tempted yet dismayed by the Devil's promises in the Rachmaninoff/Fokine ballet *Paganini*, 1939.

Like the *Rhapsody*, the *Dies Irae* features prominently in the symphony. Hinted at in the opening movement's first theme, in the third movement it reappears alongside thematic material drawn from the first movement. In an *allegro vivace* fugue, which serves as the high point of the finale, the *Dies Irae* appears, first as a brief reference in the main melodic line, but growing more and more prominent as the fugue develops. In Swan's description, 'the festive mood is broken up by a piercing *fugato*, which in its heart-rending despair leads once more to the gloomy sounds of the Dies Irae Sequence.'[31] Indeed, the *Dies Irae* continues in the trumpets in the calm following the fugue, before the first movement theme is reintroduced. These two themes compete for dominance in the final coda, with the *Dies Irae* closing the entire symphony. Swan concluded that the *Dies Irae* was 'not allowed to triumph here (as before, in the Corelli and Paganini variations), and everything ends in the festive A major, with a dynamic coda'.[32] Just as in the Rhapsody, however, the question of which theme ultimately triumphs is not clear-cut: Martyn notes that in the coda, the *Dies Irae* is 'fighting for supremacy with the movement's opening figure, in a blazing riot of orchestral colour', while Harrison concludes that the symphony ends with 'the Dies Irae at the end not quite triumphing'.[33]

Premiered on 6 November 1936, with Leopold Stokowski and the Philadelphia Philharmonic, the Third Symphony received a lukewarm response from audiences and critics alike, who had been expecting the Romantic, lyrical Rachmaninoff of the 18th Paganini Variation. Nonetheless, Rachmaninoff believed this was one of his greater works, writing to Vilshau in 1937, 'the reception by the public and critics was bitter. I recall one painful review: "Rachmaninoff doesn't have a Third Symphony in him".' Nonetheless, he maintained, 'I am personally firmly convinced that it is a good work.'[34] Though he believed strongly enough in the work to insist on recording it, he nevertheless subjected it, like so many other works, to cuts in his 1939 recording with the Philadelphia Philharmonic.

Amid the ongoing strain of concert and compositional activity, Rachmaninoff's health declined. Already in September 1931, he noted after playing through the 'Corelli Variations' to Swan:

> The blood-vessels on my fingertips have begun to burst,
> bruises are forming. I don't say much about it at home.
> But it can happen at any concert. Then I can't play
> with that spot for about two minutes, I have to strum
> some chords. It is probably old age. And yet take these
> concerts away from me and it will be the end of me.[35]

In addition to neuralgia and lower back pain (lumbago), in 1935 he developed arthritis in one of his fingers, and feared its spread to others. Nonetheless, he resisted suggestions to cut back on his performances. When doctors suggested he play less, Rachmaninoff responded with sudden ardour:

> this is my only joy – the concerts. If you deprive me of them,
> I shall wither away. If I have a pain, it stops when I am playing.
> Sometimes this neuralgia in the left side of my face and head
> torments me for twenty-four hours, but before a concert
> it disappears as if by magic. In St Louis I had an attack of
> lumbago. The curtain was raised when I was already on the
> platform and seated at the piano. While I was playing the pain
> did not disturb me at all, but I could not get up when I had
> finished. The curtain had to be lowered, and only then could
> I get up. No, I cannot play less. If I am not working, I wither
> away. No . . . It is best to die on the concert platform.[36]

Sophie Satin similarly recalled, '[Rachmaninoff] could not imagine life without the concert stage, without performances,' which was what drove him to continue to perform from year to year, even when it was no longer necessary monetarily.[37] In fact, he continued to expand his repertoire and experiment with different sorts of programmes, including a 1932 programme consisting of fantasias by Haydn, Beethoven, Chopin, Liszt and Scriabin.[38]

Increasing political tensions in Europe also played a role in his exhaustion. Rachmaninoff stopped giving concerts in Germany in 1933, when his manager there lost his position and had to leave the country.[39] In April 1935, Somoff reported that some of Rachmaninoff's 'pensioners' in the Soviet Union had been swept up in the recent wave of Stalinist terror.[40] Nor was the United States immune to this 'chauvinistic wave' sweeping the entire world. In July 1935, Somoff noted growing calls for the expulsion of foreigners who had not applied for u.s. citizenship after ten years of residence; in July 1936, Rachmaninoff suggested the need to apply, noting 'it is apparent that we will not be going to Russia, and to live without a passport is difficult and uncomfortable.'[41] Nonetheless, it was only in January 1939 that Rachmaninoff submitted his application.[42] At the same time, Nazi Germany increasingly cast its shadow over life in Villa Senar. As Rachmaninoff observed in a March 1938 letter to Somoff:

here in Europe we live as if on a volcano. Nobody knows what will happen tomorrow. But everyone thinks that war might begin tomorrow. And as you know, I am a very indecisive man, and don't know what to do. I realize only one thing: if we go to Senar and things begin to boil, we'll find ourselves in something of a mousetrap. But my heart won't permit me to leave Europe for America, leaving Tanyushka [Tatiana] here.[43]

In 1938, Rachmaninoff personally funded the escape from Germany to Zurich of Russian émigré philosopher Ivan Il'in, an old acquaintance and close friend of the Medtners, who had attracted the ire of the Nazi party.[44] On a personal level, Chaliapin's death on 11 April 1938 hit Rachmaninoff hard. He noted, 'Ended is the Chaliapin epoch! Never has his like been seen and never again shall we see it!'[45]

Despite international tensions, by the mid-1930s Rachmaninoff's piano works (whose fundamentally tonal style corresponded to the new aesthetic demands of Socialist Realism) had captured the imagination of a new generation of Soviet pianistic stars, including the young Sviatoslav Richter and Emil Gilels. In 1937, while listening to a radio broadcast from Moscow during his time at Senar, Rachmaninoff had the unexpected pleasure of hearing excellent performances of a number of his songs.[46] By 1939, Vilshau wrote to the composer of the frequent performances of his piano music including his more recent works: the Fourth Piano Concerto, the *Rhapsody on a Theme of Paganini*, and the 'Corelli Variations'. Vilshau concluded, 'The concert is rare when you aren't played or sung. You see how they value you.'[47]

In May 1939 Rachmaninoff mourned to Somoff that even his time at Senar was darkened by ceaseless discussions of Hitler and war, lamenting, 'when we say good night, the last words are always "what will the papers say tomorrow!?" And the next morning it all begins again.' Were it not for his daughter Tatiana, he confessed, he would leave Senar 'tomorrow'.[48]

He helped Tatiana purchase a dacha outside of Paris to afford her greater security in the event of war.[49] Despite feeling the increasing threat of war, he lingered at Senar through the summer of 1939, unable to bring himself to leave the place he had so come to love. 'When I see the sun, I walk in the garden and think, "Lord, how wonderful . . . if there is not war." But we have little sun now. Very little. The weather is Hitlerite.'[50] As the summer wore on, his sense of dread increased. In July 1939, he reflected, 'It seems that peace has left people living in Europe for a long time, even if there will not be war.'[51] Though Irina and Sophia joined the

Rachmaninoffs in America, attempts to persuade Tatiana and her family to leave France were unsuccessful. Having lingered until 23 August 1939, on the trip back aboard the *Aquitania*, 'antisubmarine precautions were taken, and portholes were blacked out.'[52] War broke out a week later. Rachmaninoff would never see his beloved Senar, or his younger daughter Tatiana, again.

10

Exile in America

As the Second World War raged in the summer of 1942,
Rachmaninoff bought a house in Beverly Hills. 'As a rule, I'm not
lucky with houses,' he observed with typical irony in a letter to his
secretary Nikolai Mandrovskii:

> In my lifetime I've bought six houses. Of these only one
> was a success in New York and I sold it successfully. The
> others I've either lost, as in Russia, or virtually lost, as in
> Germany and Switzerland. This last one here will probably
> be taken from me by the Japanese, though, frankly, I
> scarcely believe they will get here. If they do come, it will
> be only for the sake of my house. Such is fortune![1]

Exhausted from his concert activities, suffering from lumbago,
sclerosis and high blood pressure, Rachmaninoff hoped retirement
would finally allow him to devote more time to composition. He
spent free afternoons planning which trees to plant in the lot of his
new house. Evenings he often spent with fellow pianist and émigré
Vladimir Horowitz, playing two-piano works. Once they visited the
Disney studios together, where they met Walt Disney and watched
Bambi as well as Mickey Mouse performing Rachmaninoff's
famous Prelude in C-sharp minor.[2] Rachmaninoff even initiated
a collegial exchange with Igor Stravinsky: though diametrically
opposed in their compositional approaches and characters, each

had family stranded in occupied France, and Rachmaninoff hoped
Stravinsky might know how to get word from them.³ As to his
August 1939 departure from Senar, Rachmaninoff declared in an
interview, 'when I left Europe for the last time, I left the Old World
behind me for good and all. I have found a New World in America
and to it I dedicate what is left of my future.'⁴ Having applied for
u.s. citizenship in January 1939, Rachmaninoff and his wife became
citizens on 1 February 1943.

Rachmaninoff's final composition, the *Symphonic Dances*,
op. 45, were written primarily at the Honeyman estate 'Orchard
Point' in Centerport, New York, overlooking Long Island Sound,
in the summer of 1940. Recuperating from a minor operation

and still reeling from the loss of his old home, Rachmaninoff purchased a yacht that he named 'Senar' and threw himself into his compositional work.[5] Over the course of the summer, 'preparing for the upcoming season and composing at the same time, [Rachmaninoff] worked from 9 a.m. until 11 p.m., with a one-hour break for relaxation.'[6] Orchestration was completed amid his autumn concert tour, and the *Symphonic Dances* premiered in January 1941. The work was dedicated to the Philadelphia Orchestra, with whom he had had a lengthy and productive professional relationship, including a festival organized by conductor Eugene Ormandy in the autumn of 1939 to celebrate Rachmaninoff's American premiere thirty years earlier.[7]

Rachmaninoff
driving his yacht
'Senar'.

Rachmaninoff with Eugene Ormandy during the Rachmaninoff Festival, 1939.

The composer set the *Symphonic Dances* in three movements originally titled 'Noon', 'Twilight' and 'Midnight', possibly in the hope that Fokine might use them for a 'Fantastic Dances' ballet.[8] However, Fokine's 1942 death prevented further collaboration and descriptive titles were abandoned. In the first, march-like movement, Rachmaninoff expanded his orchestral colour and alluded to the composition's American context with an alto saxophone in the slow section, on the use of which he consulted Broadway orchestrator Robert Russell Bennett.[9] While the movement's rhythmic vibrancy is reminiscent of early works by Sergei Prokofiev, it ends surprisingly with a quotation from Rachmaninoff's First Symphony, transposed from C minor to C major. In contrast, the second movement is a symphonic waltz that shifts uneasily between 6/8, 3/8 and 9/8 time, giving it an off-kilter feel akin to Ravel's *La Valse* or *Valses nobles et sentimentales*. The *Dies Irae*, particularly apparent in the third movement, culminates (as in the *Rhapsody*) in a final struggle between two themes: here it competes with the Orthodox chant *Blessed Art Thou, O Lord,* from the ninth movement of Rachmaninoff's *All-Night Vigil.* In the *Vigil*, the chant marks the moment of Christ's resurrection; in the manuscript, Rachmaninoff marked with the word 'Allilyia' the point where the choral alleluias appear in the original work.[10] At the end of the score, he wrote the words 'I thank thee, Lord' – possibly an affirmation of spiritual triumph over the ill-reputed chant that had dogged his compositional work for so long.[11]

With the news of Nazi Germany's invasion of the Soviet Union on 22 June 1941, Rachmaninoff cast about for ways to assist his homeland, and ultimately dedicated the profits from his 1 November 1941 performance at Carnegie Hall to the Soviet war effort. Given the divisive nature of politics among the émigré community, as well as American suspicion of Communism, Rachmaninoff's decision to make such a public appeal on behalf of the Soviet Union was fraught. Indeed, his American manager persuaded him not to make his intentions public before the concert. But the concert programme proudly announced that the proceeds would go 'to the war sufferers of his native Russia'. For the Russian émigré community, Rachmaninoff's actions, as Sophie Satin later recalled, were electric, particularly because of the composer's general disinclination to engage in political squabbles within émigré life. Rachmaninoff shipped $3,920.29 worth of medical and surgical supplies to the USSR – the full proceeds from the concert. Siloti and others also chipped in.[12] With the Japanese bombing of Pearl Harbor on 7 December 1941, and the subsequent American entry into the war, Rachmaninoff's stance became less controversial.

The Soviet musical community embraced Rachmaninoff's commitment to the war effort. Though the fiftieth anniversary of Rachmaninoff's professional debut in 1942 received little attention in the United States, it was celebrated in the Soviet Union with concerts, an exhibition at the Moscow Conservatory and numerous articles. Wartime conditions notwithstanding, the Russian Consulate in Washington, DC, sent Rachmaninoff a number of these articles, causing him to write to Sophie Satin in August 1942, 'the Bolsheviks are the first to remember and probably the only ones who will remember . . . Their recognition is a bit late and untimely: before their perishing, as it were, which seems to me to be unavoidable. I would have preferred a whole Russia, even in their hands, to my recognition.'[13] He was nonetheless moved, and on 31 August 1942, he wrote to Mandrovskii: 'I am going to play again for Russia. To help Russia at the present time is the same as to help America. But everyone helps the latter, and not many [help] Russia. I am still Russian, and for that reason it is natural that I am drawn to her.'[14]

Rachmaninoff's health began to deteriorate rapidly in January 1943: pains in his left side, fatigue, loss of weight and a persistent cough hinted at more serious issues. When the Somoffs attended his concert in Columbus, Ohio, on 5 February, they were shocked by his 'gaunt, suffering face'.[15] His concert in Knoxville, Tennessee, on 17 February would prove to be his last. Rachmaninoff included a performance of Bach's English Suite no. 2 in A minor – the same piece he had played as a young man for Anton Rubinstein at Zverev's house in 1885. His rendition of the first half of Chopin's Sonata no. 2 (including its funeral march) was similarly indebted to Rubinstein's interpretation.[16]

On the way to Florida, ill health forced him to cancel his concert engagement and he travelled instead to New Orleans to rest before continuing his concert tour. When his condition worsened, he and Natasha (who, after her daughters were grown, always accompanied Rachmaninoff on his concert tours) travelled instead to Los Angeles. Upon his arrival on 26 February he was taken immediately to the Hospital of the Good Samaritan. At his own insistence, he was moved to his new house in Beverly Hills on 2 March, believing

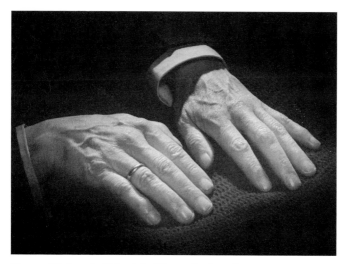

Close-up of Rachmaninoff's hands for *Life* magazine, December 1942.

that he would feel better in 'Russian surroundings' with his family around him. Listening to the radio, he asked that it be set to Moscow, as 'he wanted to hear music from Moscow.'[17] Every day he asked 'about the situation on the front, of the success of the Russians and where they were now . . . hearing that the Russians had again taken back several cities, he sighed, relieved and said "Praise God! God give them strength!"'[18] Tests revealed melanoma cancer that had already metastasized in his vital organs. His family and doctor did not tell him of his diagnosis. His condition rapidly worsened, and in the last three days of life, drifting in and out of consciousness, he would at times feverishly 'move his hands, as if he were conducting an orchestra or playing piano'.[19]

Rachmaninoff died at his home in Beverly Hills, California, on 28 March 1943, a few days short of his 70th birthday. Congratulatory birthday telegrams from the Soviet musical community arrived too late for him to consciously receive them.[20] After a small service at the Russian Orthodox church in Los Angeles, he was buried at Kensico Cemetery near Valhalla, New York. His wife Natasha, elder daughter Irina and granddaughter Sophia were in attendance through his last days, but his younger daughter Tatiana, stranded in occupied France, learned of her father's death through a radio broadcast.[21]

On 12 April 1943, *Life* magazine published the last professional pictures taken of Rachmaninoff before his death. Always reluctant to be photographed, the composer had put off photographer Eric Schaal for three years before consenting to a series of pictures in December 1942. In addition to three concert shots, one features him at work at his desk in his New York apartment. Another offers a close-up of his legendary hands with their massive span, which he had once insured against injuries.[22] A full page was dedicated to a close-up portrait of his face as he gazed off into the distance, avoiding the lens of the camera: the face of a man tired, distant yet serene.[23]

Postlude: Rachmaninoff the Modernist

In the autumn of 1974, Soviet journalist V. Bragin paid a visit to Ivanovka, now part of the collective farm 'Karl Marx'. Little remained of the manicured gardens of Rachmaninoff's former estate, apart from lilac bushes that had gone wild and wafted their fragrance through the air each spring. Wandering through the overgrown park past the muddy remnants of a pond, Bragin approached the one-time site of the outbuilding where Rachmaninoff had retreated from the noise and bustle of the large house to write many of his piano masterpieces. Suddenly, Bragin heard snatches of Rachmaninoff's light-hearted Polka drifting through the air. He quickened his step to find that 'beyond the turn stands that very outbuilding in which Rachmaninoff lived and worked.'[1] Destroyed in the Russian Civil War, this sudden manifestation of Rachmaninoff's former residence blurred the lines between memory and reality.

The reconstruction of this storied outbuilding based on descriptions from Sophie Satin was part of a longer process in the Soviet reclaiming of Rachmaninoff's legacy.[2] Although much of Rachmaninoff's music remained in the concert repertoire, he was not initially celebrated as one of the giants of Russian music like Glinka, Tchaikovsky or the Kuchka. His gesture of patriotism amid the Second World War together with his 1943 death sparked a new wave of commemorative practices. The first Rachmaninoff

Ivanovka, reconstructed as the Rachmaninoff Memorial Museum, June 1986.

exhibition was organized in Moscow in 1943. In 1945, the leading
Soviet music journal, *Sovetskaia muzyka*, dedicated an entire issue to
Rachmaninoff. His First Symphony, long buried, was reconstructed
based on orchestral parts found in Leningrad, and numerous
compositions left unpublished during Rachmaninoff's lifetime
were issued by the Soviet music publisher Muzgiz.[3] The interest in
Rachmaninoff continued to grow with the dissolution of the Soviet
Union: by 1995 the main house at Ivanovka was reconstructed.

Almost immediately after his death, Soviet officials expressed
interest in bringing his body back to Russia for burial. Rumours
that Rachmaninoff had expressed a 'desire to be buried in his
homeland' emerged at the institution in charge of cultural exchange
between the USSR and the West, VOKS (the All-Union Society for

Cultural Ties Abroad).[4] This narrative reappeared at a July 1944 meeting of Moscow musicians, where Rachmaninoff's old friend Aleksandr Gol'denveizer, noted that Rachmaninoff had 'willed that his body should be brought to Russia'.[5] In 1945, an article in *Sovetskaia muzyka* claimed that Rachmaninoff's dying wish 'was to be buried at the end of the war in Moscow's Novodevichy cemetery' where Chekhov, Scriabin and 'a whole series of people, whom [Rachmaninoff] particularly loved and valued' were also buried.[6]

This early initiative had no immediate result, however, and when Texan pianist Van Cliburn returned victorious from his triumph at the First Tchaikovsky Competition in Moscow in 1958, he planted a lilac bush in soil brought from Russia on Rachmaninoff's grave in America.[7] But in 1974, the Soviet UN representative, M. Kocharian, again raised the possibility of moving Rachmaninoff's body and requested that the Union of Composers and the Soviet Ministry of Internal Affairs take measures to accomplish this 'important ideological and political event'. Soviet musicologists were asked to find proof that Rachmaninoff had desired 'to be buried in his homeland'.[8]

The question of Rachmaninoff's burial outlived the Cold War, re-emerging in 2015, when Russian Cultural Minister Vladimir Medinskii called for Rachmaninoff's return to Russia, claiming that 'Americans have presumptuously privatized the name of Rachmaninoff, just as they have done to the names of tens and hundreds of Russians, who through the will of fate ended up abroad after the events of the revolution.'[9] Rather than Moscow, however, Medinskii envisioned a reburial in the Novgorod region at the former family estate Oneg, which he claimed would be reconstructed like Ivanovka.

The Soviet reclaiming of Rachmaninoff as an embodiment of cultural 'Russianness' stripped him of problematic political, aesthetic and religious views. His national patriotism was emphasized, while his decision to leave Russia was labelled a 'fatal error' that paralysed his creativity. This standard Soviet narrative asserted that 'Rachmaninoff longed to be buried in Moscow after the war, was uninterested in Orthodox spirituality, fascinated by Russian folk belief, and had mistakenly believed that there would be no place for music in post-1917 Russia.'[10] Indeed, when arguing for the broader distribution of a 1968 recording of Rachmaninoff's *All-Night Vigil* made by the State Academic Choir of the USSR under the baton of A. V. Sveshnikov, studio director B. Vladimirskii insisted that the *Vigil* 'cannot in any circumstance call forth any sort of specific religious emotions' and explicitly framed the work as a national, not a religious, achievement.[11]

By the 1980s, however, Rachmaninoff also began to appear in artistic narratives linking him to a 'true' Russian identity framed in opposition to the Revolution. In O. M. Lopukhov's 1981 *Portrait of S. Rachmaninoff*, the composer was depicted as a corpse-like figure, head bowed and arms crossed, while the fire of revolutionary destruction burned in the background.[12] In his 1988 painting *Eternal Russia*, nationalist painter Ilya Gerasimov even more provocatively featured Rachmaninoff alongside other historic Russian figures from Peter the Great onward. For Gerasimov, Russia's 'natural' Orthodox and ethnically Russian path was sidetracked by Communism – a view that has found considerable traction in post-Soviet Russia.[13] Alongside the renaming of streets and cities according to their pre-revolutionary names and the reconstruction of churches such as the Church of Christ the Saviour in Moscow, the bodies of leading émigrés including philosopher Ivan Il'in and White Army General Denikin have been repatriated. In its most extreme form, this kind of historical reframing has led to a complete rejection of the Soviet past as an aberration of imagined national continuities preserved across the revolutionary 1917 divide.

Any narrative that posits an eternal, unchanging 'old Russia' should be viewed with scepticism, however. As this book has shown, Rachmaninoff took active part in a profoundly dynamic and rapidly changing late imperial Russian intellectual and cultural milieu. While rejecting the compositional innovations of Scriabin, Prokofiev and Stravinsky, he nonetheless engaged with a deeply modern discourse in which music was granted metaphysical significance for its potential impact on human existence. Responding to the loss of both his fortune and homeland after 1917, he forged a new career as an international performer. He criss-crossed America (and later Europe) on a gruelling concert schedule. New recording technology allowed his music to reverberate from America across Europe, to Harbin, Istanbul and South Africa. Listeners across this newly created, inherently modern aural community responded to his music's immediate emotional appeal, inscribing their own experiences into it well beyond the bounds of 'old Russia'.

By resituating Rachmaninoff's career within a multilayered experience of innovation and uprootedness (rather than timelessly drifting outside of it), his stature as a genuinely modern figure becomes clear. When Rachmaninoff took his punctual stroll each day at 12.30 p.m. through the streets of New York in 1941, two things drew him out of his silent ruminations of concern for his daughter and her family stranded in occupied France. As his occasional walking companion and secretary Mandrovskii recalled, these were invariably

a new, little-known model of automobile or a stroller with a child. In the first case, it was the interest of a car lover. Sergei Vasil'evich drove wonderfully, loved expensive cars and always took an interest in the latest models. In the second case Sergei Vasil'evich, nodding his head, silently threw a glance at the child. His face would momentarily brighten with a smile, and he would grumble, 'Look at you'.[14]

Rachmaninoff – that nostalgic emblem of 'old Russia' – was at home in the bustle of traffic and the towering intricacies of modern construction. When he occasionally drove out of New York City to pick up his sister-in-law Sophie Satin, now a biologist who worked in the Carnegie Institute laboratory at Cold Spring Harbor, he gloried in crossing Triborough Bridge, 'a colossus of steel and concrete' that the *New York Times* described as a 'Y-shaped sky highway' at its 1936 opening.[15] The timeworn composer would gun his motor with joy and relish the sound of his perfectly tuned engine. Weaving through traffic, he sometimes recounted stories of the 'distant past' to Mandrovskii filled with 'good-natured humour, joy and tenderness'.[16]

Rachmaninoff loved modern technology, explored modern instruments like the saxophone, and had experienced late imperial Russia much as he experienced his realms of exile – as rapidly shifting maelstroms of ideas and innovation to be lived, not shunned. By the same token, he performed the part of a nostalgic embodiment of a lost nation. In his mind and music, he yearned for that transfigured Robert Sterl painting of the Kremlin at Easter in 1914 – an idealized stasis of 'old Russia' alive in his memories and a muse on his wall. Such seeming contradictions in Rachmaninoff's person constitute the very essence of modernity. Concluding his account of the modern world, Marshall Berman argued:

> to be modern, is to experience personal and social life as a maelstrom, to find one's world and oneself in perpetual disintegration and renewal, trouble and anguish, ambiguity and contradiction . . . to be a modern*ist* is to make oneself somehow at home in the maelstrom, to make its rhythms one's own, to move within its currents in search of the forms of reality, of beauty, of freedom, of justice, that its fervid and perilous flood allows.[17]

When Rachmaninoff died, tranquil in his fleeting residence at Beverly Hills in 1943, his mind was elsewhere, his hands moving restlessly over an imagined piano or conducting an invisible orchestra. But where was that piano the dying man most desired? Was it at his old estate Ivanovka? Or perhaps in his acoustically extraordinary Bauhaus-style showpiece of modern aesthetics and conveniences at Villa Senar? Most likely he imagined himself onstage, his fingers flitting over ivory keys before a rapt audience. And the keys under his fingertips were almost certainly not those of the German Bechstein piano that he had preferred in imperial Russia, but rather the responsive modernity of Steinway's accelerated action that made these instruments, in Rachmaninoff's own words in 1934, 'more perfect than ever before'.[18]

References

Archival Abbreviations

LCRA   Library of Congress Rachmaninoff Archive, Washington, DC

GTSMMK   State Central Museum of Musical Culture, Moscow
(Gosudarstvennyi tsentral'nyi muzei muzykal'noi kultury)

Prelude: In Search of Rachmaninoff

1   Leonard Liebling, 'Variations', *Musical Courier*, CXXVII/7 (1943),
    p. 17.
2   Leonid Sabaneev, 'Moi vstrechi s Rakhmaninovym', *Muzykal'naia
    akademiia*, 2 (1993), pp. 209–11 (p. 211).
3   Katherine Swan and A. J. Swan, 'Rachmaninoff: Personal Reminiscences,
    Part One', *Musical Quarterly*, XXX/1 (1944), pp. 1–19 (p. 3).
4   Robert Craft, *Conversations with Stravinsky* (New York, 1959), p. 42.
5   Liebling, 'Variations', p. 17.
6   Barrie Martyn, *Rachmaninoff: Composer, Pianist, Conductor* (Aldershot,
    1990), p. 84.
7   Eric Blom, 'Sergey Vassilievich Rakhmaninov', in *Grove's Dictionary of
    Music and Musicians*, 5th edn (New York, 1954), vol. VII, p. 27.
8   Bernard Holland, 'Basking in the Glow of the Golden Arches', *New York
    Times* (22 December 1996), p. H42.
9   Leonid Sabaneev, 'Skriabin i Rakhmaninov', *Muzyka*, 75 (1912),
    pp. 390–95 (pp. 390–91).
10 Quoted in Richard Taruskin, *Oxford History of Western Music*, vol. IV
    (Oxford and New York, 2005), p. 553.

11 Glen Carruthers, 'The (Re)appraisal of Rachmaninov's Music', *Musical Times*, CXLVII/1896 (2006), pp. 44–50.

12 Sergei Rachmaninoff, 'Music Should Speak from the Heart', *The Etude*, LIX/12 (1941), pp. 804, 848 (p. 804).

13 Quoted in Robin Gehl, 'Reassessing a Legacy: Rachmaninoff in America, 1918–43', PhD dissertation, University of Cincinnati, 2008, p. 238.

14 'Music's Moneybags', *TIME*, 21 September 1942, http://content.time.com, accessed 5 October 2021.

15 Pauline Fairclough, '"Don't Sing It on a Feast Day"', *Journal of the American Musicological Society*, LXV/1 (2012), pp. 67–111 (p. 87).

16 Rachmaninoff, 'National and Radical Impressions in the Music of Today and Yesterday', *The Etude*, XXXVII/10 (1919), pp. 615–16.

17 Elger Niels and Wouter de Voogd, compilers, *Inventory of Books from Sergei Rachmaninoff's Cabinet at SENAR* (Rachmaninoff Network, 2017/ updated 2019).

18 Richard Taruskin, *Russian Music at Home and Abroad* (Berkeley, CA, 2016), p. 121.

19 Marshall Berman, *All That Is Solid Melts into Air* (New York, 1988), p. 5.

20 Ibid., p. 15.

21 Rebecca Mitchell, 'In Search of Russia', *Slavonic and East European Review*, XCVII/1 (2019), pp. 136–68.

22 Berman, *All That Is Solid*, p. 6.

23 Rachmaninoff, 'Music Should Speak', p. 804.

24 'Melodie, op. 3, no. 3', *The Etude*, XXXVII/10 (1919), p. 632; Sergei Rachmaninoff, 'New Light on the Art', *The Etude*, XLI/4 (1923), pp. 223–4.

25 Letter 1939, in *S. Rakhmaninov: Literaturnoe nasledie*, ed. Z. A. Apetian (Moscow, 1978–80), vol. III, pp. 171–2.

1 The Making of a Moscow Musician

1 'Vospominaniia', in *S. Rakhmaninov: Literaturnoe nasledie*, ed. Z. A. Apetian (Moscow, 1978–80), vol. I, p. 51.

2 Gary M. Hamburg, 'The Russian Nobility on the Eve of the 1905 Revolution', *Russian Review*, XXXVIII/3 (1979), pp. 323–38; Roberta

Manning, *The Crisis of the Old Order in Russia* (Princeton, NJ, 1982). A desiatin is roughly equivalent to 1.09 hectares (2.7 ac).

3 Max Harrison, *Rachmaninoff: Life, Works, Recordings* (London and New York), pp. 5–8.

4 Anton Rubinstein, *Autobiography* (Boston, MA, 1890), pp. 91–2.

5 Lev Tolstoi, *Anna Karenina*, in *Sobranie sochinenii* (Moscow, 1958), vol. VIII, p. 7.

6 Sofiia Satina, 'Zapiska o S. V. Rakhmaninove', in *Vospominaniia o Rakhmaninove*, ed. Z. A. Apetian (Moscow, 1988), vol. I, pp. 12–115 (pp. 16–17).

7 Letter 11 June 1891, in *Rakhmaninov: Literaturnoe nasledie*, vol. I, p. 171.

8 Letter 7 February 1893, ibid., p. 211.

9 Katherine Swan and A. J. Swan, 'Rachmaninoff: Personal Reminiscences, Part II', *Musical Quarterly*, XXX/2 (1944), pp. 174–91 (p. 181).

10 Satina, 'Zapiska', pp. 18–19.

11 Matvei Presman, 'Ugolok muzykal'noi Moskvy', in *Vospominaniia o Rakhmaninove*, vol. I, pp. 177–241 (pp. 149–52).

12 Satina, 'Zapiska', p. 21.

13 Sergei Rachmaninoff, 'Some Critical Moments in My Career', *Musical Times*, LXXI (1930), pp. 557–8 (p. 557).

14 Alfred Rieber, *Merchants and Entrepreneurs in Imperial Russia* (Chapel Hill, NC, 1982), pp. 133–77; Rebecca Mitchell, 'Rachmaninoff and Moscow Musical Life', forthcoming in *Rachmaninoff and His World*, ed. Philip Ross Bullock (Chicago, IL, 2022).

15 Sofiia Satina, 'Vospominaniia', *Muzykal'naia akademiia*, II (1993), pp. 204–8 (p. 206).

16 Quoted in Sergei Bertensson and Jay Leyda, *Sergei Rachmaninoff: A Lifetime in Music* (Bloomington and Indianapolis, IN, 2001), p. 16.

17 Presman, 'Ugolok', p. 150.

18 Florence Leonard, 'Interpretation Depends on Talent and Personality', *The Etude*, L/4 (1932), pp. 239–40.

19 Satina, 'Vospominaniia', p. 206.

20 Presman, 'Ugolok', p. 158.

21 Philip S. Taylor, *Anton Rubinstein: A Life in Music* (Bloomington and Indianapolis, IN, 2007), pp. 205–6.

22 Leonard, 'Interpretation Depends on Talent and Personality', p. 240.

23 Taylor, *Anton Rubinstein*, pp. 194–9.

24 Presman, 'Ugolok', p. 194.

25 S. V. Rachmaninoff, 'New Light on the Art of the Piano', *The Etude*, XLI/4 (1923), pp. 223–4.

26 Rachmaninoff, 'Ten Important Attributes of Beautiful Pianoforte Playing', *The Etude*, XXVIII/3 (1910), pp. 153–4.

27 Rachmaninoff, 'National and Radical Impressions in the Music of Today and Yesterday', *The Etude*, XXXVII/10 (1919), pp. 615–16.

28 Barrie Martyn, 'The Legacy of Rachmaninoff', *Clavier*, XXXII/3 (March 1993), pp. 15–17 (p. 15).

29 N. A. Rakhmaninova, 'S. V. Rakhmaninov', in *Vospominaniia o Rakhmaninove*, vol. II, pp. 292–332 (p. 312).

30 Presman, 'Ugolok', pp. 178–9; *Sergei Rachmaninoff: The Complete Recordings* (RCA Victor Gold Seal: 09026-6126502).

31 Satina, 'Zapiska', p. 20.

32 Letter 10 January 1891, in *Rakhmaninov: Literaturnoe nasledie*, vol. I, p. 163.

33 Letter 14 December 1892, ibid., p. 205.

34 Letter 17 December 1893, ibid., p. 229.

35 Barrie Martyn, *Rachmaninoff: Composer, Pianist, Conductor* (Abingdon-on-Thames, 1990), pp. 86–7.

36 Katherine Swan and A. J. Swan, 'Rachmaninoff: Personal Reminiscences, Part One', *Musical Quarterly*, XXX/1 (1944), pp. 1–19 (p. 13).

37 N. A. Rakhmaninova, 'Rakhmaninov', p. 303.

38 Cited in Geoffrey Norris, 'Rakhmaninov's Apprenticeship', *Musical Times*, CXXIV/1688 (1983), pp. 602–3, 605 (p. 603).

39 Letter 26 February 1930, in *Rakhmaninov: Literaturnoe nasledie*, vol. II, pp. 296–7.

40 Satina, 'Vospominaniia', p. 204.

41 Cited in Bertensson and Leyda, *Rachmaninoff*, p. 20; Presman, 'Ugolok', p. 202.

42 Oskar von Riesemann, *Rachmaninoff's Recollections* (New York, 1934), p. 52.

43 Victor I. Seroff, *Rachmaninoff* (London, 1951), pp. 31–2; Leonid Sabaneev, *Vospominaniia o Rossii* (Moscow, 2005), p. 73.

44 Satina, 'Zapiska', p. 22.

2 Ivanovka

1   S. V. Rakhmaninov, 'Ivanovka', in *S. Rakhmaninov: Literaturnoe nasledie*, ed. Z. A. Apetian (Moscow, 1978–80), vol. I, p. 52.

2   Ibid.

3   Ibid.

4   Sofiia Satina, 'Vospominaniia', *Muzykal'naia akademiia*, II (1993), pp. 204–8 (p. 206).

5   L. D. Rostovtsova, 'Vospominaniia', in *Vospominaniia o Rakhmaninove*, 5th edn, ed. Z. A. Apetian (Moscow, 1988), vol. I, pp. 232–50 (p. 233).

6   A. I. Ermakov, 'V Ivanovku ia vsegda stremilsia', in *Rakhmaninov i mirovaia kultura*, ed. I. N. Vanovskaia (Ivanovka, 2014), p. 267.

7   Rostovtsova, 'Vospominaniia', p. 233.

8   V. D. Skalon, 'Dnevnik', in *Vospominaniia o Rakhmaninove*, vol. II, pp. 431–66 (p. 434).

9   Ibid.

10 E. Iu. Zhukovskaia, 'Vospominaniia', in *Vospominaniia o Rakhmaninove*, vol. I, pp. 251–342 (p. 254).

11 Rostovtsova, 'Vospominaniia', p. 235.

12 Richard D. Sylvester, *Rachmaninoff's Complete Songs* (Bloomington and Indianapolis, IN, 2014), pp. 35–6.

13 Zhukovskaia, 'Vospominaniia', pp. 258–9; N. A. Rakhmaninova, 'S. V. Rakhmaninov', in *Vospominaniia o Rakhmaninove*, vol. II, pp. 292–332 (pp. 302–4).

14 E. F. Gnesina, 'O Rakhmaninove', ibid., vol. I, pp. 205–11 (p. 205).

15 O. N. Konius, [Untitled], ibid., vol. I, pp. 227–31 (p. 229).

16 M. E. Bukinik, [Untitled], ibid., vol. I, pp. 213–26 (p. 214).

17 Ibid.

18 E. K. Somova, [Untitled], ibid., vol. II, pp. 231–7 (p. 236).

19 GTSMMK, fol. 18, no. 34.

20 Geoffrey Norris, 'Rakhmaninov's Apprenticeship', *Musical Times*, CXXIV/1688 (1983), pp. 602–3, 605 (p. 602).

21 Letter 20 July 1891, in *Rakhmaninov: Literaturnoe nasledie*, vol. I, pp. 178–9 (p. 178).

22 *Rakhmaninov: Literaturnoe nasledie*, vol. I, p. 512.

23 Geoffrey Norris, 'Rakhmaninov's Second Thoughts', *Musical Times*, cxiv/1562 (1973), pp. 364–8; David Cannata, *Rachmaninoff and the Symphony* (Innsbruck, 1999).

24 I. F. Shaliapina, 'Pamiati S. V. Rakhmaninova', in *Vospominaniia o Rakhmaninove*, vol. ii, pp. 173–8 (pp. 177–8).

25 Rostovtsova, 'Vospominaniia', p. 239.

26 Shaliapina, 'Pamiati S. V. Rakhmaninova', p. 178.

27 Rostovtsova, 'Vospominaniia', p. 239.

28 Sofiia Satina, 'Zapiska o S. V. Rakhmaninove', in *Vospominaniia o Rakhmaninove*, vol. i, pp. 12–115 (p. 68); Rebecca Mitchell, 'Rachmaninoff and Moscow Musical Life', forthcoming in *Rachmaninoff and His World*, ed. Philip Ross Bullock (Chicago, il, 2022).

29 Rostovtsova, 'Vospominaniia', p. 239.

30 Apetian, ed., *Rakhmaninov: Literaturnoe nasledie*, vol. i.

31 Ibid., p. 518.

32 Geoffrey Norris, *Rakhmaninov* (London, 1976), p. 83.

33 Serge Rachmaninoff, 'My Prelude in C-sharp Minor', *Delineator*, 75 (1910), p. 127.

34 Letter 25 January 1930 (Edward Borgers to Rachmaninoff), lcra, Box 42, file 65; Benno Moiseiwitsch, 'Sergei Rachmaninoff', *Gramophone*, xx (1943), pp. 169–70; Max Harrison, *Rachmaninoff: Life, Works, Recordings* (London and New York, 2005), pp. 227–9.

35 Later publications of Rachmaninoff's music were jointly produced by Gutheil and Breitkopf & Härtel.

36 Leonid Sabaneev, 'Moi vstrechi s Rakhmaninovym', *Muzykal'naia akademiia*, 2 (1993), pp. 209–11 (p. 210).

37 Geoffrey Norris, 'Rachmaninoff in London', *Musical Times*, cxliii/1902 (1993), pp. 186–8 (p. 187).

38 Ibid.

39 *The Opry House*, directed and produced by Walt Disney (Celebrity Pictures, 1929).

40 Charles Cooke, 'Let's Give them a Rest!', The *Etude*, lxix/1 (1951), p. 17.

41 Barrie Martyn, *Rachmaninoff: Composer, Pianist, Conductor* (Aldershot, 1990), p. 74.

42 See Richard Taruskin, *Defining Russia Musically* (Berkeley, ca, 1997), pp. 152–85.

43 Sylvester, *Rachmaninoff's Complete Songs*, p. 42.

44 Ibid.

45 Rostovtsova, 'Vospominaniia', p. 236.

46 Katherine Swan and A. J. Swan, 'Rachmaninoff: Personal Reminiscences, Part Two', *Musical Quarterly*, xxx/2 (1944), pp. 174–91 (p. 177).

47 Letter 2 September 1895, in *Rakhmaninov: Literaturnoe nasledie*, vol. i, p. 243.

48 Ts. Kiui, 'Tretyi russkii simfonicheskii kontsert,' *Novosti i birzhevaia gazeta* (17 March 1897), p. 3.

49 Leonid Sabaneev, 'Moi vstrechi s Rakhmaninovym', *Muzykal'naia akademiia*, 2 (1993), pp. 209–11 (p. 210).

50 Rostovtsova, 'Vospominaniia', p. 242.

51 Swan and Swan, 'Rachmaninoff: Personal Reminiscences, Part Two', p. 185.

52 Marietta Shaginian, 'Vospominaniia', in *Vospominaniia o Rakhmaninove*, vol. ii, pp. 90–158 (pp. 101–2).

53 Ts. Kiui, 'Tretyi russkii simfonicheskii kontsert', p. 3.

54 Rostovtsova, 'Vospominaniia', pp. 240, 245.

55 Bertensson and Leyda, *Rachmaninoff*, p. 68.

56 Ibid., p. 71.

57 Letter 6 May 1897, in *Rakhmaninov: Literaturnoe nasledie*, vol. i, p. 262.

58 Shaginian, 'Vospominaniia', pp. 151–2.

59 Ibid., pp. 101–2.

60 Martyn, *Rachmaninoff*, pp. 98–9.

61 Zhukovskaia, 'Vospominaniia', p. 256.

62 Ibid., p. 266.

63 Apetian, ed., *Rakhmaninov: Literaturnoe nasledie*, vol. i, pp. 550–52.

64 Letter 6 May 1897, ibid., pp. 261–2.

65 Geoffrey Norris, 'Rachmaninoff', www.oxfordmusiconline.com/grovemusic, 20 January 2001.

66 Harrison, *Rachmaninoff*, p. 78; Elger Niels, 'Nikolai Dahl's Cure – Good Luck or Good Practicing?', www.rachmaninoff.org, 14 October 2020.

67 Rostovtsova, 'Vospominaniia', p. 241.

68 Letter 6 December 1897, in *Rakhmaninov: Literaturnoe nasledie*, vol. i, p. 274.

69 Letter 9 June 1893, ibid., p. 218.

70 Shaginian, 'Vospominaniia', p. 145.

71 Liudmila Kovaleva-Ogorodnova, *Sergei Rakhmaninov: Biografiia* (St Petersburg, 2015), pp. 139–40.

72 Letter 6 December 1897, in *Rakhmaninov: Literaturnoe nasledie*, vol. I, p. 274.

73 Rostovtsova, 'Vospominaniia', p. 247.

74 Harrison, *Rachmaninoff*, p. 82.

3 'My Muse Has Not Died'

1 Sergei Rachmaninoff, 'Some Critical Moments in My Career', *Musical Times*, LXXI/71 (1930), pp. 557–8.

2 Rachmaninoff, 'The Artist and the Gramophone', *Gramophone*, VIII/95 (1931), pp. 525–6.

3 Pål Kolstø, 'The Elder at Iasnaia Poliana', *Kritika*, IX/3 (2008), pp. 533–54 (p. 536).

4 Z. A. Apetian, ed., *S. Rakhmaninov: Literaturnoe nasledie* (Moscow, 1978–80), vol. I, pp. 551–2.

5 Katherine Swan and A. J. Swan, 'Rachmaninoff: Personal Reminiscences, Part Two', *Musical Quarterly*, XXX/2 (1944), pp. 174–91 (pp. 184–5).

6 Richard D. Sylvester, *Rachmaninoff's Complete Songs: A Companion with Texts and Translations* (Bloomington and Indianapolis, IN, 2014), p. 95.

7 A. F. Gedike, 'Pamiatnyi vstrechi', in *Vospominaniia o Rakhmaninove*, 5th edn, ed. Z. A. Apetian (Moscow, 1988), vol. II, pp. 4–17 (p. 6); Sofiia Satina, 'Zapiska o S. V. Rakhmaninove', in *Vospominaniia o Rakhmaninove*, vol. I, pp. 12–115 (p. 33).

8 Letter 8 May 1912, in *Rakhmaninov: Literaturnoe nasledie*, vol. II, pp. 47–9.

9 Letter 3 September 1928, ibid., p. 241.

10 Letter 13 May 1938, ibid., vol. III, p. 130.

11 Geoffrey Norris, 'Rachmaninoff', www.oxfordmusiconline.com/ grovemusic, 20 January 2021.

12 Aleksei Naumov, 'V mire muzykal'nykh rukopisei Rakhmaninova', *Novoe o Rakhmaninove*, ed. M. P. Rakhmanova and M. V. Esipova (Moscow, 2006), pp. 173–80 (pp. 176–7). Speculation focuses on a young woman named Elena Dahl, based on an interview with Rachmaninoff's grandson, Alexandre, who claimed the two met at Dahl's apartment in November–December 1898 and fell in love.

13 Julia Mannherz, *Modern Occultism in Late Imperial Russia* (Dekalb, 2012), p. 66.

14 Ibid., p. 74.

15 Ibid., pp. 73–5.

16 N. A. Teleshov, 'Iz "Zapisok pisatelia"', in *Vospominaniia o Rakhmaninove*, vol. II, pp. 37–8.

17 Quoted in Max Harrison, *Rachmaninoff: Life, Works, Recordings* (London and New York, 2005), p. 86.

18 E. Iu. Zhukovskaia, 'Vospominaniia', in *Vospominaniia o Rakhmaninove*, vol. II, pp. 293–4.

19 Letter [15]/28 April 1906, in *Rakhmaninov: Literaturnoe nasledie*, vol. I, p. 375.

20 Letter 18 June 1898, ibid., p. 277.

21 Letter 14 August 1898, ibid., p. 278.

22 E. R. Vinter-Rozhanskaia, 'Iz vospominanii', in *Vospominaniia o Rakhmaninove*, vol. II, pp. 18–24 (p. 21).

23 Zhukovskaia, 'Vospominaniia', p. 282.

24 Ibid., p. 287; *Vospominaniia o Rakhmaninove*, vol. II, pp. 493–4.

25 Ibid., p. 295.

26 Sylvester, *Rachmaninoff's Complete Songs*, pp. 95–8.

27 Zhukovskaia, 'Vospominaniia', pp. 294–5.

28 Sylvester, *Rachmaninoff's Complete Songs*, pp. 26–7.

29 Ibid., pp. 124–5.

30 Barrie Martyn, *Rachmaninoff: Composer, Pianist, Conductor* (Aldershot, 1990), p. 126.

31 *Vospominaniia o Rakhmaninove*, vol. I, pp. 506–7.

32 A. Gol'denveizer, 'Iz lichnykh vospominanii', in *Vospominaniia o Rakhmaninove*, vol. II, pp. 405–26 (p. 415).

33 Satina, 'Zapiska', pp. 33–4.

34 'Iz Moskvy', *Russkaia muzykal'naia gazeta*, 50 (1900), p. 1250.

35 Harrison, *Rachmaninoff*, p. 94.

36 Gol'denveizer, 'Iz lichnykh vospominanii', p. 415.

37 Quoted in Leonid Sabaneev, 'Moi vstrechi s Rakhmaninovym', *Muzykal'naia akademiia*, 2 (1993), pp. 209–11 (p. 210).

38 M. L. Chelishcheva, 'S. V. Rakhmaninov v Mariinskom uchilishche', in *Vospominaniia o Rakhmaninove*, vol. I, pp. 386–9 (p. 389).

39 A. A. Trubnikova, 'Sergei Rakhmaninov', ibid., pp. 116–45 (pp. 125–6).

40 Zhukovskaia, 'Vospominaniia', p. 312.

41 L. D. Rostovtsova, 'Vospominaniia', in *Vospominaniia o Rakhmaninove*, vol. I, pp. 232–50 (p. 247).

42 Sylvester, *Rachmaninoff's Complete Songs*, pp. 88–123.

43 Zhukovskaia, 'Vospominaniia', p. 312.

44 Rostovtsova, 'Vospominaniia', p. 247; Marietta Shaginian, 'Vospominaniia o S. V. Rakhmaninove', in *Vospominaniia o Rakhmaninove*, vol. II, pp. 90–158 (p. 145).

4 In Russia's Silver Age

1 Quoted in V. V. Bychkov, *Russkaia teurgicheskaia estetika* (Moscow, 2007), p. 8.

2 Quoted in Avril Pyman, *A History of Russian Symbolism* (Cambridge and New York, 1994), p. 1.

3 Bychkov, *Russkaia teurgicheskaia estetika*, pp. 7–9.

4 Erich Lippman, 'God-Seeking, God-Building, and the New Religious Consciousness', in *The Oxford Handbook of Russian Religious Thought*, ed. Caryl Emerson, George Pattison and Randall A. Poole (Oxford, 2020), pp. 223–39 (p. 224).

5 Ibid., p. 226.

6 Quoted in Rebecca Mitchell, '"Musical Metaphysics" in Late Imperial Russia', in *The Oxford Handbook of Russian Religious Thought*, pp. 379–95 (pp. 382–3).

7 Ibid., p. 385.

8 The State Tret'iakov Gallery, https://web.archive. orgweb/20140523230543/http://www.tretyakovgallery.ru/ru/ collection/_show/image/_id/252, accessed 3 August 2021.

9 B. V. Asaf'ev, 'S. V. Rakhmaninov', in *Vospominaniia o Rakhmaninove*, ed. Z. A. Apetian (Moscow, 1988), vol. II, pp. 373–400 (p. 386).

10 Ibid.

11 Ibid. Italics added.

12 L., 'Sovremennye muzykal'nye deiateli', *Russkaia muzykal'naia gazeta*, 1 (1905), pp. 1–6 (p. 4).

13 G. Prokof'ev, 'Pevets intimnykh nastroenii', *Russkaia muzykal'naia gazeta*, 37 (1910), pp. 750–54.

14 Barrie Martyn, *Rachmaninoff: Composer, Pianist, Conductor* (Aldershot, 1990), p. 151.

15 Prokof'ev, 'Pevets intimnykh nastroenii', *Russkaia muzykal'naia gazeta*, pp. 750–54.

16 Ibid.

17 Sergei Rachmaninoff, 'My Prelude in C-Sharp Minor', *Delineator*, 75 (1910), p. 127.

18 E. F. Gnesina, 'O Rakhmaninove', in *Vospominaniia o Rakhmaninove*, vol. I, pp. 205–11 (p. 208).

19 L. D. Rostovtsova, 'Vospominaniia', ibid., pp. 232–50 (p. 248).

20 E. Iu. Zhukovskaia, 'Vospominaniia', ibid., pp. 251–342 (p. 313).

21 Z. A. Apetian, ed., *S. Rakhmaninov: Literaturnoe nasledie* (Moscow, 1978–80), vol. I, pp. 57–61.

22 N. A. Rakhmaninova, 'S. V. Rakhmaninov', in *Vospominaniia o Rakhmaninove*, vol. II, pp. 292–332 (p. 316).

23 Ibid., p. 54.

24 A. Livin, 'Novye opery S. Rakhmaninova', *Russkaia muzykal'naia gazeta*, 4–5 (1906), pp. 123–6.

25 G. P-ch, 'Skupoi rytsar' i "Francheska da Rimini" S. V. Rakhmaninova', *Russkaia muzykal'naia gazeta*, 4 (1907), pp. 121–30.

26 'Modernism Is Rachmaninoff's Bane', *Musical America*, XI/2 (1909), p. 23.

27 A. V. Ossovskii, 'S. V. Rakhmaninov', in *Vospominaniia o Rakhmaninove*, vol. I, pp. 343–85 (p. 359).

28 Rachmaninoff, 'Some Critical Moments in My Career', *Musical Times*, LXXI (1930), pp. 557–8.

29 Rebecca Mitchell, 'Rachmaninoff and Moscow Musical Life', forthcoming in *Rachmaninoff and His World*, ed. Philip Ross Bullock (Chicago, IL, 2022).

30 Charles F. Barber, *Lost in the Stars: The Forgotten Musical Life of Alexander Siloti* (Lanham and Oxford, 2002), pp. 85–96.

31 V. G. Karatygin, 'Skriabin i molodye moskovskie kompozitory', *Apollon*, 5 (1912), pp. 25–38.

32 Marietta Shaginian, 'Vospominaniia', in *Vospominaniia o Rakhmaninove*, vol. II, pp. 90–158 (p. 145).

33 L., 'Sovremennye muzykal'nye deiateli', p. 1.

34 R. Khazarnufsky, 'Introduction', in *Landmarks*, ed. Boris Shragin and Albert Todd (New York, 1977), pp. v–lv (p. xxviii).

35 *Russkaia muzykal'naia gazeta*, 7 (1905), pp. 201–2.

36 Lynn Sargeant, *Harmony and Discord: Music and the Transformation of Russian Cultural Life* (Oxford, 2011), pp. 219–60.

37 Iv. Lipaev, 'Moskovskie pis'ma', *Russkaia muzykal'naia gazeta*, 3 (1906), p. 88.

38 Abraham Ascher, *The Revolution of 1905: Russia in Disarray* (Stanford, CA, 1988), pp. 304–23.

39 Quoted in Sylvester, *Rachmaninoff's Complete Songs*, p. 135; Sergei Bertensson and Jay Leyda, *Sergei Rachmaninoff: A Lifetime in Music* (Bloomington and Indianapolis, IN, 2001), p. 117.

40 Bertensson and Leyda, *Rachmaninoff*, p. 128.

41 Letter 21 August 1906, in *Rakhmaninov: Literaturnoe nasledie*, vol. I, pp. 397–9 (p. 398).

42 Sylvester, *Rachmaninoff's Complete Songs*, p. 135.

43 Letter 2 August 1906, in *Rakhmaninov: Literaturnoe nasledie*, vol. I, pp. 396–7.

44 Apetian, ed., *Rakhmaninov: Literaturenoe nasledie*, vol. I, pp. 521, 546.

45 E. K. Somova, [Untitled], in *Vospominaniia o Rakhmaninove*, vol. II, pp. 231–7 (p. 233).

46 Victor Seroff, 'The Great Rachmaninoff', *Vogue*, 101 (April 1943), pp. 43, 88.

47 Apetian, ed., *Rakhmaninov: Literaturnoe nasledie*, vol. I, p. 555.

48 Ibid., p. 576.

49 Letter 14/[27] September 1908, ibid., pp. 454–61; N. A. Rakhmaninova, 'S. V. Rakhmaninov', in *Vospominaniia o Rakhmaninove*, vol. II, pp. 292–332 (p. 296).

50 Sofiia Satina, 'Zapiska o S. V. Rakhmaninove', in *Vospominaniia o Rakhmaninove*, vol. I, pp. 12–115 (pp. 67–8); Apetian, ed., *Rakhmaninov: Literaturnoe nasledie*, vol. II, pp. 438–9.

51 Apetian, ed., *Rakhmaninov: Literaturnoe nasledie*, vol. I, p. 546; Sylvester, *Rachmaninoff's Complete Songs*, pp. 141–3.

52 Sylvester, *Rachmaninoff's Complete Songs*, p. 142.

53 Bernice Glatzer Rosenthal, *Dmitri Sergeevich Merezhkovsky and the Silver Age* (The Hague, 1975), p. 87.

54 [Anonymous], 'Romansy S. Rakhmaninova', *Russkaia muzykal'naia gazeta*, 42–3 (1914), pp. 762–7 (p. 765).

55 Letter 18 February/3 March 1907, in *Rakhmaninov: Literaturnoe nasledie*, vol. I, pp. 425–6.

56 Sylvester, *Rachmaninoff's Complete Songs*, p. 94.

5 Dresden

1 N. Kardinar, 'Neizvestnaia stranitsa biografii S. V. Rakhmaninova', in *Sovetskaia muzyka*, 2 (1979), pp. 102–6.

2 N. A. Rakhmaninova, 'S. V. Rakhmaninov', in *Vospominaniia o Rakhmaninove*, ed. Z. A. Apetian (Moscow, 1988), vol. II, pp. 292–332 (p. 295).

3 Letter 9 November 1920, in *Rakhmaninov: Literaturnoe nasledie*, ed. Z. A. Apetian (Moscow, 1978–80), vol. II, p. 110.

4 A. V. Ossovskii, 'S. V. Rakhmaninov', in *Vospominaniia o Rakhmaninove*, vol. I, pp. 343–85 (pp. 379–80); A. F. Gedike, 'Pamiatnyi vstrechi', ibid., vol. II, pp. 4–17 (p. 16); V. A. Iuzefovich, *Sergei Kusevitskii: Russkie gody* (Moscow, 2004), pp. 85, 130–31.

5 Ossovskii, 'S. V. Rakhmaninov', pp. 372–3.

6 Philipp Ther, *Center Stage*, trans. Charlotte Hughes-Kreutzmuller (West Lafayette, IN, 2014), p. 243.

7 Ibid., p. 243.

8 Letter [27 October]/9 November 1906, in *Rakhmaninov: Literaturnoe nasledie*, vol. I, pp. 403–5.

9 Letter [8]/21 November 1906, ibid., p. 408.

10 Charlotte Kratz, 'Die Rezeption von Sergej Rachmaninovs Konzerttätigkeit in Deutschland', PhD dissertation, Philipps-Universität Marburg, 2008, p. 10.

11 Letter [27 October]/9 November 1906, in *Rakhmaninov: Literaturnoe nasledie*, vol. I, pp. 404–5.

12 Letter [8]/21 December 1906, ibid., p. 414.

13 'Modernism Is Rachmaninoff's Bane', *Musical America*, XI/2 (1909), p. 23.

14 Ibid.

15 David Cannata, *Rachmaninoff and the Symphony* (Innsbruck, 1999), p. 132.

16 Ther, *Center Stage*, p. 242.

17 Barrie Martyn, *Rachmaninoff: Composer, Pianist, Conductor* (Aldershot, 1990), pp. 199–200.

18 Apetian, ed., *S. Rakhmaninov: Literaturnoe nasledie*, vol. I, p. 628.

19 Martyn, *Rachmaninoff*, p. 199.

20 Letter [29 January]/11 February 1907, in *Rakhmaninov: Literaturnoe nasledie*, vol. I, p. 422.

21 Letter [31 March]/13 April 1907, ibid., pp. 430–31.

22 Rakhmaninova, 'Rakhmaninov', p. 296.

23 Harrison, *Rachmaninoff*, pp. 135–40

24 Martyn, *Rachmaninoff*, pp. 179–87.

25 G. Prokof'ev, 'Pevets intimnoi nastroenii', *Russkaia muzykal'naia gazeta*, 38 (1910), p. 783.

26 'Modernism Is Rachmaninoff's Bane', p. 23.

27 Basanta Koomar Roy, 'Rachmaninoff Is Reminiscent', *Musical Observer*, 26 (1927), pp. 16, 41 (p. 16).

28 Ibid.

29 Vladimir Nabokov, *Despair* (New York, 1989), p. 56.

30 Letter 20 April 1925, in *Rakhmaninov: Literaturnoe nasledie*, vol. II, p. 167.

31 Viktor Val'ter, 'Muzyka', *Rech*, 44 (1911), p. 3.

32 Letter [18 February]/3 March 1909, in *Rakhmaninov: Literaturnoe nasledie*, vol. I, p. 472.

6 The Twilight of Old Russia

1 Barrie Martyn, *Rachmaninoff: Composer, Pianist, Conductor* (Aldershot, 1990), p. 214.

2 Richard Taruskin, *Russian Music at Home and Abroad* (Berkeley, CA, 2016), p. 135.

3 Max Harrison, *Rachmaninoff: Life, Works, Recordings* (London and New York, 2005), p. 270. Rachmaninoff's acquaintance Cyril Smith claimed Rachmaninoff 'could with his left hand stretch C-E-flat-G-C-G and the right could manage C (second finger)-E-G-C-E (thumb under)'.

4 Taruskin, *Russian Music*, pp. 135–6.

5 Quoted ibid., p. 134.

6 Robin Gehl, 'Reassessing a Legacy: Rachmaninoff in America, 1918–43', PhD dissertation, University of Cincinnati, 2008, p. 252.

7 V. N. Briantseva, *S. V. Rakhmaninov* (Moscow, 1976), p. 409.

8   Ibid.

9   Quoted in Sergei Bertensson and Jay Leyda, *Sergei Rachmaninoff: A Lifetime in Music* (Bloomington and Indianapolis, IN, 2001), p. 166.

10 Iu. Engel, 'Muzyka', *Russkie vedomosti*, 1 (1910), pp. 14–15.

11 Rebecca Mitchell, *Nietzsche's Orphans* (New Haven, CT, 2015).

12 Shaginian, 'Vospominaniia', in *Vospominaniia o Rakhmaninove*, ed. Z. A. Apetian (Moscow, 1988), vol. II, pp. 90–158 (p. 90).

13 Mitchell, *Nietzsche's Orphans*, pp. 61–103.

14 'M. Ippolitov-Ivanov o sovremennom tvorchestve', *Russkaia muzykal'naia gazeta*, 6 (1914), pp. 167–8.

15 Statistik, 'Samoubiistva v Moskve za 1910 god', *Russkie vedomosti*, 84 (1911), p. 4.

16 Mark Steinberg, *Petersburg Fin-de-Siecle* (New Haven, CT, 2011), pp. 234–67.

17 Z. A. Apetian, ed., *S. Rakhmaninov: Literaturnoe nasledie* (Moscow, 1978–80), vol. I, p. 631.

18 A. V. Ossovskii, 'S. V. Rakhmaninov', in *Vospominaniia o Rakhmaninove*, vol. I, pp. 343–85 (pp. 370–71). Other board members were A. F. Gedike, Leonid Sabaneev and A. V. Ossovskii.

19 Ossovskii, 'Rakhmaninov', p. 375; V. A. Iuzefovich, *Sergei Kusevitskii: Russkie gody* (Moscow, 2004), pp. 148–54.

20 Apetian, ed., *Rakhmaninov: Literaturnoe nasledie*, vol. II, pp. 384–5.

21 N. B. Mandrovskii, [Untitled], *Vospominaniia o Rakhmaninove*, vol. II, pp. 243–5.

22 Sofiia Satina, 'Zapiska o S. V. Rakhmaninove', in *Vospominaniia o Rakhmaninove*, vol. I, pp. 12–115 (p. 40).

23 Letter 30 July 1912, in *Rakhmaninov: Literaturnoe nasledie*, vol. II, p. 53.

24 Liudmila Kovaleva-Ogorodnova, *Sergei Rakhmaninov: Biografiia* (St Petersburg, 2015), pp. 258–9.

25 Richard D. Sylvester, *Rachmaninoff's Complete Songs: A Companion with Texts and Translations* (Bloomington and Indianapolis, IN, 2014), p. 203.

26 See for instance Robert Cunningham, 'Harmonic Prolongation in Selected Works of Rachmaninoff, 1910–1931', PhD dissertation, Florida State University, 1999; Blair Johnston, 'Harmony and Climax in the Late Works of Sergei Rachmaninoff', PhD dissertation, University of Michigan, 2009.

27   Anthony J. La Magra, 'A Source Book for the Study of Rachmaninoff's
     "Preludes"', PhD dissertation, Columbia University, 1966, p. 135; Glenn
     R. Winters, 'An Analysis of Sergei Rachmaninoff's "Preludes" Opus
     23 and Opus 32, and "Etudes-Tableaux" Opus 33 and Opus 39', DMA
     dissertation, Northwestern University, Illinois, 1986, p. 49.

28   Patricia Brady, 'Rachmaninoff's *Etudes-Tableaux*', PhD dissertation,
     Indiana University, 1986, p. 120. Originally written as a group of nine
     pieces in 1911, the composer was dissatisfied with three of the pieces
     (3, 4 and 5) in op. 33 and withdrew them before their 1914 publication.
     The six pieces submitted to Gutheil, however, retained their original
     numbering (1, 2, 6, 7, 8 and 9). One of the withdrawn pieces was later
     published as op. 39, no. 6, while the remaining two etudes were first
     published by the Soviet publisher Muzgiz in 1948 and posthumously
     reinserted into the op. 33 set in 1950. See ibid., p. 60.

29   Morton Estrin, 'Playing the Preludes, Opus 32', *Clavier* (October 1973),
     p. 20; Winters, 'Rachmaninoff's "Preludes"', pp. 44–96.

30   Winters, 'Rachmaninoff's "Preludes"', p. 91.

31   Letter 31 July 1910, in *Rakhmaninov: Literaturnoe nasledie*, vol. II,
     pp. 18–19.

32   Rachmaninoff, 'Music Should Speak from the Heart', *The Etude*, LIX/12
     (1941), pp. 804, 848.

33   Rachmaninoff, 'How Russian Piano Students Work', *The Etude*, XXXX/5
     (1923), p. 298.

34   Rachmaninoff, 'My Prelude in C-Sharp Minor', *Delineator*, 75 (1910), p. 127.

35   K. Eiges, 'Rikhard Vagner i ego khudozhestvennoe reformatorstvo',
     Russkaia mysl, VI (1913), pp. 56–68 (pp. 64–5).

36   K. Eiges, 'Moi vstrechi s S. V. Rakhmaninovyn', *Novoe o Rakhmaninove*,
     ed. M. P. Rakhmanova and M. V. Esipova (Moscow, 2006), pp. 49–54.

37   Brady, 'Rachmaninoff's *Etudes-Tableaux*', p. 89.

38   Benno Moiseiwitsch, 'Sergei Rachmaninoff', *Gramophone*, XX (1943),
     pp. 169–70.

39   William Richardson, *Zolotoe Runo and Russian Modernism* (Ann Arbor,
     MI, 1986), p. 29.

40   Gr. Pr., 'Kontserty v Moskve', *Russkaia muzykal'naia gazeta* (1914), pp. 27–8.

41   Shaginian, 'Vospominaniia', p. 100; on Rachmaninoff's use of
     Bechstein pianos, see G. M. Kogan, 'Iz stat'i "Rakhmaninov i
     Skriabin"', in *Vospominaniia o Rakhmaninove*, vol. I, pp. 433–9 (p. 433).

42 A. A. Trubnikova, 'Sergei Rakhmaninov', in *Vospominaniia o Rakhmaninove*, vol. I, pp. 116–45 (p. 133); E. Iu. Zhukovskaia, 'Vospominaniia', ibid., pp. 251–342 (pp. 329–30).

43 Trubnikova, 'Rakhmaninov', ibid., pp. 131–2.

44 M. L. Chelishcheva, 'S. V. Rakhmaninov v Mariinskom uchilishche', ibid., pp. 402–6 (pp. 405–6).

45 A. V. Nezhdanova, 'O Rakhmaninove', ibid., vol. II, pp. 27–32 (p. 28).

46 Shaginian, 'Vospominaniia', p. 103.

47 Ibid., p. 104.

48 Ibid., p. 107.

49 Marietta Shaginian, 'S. V. Rakhmaninov', *Trudy i dni*, 4–5 (1912), pp. 97–114 (p. 112).

50 Ibid., p. 104.

51 Ibid., p. 108.

52 A. F. Gedike, 'Pamiatnyi vstrechi', in *Vospominaniia o Rakhmaninove*, vol. II, pp. 4–17 (p. 15).

53 A. V. Ossovskii, 'S. V. Rakhmaninov', ibid., vol. I, pp. 343–85 (p. 372).

54 Shaginian, 'Vospominaniia', p. 116.

55 Ibid., pp. 56–7.

56 Sylvester, *Rachmaninoff's Complete Songs*, p. 18; Martyn, *Rachmaninoff*, p. 236.

57 Sylvester, *Rachmaninoff's Complete Songs*, p. 195.

58 Ellen Bakulina, 'Tonal Pairing in Two of Rachmaninoff's Songs', in *Analytical Approaches to 20th-Century Music*, ed. Inessa Bazayev and Christopher Segall (New York and London, 2020), p. 20.

59 Sylvester, *Rachmaninoff's Complete Songs*, pp. 205–6.

60 M. E. Bukinik, [Untitled], in *Vospominaniia o Rakhmaninove*, vol. I, pp. 213–26 (p. 226).

61 Bertensson and Leyda, *Rachmaninoff*, p. 191.

62 Quoted ibid., pp. 184–5.

63 Mitchell, *Nietzsche's Orphans*, p. 158.

64 David Cannata, *Rachmaninoff and the Symphony* (Innsbruck, 1999), pp. 60–61.

65 N. A. Rakhmaninova, 'S. V. Rakhmaninov', in *Vospominaniia o Rakhmaninove*, vol. II, pp. 292–332 (p. 304).

66 Satina, 'Zapiska', p. 44.

7 'All That Is Solid Melts into Air'

1 Letter 22 July 1914, in *S. Rakhmaninov: Literaturnoe nasledie*, ed. Z. A. Apetian (Moscow, 1978–80), vol. II, pp. 71–2.

2 Peter Gatrell, *Russia's First World War* (New York, 2005), pp. 22–3.

3 Letter 2 September 1914, in *Rakhmaninov: Literaturnoe nasledie*, vol. II, p. 73.

4 Letter 1 October 1914, ibid., p. 74.

5 Letter 8 January 1915, ibid., p. 76.

6 L. Sabaneev, *Vospominaniia o Rossii* (Moscow, 2005), pp. 15–16.

7 Quoted in V. A. Iuzefovich, *Sergei Kusevitskii: Russkie gody* (Moscow, 2004), p. 140.

8 Apetian, ed., *Rakhmaninov: Literaturnoe nasledie*, vol. I, p. 514.

9 Rebecca Mitchell, *Nietzsche's Orphans* (New Haven, CT, 2015), p. 192.

10 I. A. Bunin, V. V. Veresaeva and N. D. Meleshova, eds, *Den' pechati* (Moscow, 1915).

11 Richard D. Sylvester, *Rachmaninoff's Complete Songs: A Companion with Texts and Translations* (Bloomington and Indianapolis, IN, 2014), p. 233.

12 Ellen Bakulina, 'Tonality and Mutability in Sergei Rachmaninoff's *All-Night Vigil*, Movement 12', *Journal of Music Theory*, LIX/1 (2015), pp. 63–97 (p. 66).

13 A. F. Gedike, 'Pamiatnyi vstrechi', in *Vospominaniia o Rakhmaninove*, ed. Z. A. Apetian (Moscow, 1988), vol. II, pp. 4–17 (pp. 11–12).

14 Marina Frolova-Walker, *Russian Music and Nationalism* (New Haven, CT, and London, 2007), pp. 265–97.

15 Letter 19 June 1910, in *Rakhmaninov: Literaturnoe nasledie*, vol. II, p. 14.

16 Ibid.

17 Letter 31 July 1910, ibid., pp. 18–19.

18 Oskar von Riesemann reports that Rachmaninoff was inspired to return to Orthodox liturgical settings after hearing a performance of his *Liturgy* with which he was increasingly dissatisfied. See Oskar von Riesemann, *Rachmaninoff's Recollections* (New York, 1934), p. 176.

19 Sergei Bertensson and Jay Leyda, *Sergei Rachmaninoff: A Lifetime in Music* (Bloomington and Indianapolis, IN, 2001), p. 191; Letter 30 April 1935, in *Rakhmaninov: Literaturnoe nasledie*, vol. III, pp. 49–50.

20 Frolova-Walker, *Russian Music*, pp. 297–9.

21 Bakulina, 'Tonality and Mutability', pp. 63–4.

22 Olga Ellen Bakulina, 'The Problem of Tonal Disunity in Sergei Rakhmaninoff's *All-Night Vigil*, op. 37', PhD dissertation, City University of New York, 2015, pp. 197, 205.

23 Frolova-Walker, *Russian Music*, pp. 298–9.

24 Barrie Martyn, *Rachmaninoff: Composer, Pianist, Conductor* (Aldershot, 1990), p. 257.

25 Riesemann, *Rachmaninoff's Recollections*, p. 177.

26 G. Ch. 'Vsenoshchnoe bdenie S. V. Rakhmaninova', *Moskovskie vedomosti*, 62 (1915), p. 2.

27 L. Sabaneev, 'Vsenoshchnoe bdenie Rakhmaninova', *Golos Moskvy*, 58 (1915), p. 5.

28 Iurii Sakhnovskii, 'Vsenoshchnoe bdenie', *Russkoe slovo*, 57 (1915), p. 7.

29 Bertensson and Leyda, *Rachmaninoff*, p. 191.

30 Martyn, *Rachmaninoff*, p. 84.

31 Sylvester, *Rachmaninoff's Complete Songs*, p. 222.

32 Ibid., pp. 227–8.

33 Sergei Prokofiev, *Autobiography, Articles, Reminiscences* (Moscow, 1960), p. 41.

34 Rebecca Mitchell, 'Scriabin and the Silver Age', in *Interpreting Scriabin*, ed. Kenneth Fokert-Smyth and Vasilis Kallis (Woodbridge, 2021).

35 Letter 22 June 1915, in *Rakhmaninov: Literaturnoe nasledie*, vol. ii, pp. 81–2.

36 Ibid., p. 404.

37 Marietta Shaginian, 'Vospominaniia', in *Vospominaniia o Rakhmaninove*, vol. ii, pp. 90–158 (pp. 140–41).

38 Ibid.

39 Apetian, ed., *Rakhmaninov: Literaturnoe nasledie*, vol. ii, p. 404.

40 Shaginian, 'Vospominaniia', p. 152.

41 Ibid., pp. 148–53.

42 Ibid., p. 154.

43 Sylvester, *Rachmaninoff's Complete Songs*, p. 239

44 Apetian, ed., *Vospominaniia o Rakhmaninove*, vol. ii, p. 494.

45 Letter 1 September 1916, in *Rakhmaninov: Literaturnoe nasledie*, vol. ii, p. 88.

46 Ibid., p. 407.

47 Shaginian, 'Vospominaniia', p. 153.

48 Ibid.

49 Sergei Prokof'ev, *Dnevnik 1907–1918* (Paris, 2002), pp. 623, 664.

50 Ibid., p. 664.

51 Ibid.

52 Letter 4 November 1921, in *Rakhmaninov: Literaturnoe nasledie*, vol. II, pp. 117–18.

53 Brady, 'Rachmaninoff's *Etudes-Tableaux*', p. 81.

54 Letter 2 January 1930, in *Rakhmaninov: Literaturnoe nasledie*, vol. II, pp. 270–71.

55 Ibid.

56 Quoted in Patricia Brady, 'Rachmaninoff's *Etudes-Tableaux*', PhD dissertation, Indiana University, 1986, p. 63.

57 Quoted in Bertensson and Leyda, *Rachmaninoff*, pp. 201–2.

58 Martyn, *Rachmaninoff*, p. 276.

59 Brady, 'Rachmaninoff's *Etudes-Tableaux*', p. 65.

60 Letter 1 June 1917, in *Rakhmaninov: Literaturnoe nasledie*, vol. II, pp. 101–2.

61 Letter 22 June 1917, ibid., pp. 102–3.

62 Sergei Rachmaninoff, 'Recollections of a Vanished World', LCRA, Box 50, file 2.

63 See https://ivanovka-museum.ru; A. I. Ermakov, '"V Ivanovku ia vsegda stremilsia"', in *Rakhmaninov i mirovaia kultura*, ed. I. N. Vanovskaia (Ivanovka, 2014), pp. 266, 268; N. A. Rakhmaninova, 'S. V. Rakhmaninov', in *Vospominaniia o Rakhmaninove*, vol. II, pp. 292–332 (p. 298).

64 Boris Sennikov, *Tambovskoe vosstanie 1918–1921 i raskrest'ianivanie Rossii 1929–1933* (Moscow, 2004).

65 Shaginian, 'Vospominaniia', p. 155.

66 Apetian, ed., *Rakhmaninov: Literaturnoe nasledie*, vol. II, p. 415.

67 Rakhmaninova, 'Rakhmaninov', p. 299.

68 Bertensson and Leyda, *Rachmaninoff*, pp. 203–7.

69 Rachmaninoff, 'Recollections of a Vanished World'.

70 Letter 18 August 1922, in *Rakhmaninov: Literaturnoe nasledie*, vol. III, p. 231.

8 The Virtuoso in Emigration

1   Letter 15 April 1922, in *Rakhmaninov: Literaturnoe nasledie*, ed. Z. A.
    Apetian (Moscow, 1978–80), vol. III, pp. 399–400.
2   Letter 3 April 1925, ibid., p. 405.
3   Marc Raeff, *Russia Abroad* (Oxford and New York, 1990), p. 10.
4   David Lowenthal, 'Past Time, Present Place: Landscape and Memory',
    Geographical Review, LXV/1 (1975), pp. 1–36 (p. 28).
5   'Rachmaninoff Is a Master Pianist', *Boston Daily Globe* (16 December
    1918), p. 6.
6   Svetlana Boym, *The Future of Nostalgia* (New York, 2001), pp. 11, 13.
7   David Cannata, *Rachmaninoff and the Symphony* (Innsbruck, 1999), p. 21.
8   N. A. Rakhmaninova, 'S. V. Rakhmaninov', in *Vospominaniia o
    Rakhmaninove*, ed. Z. A. Apetian (Moscow, 1988), vol. II, pp. 292–332
    (p. 300).
9   *Christian Science Monitor* (14 November 1918), p. 8.
10 Rakhmaninova, 'Rakhmaninov', p. 301.
11 'Rachmaninoff Is Here', *New York Times* (13 November 1918), p. 5.
12 Robin Gehl, 'Reassessing a Legacy: Rachmaninoff in America,
    1918–43', PhD dissertation, University of Cincinnati, 2008, pp. 45,
    52; M. P. Rakhmanova and M. V. Esipova, eds, *Novoe o Rakhmaninove*
    (Moscow, 2006), p. 57; N. A. Rakhmaninova, 'Rakhmaninov', p. 301.
13 D. W. Fostle, *The Steinway Saga* (New York, 1995), pp. 451–3.
14 Voytek Matushevski, 'Rachmaninoff's Last Tour', *Clavier*, 32 (1993),
    pp. 18–25 (p. 20).
15 Gehl, 'Reassessing a Legacy', pp. 48–9; Fostle, *Steinway Saga*, p. 465.
16 Sergei Rachmaninoff, 'National and Radical Impressions in the Music
    of Today and Yesterday', *The Etude*, XXXVII/10 (1919), pp. 615–16.
17 Ibid.
18 Ibid., p. 630.
19 Gehl, 'Reassessing a Legacy'.
20 'Composers and the Pianola – Sergei Rachmaninoff', www.pianola.
    org, accessed 3 August 2021.
21 Sergei Bertensson and Jay Leyda, *Sergei Rachmaninoff: A Lifetime in
    Music* (Bloomington and Indianapolis, IN, 2001), p. 215.
22 Rick Robertson, '88s on 78s: Pianists on Record from 1903 to 1925',
    American Music Teacher, LII/5 (2003), pp. 30–32.

23 Emily Thompson, 'Machines, Music, and the Quest for Fidelity',
   Musical Quarterly, LXXIX/1 (1995), p. 169.

24 Rachmaninoff, 'The Artist and the Gramophone', *Gramophone*, VIII/95
   (1931), pp. 525–6.

25 Jonathan Summers, 'Sergey Rachmaninov', *Great Pianists:
   Rachmaninov* (Naxos Historical Recordings), 2017.

26 Nick Seaver, '"This Is Not a Copy": Mechanical Fidelity and the
   Re-enacting Piano', *differences: A Journal of Feminist Cultural Studies*
   XXII/2–3 (2011), pp. 54–72 (p. 55).

27 Ibid., p. 54.

28 'Rachmaninoff Returns after Nine Years and Draws Record Crowd',
   Chicago Daily Tribune (10 March 1919), p. 15.

29 Olin Downes, 'Rachmaninoff Concert', *New York Times* (1 April 1928),
   p. 32.

30 Rachmaninoff, 'The Artist and the Gramophone', pp. 525–6.

31 Letter 18 July 1939 (Vilshau to Rachmaninoff), LCRA, Box 49, file 6.

32 Letter 23 December 1928 (Gumeniuk to Rachmaninoff), LCRA, Box 44,
   file 29.

33 Rebecca Mitchell, 'In Search of Russia', *Slavonic and East European
   Review*, XCVII/1 (2019), pp. 136–68 (p. 146).

34 Letter 1943 (Sadie Battle to Rachmaninoff), LCRA, Box 42, file 62.

35 Letter 13 May 1938 (E. Somoff to Rachmaninoff), LCRA, Box 47, file 62.

36 Letter [undated] (Ulya Shakir to Rachmaninoff), LCRA, Box 48, file 14.

37 Cannata, *Rachmaninoff and the Symphony*, p. 23.

38 Gehl, 'Reassessing a Legacy', p. 57

39 Letter 2 November 1922, LCRA, Box 42, file 16. This is equivalent to
   almost U.S.$72,000 in 2020.

40 Letter 27 January 1923, in *Rakhmaninov: Literaturnoe nasledie*, vol. II,
   pp. 136–7.

41 Letter 9 September 1922, ibid., pp. 128–9.

42 Rakhmanova and Esipova, eds, *Novoe o Rakhmaninove*, p. 46.

43 Letter 9 September 1922, in *Rakhmaninov: Literaturnoe nasledie*, vol. II,
   pp. 128–9.

44 Cannata, *Rachmaninoff and the Symphony*, pp. 21–2.

45 Bertensson and Leyda, *Rachmaninoff*, pp. 240–41.

46 Letter 27 August 1924, in *Rakhmaninov: Literaturnoe nasledie*, vol. II,
   pp. 157–8.

47 Letter 2 September 1925, ibid., pp. 180–81.

48 Cannata, *Rachmaninoff and the Symphony*, pp. 22–3.

49 Letter 8 December 1934, in *Rakhmaninov: Literaturnoe nasledie*, vol. III, pp. 33–4.

50 Letter 29 October 1921, ibid., vol. II, p. 116.

51 Letter 28 December 1921, ibid., p. 119.

52 Katherine Swan and A. J. Swan, 'Rachmaninoff: Personal Reminiscences, Part One', *Musical Quarterly* XXX/1 (1944), pp. 1–19 (p. 2).

53 Nikolai Metner, *Pis'ma*, ed. Z. A. Apetian (Moscow, 1973), p. 358.

54 Barrie Martyn, *Rachmaninoff: Composer, Pianist, Conductor* (Aldershot, 1990), p. 255.

55 Ibid., p. 260.

56 Olin Downes, 'Music', *New York Times* (23 March 1927), p. 28.

57 'Rachmaninoff Wins Acclaim with New Piece', *Washington Post* (30 March 1927), p. 22.

58 Letter 9 September 1926, in *Rakhmaninov: Literaturnoe nasledie*, vol. II, pp. 197–8.

59 Letter 13 September 1926 (Medtner to Rachmaninoff), in Metner, *Pis'ma*, p. 337.

60 Harrison, *Rachmaninoff*, pp. 254–7.

61 Olin Downes, 'Music', p. 28.

62 Pamela Jordan, *Stalin's Singing Spy: The Life and Exile of Nadezhda Plevitskaya* (Lanham, MD, 2016).

63 Bertensson and Leyda, *Rachmaninoff*, p. 258.

64 Rachmaninov, 'Some Critical Moments in My Career', *Musical Times*, LXXI/1048 (June 1930), pp. 557–8.

65 Bertensson and Leyda, *Rachmaninoff*, p. 270.

66 'Recollections of a Vanished World', LCRA, Box 50, file 1; Box 50, file 2; Box 83, file 9; Box 83, file 10.

67 Apetian, ed., *Rakhmaninov: Literaturnoe nasledie*, vol. II, pp. 561–3; Letter 15 April 1936, in *Rakhmaninov: Literaturnoe nasledie*, vol. III, pp. 76–7.

68 Bertensson and Leyda, *Rachmaninoff*, p. 270.

9 Villa Senar

1 Letter 11 April 1934, in *Rakhmaninov: Literaturnoe nasledie*, ed. Z. A. Apetian (Moscow, 1978–80), vol. III, pp. 16–18,

2 Sergei Rachmaninoff Foundation, ed., *Villa Senar: Sergei Rachmaninoff's Dream of a House* (Hertenstein, 2016), p. 29.

3 Ibid., p. 19.

4 Ibid., p. 11.

5 Elger Niels and Wouter de Voogd, compilers, *Inventory of Books from Sergei Rachmaninoff's Cabinet at SENAR* (Rachmaninoff Network, 2017/ updated 2019); Sergei Bertensson and Jay Leyda, *Sergei Rachmaninoff: A Lifetime in Music* (Bloomington and Indianapolis, IN, 2001), p. 358.

6 Letter 7 June 1937, in *Rakhmaninov: Literaturnoe nasledie*, vol. III, pp. 108–11 (p. 110); I. Ilf and E. Petrov, *Odnoetazhnaia Amerika* (Moscow, 1937), p. 148.

7 Richard James Burgess, *History of Music Production* (Oxford, 2014), pp. 34, 39.

8 Letter 7 June 1937, in *Rakhmaninov: Literaturnoe nasledie*, vol. III, p. 109.

9 Bertensson and Leyda, *Rachmaninoff*, p. 371.

10 El, '"Kolokola" S. V. Rakhmaninova v Moskve', *Rossiia i slavianstvo*, 121 (1931), p. 3.

11 '"Class War" in Music: Bolshevist Boycott of M. Rachmaninoff', *Times* (20 March 1931), p. 13.

12 Pauline Fairclough, '"Don't Sing it on a Feast Day"', *Journal of the American Musicological Society*, LXV/1 (2012), pp. 67–111 (pp. 92–3).

13 Letter 16 July 1931, in *Rakhmaninov: Literaturnoe nasledie*, vol. II, pp. 307–8.

14 Letter 15 April 1936, ibid., vol. III, p. 77.

15 Sergei Rachmaninoff, 'The Artist and the Gramophone', *Gramophone*, VIII/95 (1931), pp. 525–6.

16 Katherine Swan and A. J. Swan, 'Rachmaninoff: Personal Reminiscences: Part One', *Musical Quarterly*, XXX/1 (1944), pp. 1–19 (p. 9).

17 Letter 21 December 1931, in *Rakhmaninov: Literaturnoe nasledie*, vol. III, pp. 321–2.

18 I. S. Iasser, 'Moe obshchenie s Rakhmaninovym', in *Vospominaniia o Rakhmaninove*, ed. Z. A. Apetian (Moscow, 1988), vol. II, pp. 352–72 (p. 358).

19 Ibid., pp. 524–5.

20 A. V. Liakhovich, *Simvolia v pozdnikh proizvedeniiakh Rakhmaninova* (Tambov, 2013), p. 85. See also Philip Ross Bullock, ed., *Rachmaninoff and His World* (Chicago, IL, 2022).

21 Letter 19 August 1934, in *Rakhmaninov: Literaturnoe nasledie*, vol. III, p. 27.

22 David Cannata, *Rachmaninoff and the Symphony* (Innsbruck, 1999), pp. 55–7.

23 Letter 20 January 1935, in *Rakhmaninov: Literaturnoe nasledie*, vol. III, p. 37.

24 Letter 1 November 1914, ibid., vol. II, p. 76; p. 402; Marietta Shaginian, 'Vospominaniia', in *Vospominaniia o Rakhmaninove*, vol. II, pp. 90–158 (pp. 148–50).

25 Apetian, ed., *Rakhmaninov: Literaturnoe nasledie*, vol. III, p. 304.

26 Letter 29 August 1937, ibid., p. 114.

27 Letter 29 August 1937, in *Rakhmaninov: Literaturnoe nasledie*, vol. III, p. 114.

28 Letter 4 July 1939, ibid., p. 156.

29 Quoted in Harrison, *Rachmaninoff*, p. 314.

30 Katherine Swan and A. J. Swan, 'Rachmaninoff: Personal Reminiscences, Part Two', *Musical Quarterly*, XXX/2 (1944), pp. 174–91 (p. 190).

31 Ibid.

32 Ibid.

33 Harrison, *Rachmaninoff*, p. 312; Martyn, *Rachmaninoff*, pp. 342–3.

34 Letter 7 June 1937, in *Rakhmaninov: Literaturnoe nasledie*, vol. III, pp. 109–10.

35 Swan and Swan, 'Rachmaninoff: Reminiscences, Part One', p. 9.

36 Swan and Swan, 'Rachmaninoff: Reminiscences, Part Two', pp. 186–7.

37 Sofiia Satina, 'Zapiska o S. V. Rakhmaninove', in *Vospominaniia o Rakhmaninove*, vol. I, pp. 12–115 (p. 60).

38 Harrison, *Rachmaninoff*, p. 297.

39 Charlotte Kratz, 'Die Rezeption von Sergej Rachmaninovs Konzerttätigkeit in Deutschland', PhD dissertation, Philipps-Universität Marburg, 2008, p. 18.

40 Letter 19 April 1935 (Somoff to Rachmaninoff), LCRA, Box 47, file 61.

41 Letter 3 July 1935 (Somoff to Rachmaninoff), LCRA, Box 47, file 61; Letter 11 July 1936 (Rachmaninoff to Somoff), LCRA, Box 41, file 24.

42 'Sergei Rachmaninoff Application for American Citizenship 1939',
www.rachmaninoff.org, accessed 3 August 2021.

43 Letter 27 March 1938, in *Rakhmaninov: Literaturnoe nasledie*, vol. III, p. 124.

44 Catalogue number 0000107, ©2017 from the Serge Rachmaninoff
Archives at Villa Senar – Courtesy of Serge Rachmaninoff Foundation/
Rachmaninoff Network.

45 Bertensson and Leyda, *Rachmaninoff*, p. 342.

46 Letter 8 September 1937, in *Rakhmaninov: Literaturnoe nasledie*, vol. III,
p. 115.

47 Letter 18 July 1939 (Vilshau to Rachmaninoff), LCRA, Box 49, file 6.

48 Letter 2 May 1939, in *Rakhmaninov: Literaturnoe nasledie*, vol. III, p. 149.

49 Bertensson and Leyda, *Rachmaninoff*, p. 357.

50 Letter 20 May 1939, in *Rakhmaninov: Literaturnoe nasledie*, vol. III,
pp. 151–2.

51 Letter 5 July 1939, ibid., p. 157.

52 Bertensson and Leyda, *Rachmaninoff*, p. 353–4.

10 Exile in America

1 Letter 29 June 1942, in *Rakhmaninov: Literaturnoe nasledie*, ed. Z. A.
Apetian (Moscow, 1978–80), vol. III, p. 208.

2 Leonard Liebling, 'Variations', *Musical Courier*, CXXVI/1 (1942), p. 23.

3 Sergei Bertensson and Jay Leyda, *Sergei Rachmaninoff: A Lifetime in
Music* (Bloomington and Indianapolis, IN, 2001), p. 374.

4 Leonard Liebling, 'Variations', *Musical Courier*, CXXVII/7 (1943), p. 17.

5 Bertensson and Leyda, *Rachmaninoff*, pp. 358–9.

6 Satina, 'Zapiska o S. V. Rakhmaninove', in *Vospominaniia o
Rakhmaninove*, ed. Z. A. Apetian (Moscow, 1988), p. 102.

7 Joseph Reither, 'Chronicle of Exile', *Tempo*, 22 (1951–2), pp. 28–36.

8 Ibid.

9 Max Harrison, *Rachmaninoff: Life, Works, Recordings* (London and New
York, 2005), pp. 332–4.

10 Ibid., p. 334.

11 Barrie Martyn, *Rachmaninoff: Composer, Pianist, Conductor* (Aldershot,
1990), p. 353.

12 Apetian, ed., *Rakhmaninov: Literaturnoe nasledie*, vol. III, p. 336.

13 Letter 29 August 1942, ibid., pp. 218–19.
14 Letter 31 August 1942, ibid., pp. 220–21.
15 E. K. Somova, [Untitled], in *Vospominaniia o Rakhmaninove*, vol. II, pp. 231–7 (p. 236).
16 Harrison, *Rachmaninoff*, p. 346.
17 O. G. Mordovskaia, [Untitled], in *Vospominaniia o Rakhmaninove*, vol. II, pp. 333–9 (p. 334).
18 Ibid., p. 336.
19 A. V. Golitsyn, 'Bolezn' i smert' S. V. Rakhmaninova', ibid., pp. 421–3.
20 Mordovskaia, [Untitled], p. 337.
21 Apetian, ed., *Rakhmaninov: Literaturnoe nasledie*, vol. III, p. 331.
22 'Ruki Rakhmaninova', *Vozrozhdenie*, MMMCCXVI/9 (1934), p. 3.
23 'Speaking of Pictures', *Life* (12 April 1943), pp. 4–5, 7.

Postlude: Rachmaninoff the Modernist

1 V. Bragin, 'Vozvrashchenie v Ivanovku', LCRA, Box 88, file 12; N. Emel'ianova, 'Novyi muzei', *Sovetskaia muzyka*, 10 (1968), pp. 158–9.
2 See https://ivanovka-museum.ru/o-muzee/hystory, accessed 5 October 2021.
3 Pauline Fairclough, *Classics for the Masses* (New Haven, CT, 2016), p. 190.
4 Z. A. Apetian, ed., *S. Rakhmaninov: Literaturnoe nasledie* (Moscow, 1978–80), vol. III, p. 392.
5 A. Gol'denveizer, 'Doklad, posviashchennye pamiati S. V. Rakhmaninova', GTSMMK, fol. 18, no. 2694, ll. 1–2.
6 K. Kuznetsov, 'Tvorcheskaia zhizn' S. V. Rakhmaninova', *Sovetskaia muzyka*, 4 (1945), pp. 25–51 (p. 42).
7 'Cliburn in Salute to Rachmaninoff', *New York Times* (1 June 1958), p. 74.
8 Leonid Maksimenkov, ed., *Muzyka vmesto sumbura* (Moscow, 2013), p. 430.
9 'Medinskii vystupaet za vozvrashchenie prakha Rakhmaninova', https://tass.ru/kultura/2188793, accessed 3 August 2021.
10 Rebecca Mitchell, 'In Search of Russia', *Slavonic and East European Review*, XCVII/1 (2019), pp. 136–68 (p. 162).
11 Maksimenkov, *Muzyka vmesto sumbura*, pp. 620–21.

12 O. M. Lopukhov, 'Portrait of S. Rachmaninoff', www.izmailtv.com/
gallery/portret-s-rakhmaninova, accessed 3 August 2021.

13 Ilya Glazunov, 'Eternal Russia', http://glazunov.ru/en/art/
monumental-works/works/63-eternal-russia, accessed 3 August 2021.

14 N. B. Mandrovskii, [Untitled], in *Vospominaniia o Rakhmaninove*,
vol. II, pp. 243–5 (p. 243).

15 'Great Link Is Acclaimed', *New York Times* (12 July 1936), p. 1.

16 Mandrovskii, [Untitled], p. 244.

17 Marshall Berman, *All That Is Solid Melts into Air* (New York, 1988),
p. 346.

18 Advertisement, *New York Times* (30 September 1934), p. RP10.

Further Reading

Apetian, Z. A., ed., *S. Rakhmaninov: Literaturnoe nasledie*, 3 vols (Moscow, 1978–80)

——,*Vospominaniia o Rakhmaninove*, 2 vols, 5th edn (Moscow, 1988)

Barber, Charles, *Lost in the Stars: The Forgotten Musical Life of Alexander Siloti* (Lanham, MD, 2002)

Berman, Marshall, *All That Is Solid Melts into Air: The Experience of Modernity* (New York, 1988)

Bertensson, Sergei, and Jay Leyda, *Sergei Rachmaninoff: A Lifetime in Music* (Bloomington and Indianapolis, IN, 2001)

Bullock, Philip Ross, ed., *Rachmaninoff and His World* (Chicago, IL, 2022)

Cannata, David, *Rachmaninoff and the Symphony* (Innsbruck, 1999)

Emerson, Caryl, George Pattison and Randall A. Poole, eds, *The Oxford Handbook of Russian Religious Thought* (Oxford, 2020)

Frolova-Walker, Marina, *Russian Music and Nationalism from Glinka to Stalin* (New Haven, CT, 2008)

Harrison, Max, *Rachmaninoff: Life, Works, Recordings* (London and New York, 2005)

Iuzefovich, V. A., *Sergei Kusevitskii: Russkie gody* (Moscow, 2004)

Kovaleva-Ogorodnova, Liudmila, *Sergei Rakhmaninov: Biografiia* (St Petersburg, 2015)

Martyn, Barrie, *Rachmaninoff: Composer, Pianist, Conductor* (Aldershot, 1990)

Mitchell, Rebecca, *Nietzsche's Orphans: Music, Metaphysics and the Twilight of the Russian Empire* (New Haven, CT, 2015)

Prokofiev, Sergei, *Prodigious Youth: Diaries, 1907–1914* (London, 2006)

——, *Behind the Mask: Diaries, 1915–1923* (London, 2008)

Pyman, Avril, *A History of Russian Symbolism* (Cambridge and New York, 1994)

Raeff, Marc, *Russia Abroad: A Cultural History of the Russian Emigration, 1919–1939* (Oxford and New York, 1990)

Rakhmanova, M. P., and M. V. Esipova, eds, *Novoe o Rakhmaninove* (Moscow, 2006)

Rubinstein, Anton, *Autobiography*, trans. Aline Delano (Boston, MA, 1890)

Sargeant, Lynn, *Harmony and Discord: Music and the Transformation of Russian Cultural Life* (Oxford, 2011)

Steinberg, Mark, *Petersburg Fin-de-Siecle* (New Haven, CT, 2011)

Sylvester, Richard D., *Rachmaninoff's Complete Songs: A Companion with Texts and Translations* (Bloomington and Indianapolis, IN, 2014)

Taruskin, Richard, *Russian Music at Home and Abroad* (Berkeley, CA, 2016)

——, *Defining Russia Musically* (Berkeley, CA, 1997)

Taylor, Philip S., *Anton Rubinstein: A Life in Music* (Bloomington and Indianapolis, IN, 2007)

Select Discography

Great Pianists: Rachmaninov, Vols IV–V includes Rachmaninoff's Edison
   recordings (Naxos Historical: 8.111407-8)

Rachmaninoff: Complete Solo Piano Music, Michael Ponti, piano (Musical
   Concepts: 0851950001988, 6 CDs)

Rachmaninoff Plays Symphonic Dances includes Rachmaninoff's impromptu
   1940 performance of sections of the *Symphonic Dances* to Eugene
   Ormandy (Marston Records: 53022-2, 3 CDs)

Rachmaninov: The Complete Works is a comprehensive survey of the
   composer's works, many of them in historic performances (Decca
   Classics: 4786765, 32 CDs)

Sergei Rachmaninoff: The Complete Recordings is a complete reissue of
   Rachmaninoff's RCA/Victor recordings and select Edison recordings
   (RCA Victor Gold Seal: 09026-6126502, 10 CDs)

Acknowledgements

A published book is the final crystallization of countless hours of research, writing and conversation. I have been fortunate enough to benefit from the support and encouragement of many colleagues and friends. First, a particular thank you to Michael Leaman of Reaktion Books, whose suggestion it was that I write this Critical Lives biography. Special thanks are also due to Ettore F. Volontieri, Elger Niels and Wouter de Voogd of the Sergei Rachmaninoff Foundation, who generously offered me a personal tour of Villa Senar and answered multiple queries. It is my hope that this biography will do its small part in supporting their important goal of preserving Rachmaninoff's legacy for future generations of performers, scholars and audiences. The Sergei Rachmaninoff Archive at the Library of Congress in Washington, DC, and the Glinka Museum of Musical Culture in Moscow provided access to key sources, while Middlebury College's tireless librarians obtained a vast number of books and articles via interlibrary loan that made writing this work possible. *The Etude* magazine was made available to me by Dr Pam Dennis of Gardner-Webb University at https://digitalcommons.gardner-webb.edu/etude. Middlebury College provided the financial and logistical support required to make writing this book possible, as well as valuable research time. Numerous friends and colleagues have supported my work in various ways over the past three years, including Philip Bullock, Pauline Fairclough, Lisa Larson, James Taylor and Elina Viljanen. Polina Dimova kept me on task amid the unique challenges of writing a book during the COVID-19 pandemic, while Olga Panteleeva helped me avoid numerous errors. Thanks are also due to my students at Middlebury's ESI College, who graciously read and discussed an earlier draft of this work. My parents, Karen and Archie Mitchell, read and commented on the entire manuscript, improving several chapter titles. My brother Matthew and his family (Suzanne, Jamie) have inspired me with their humanity and perseverance. Most of all, thank you to my partner Andrew Demshuk and son Archie Ray, who have both accompanied me on this journey into Rachmaninoff's life and work, providing much-needed love, support and writing time.

Photo Acknowledgements

The author and publishers wish to express their thanks to the below sources of illustrative material and/or permission to reproduce it.

Alamy: pp. 28 (Album), 65, 72 (Heritage Image Partnership), 20, 21, 24, 57 (Lebrecht Music and Arts), 42, 78, 196 (Sputnik); author's collection: pp. 105, 122, 151; Lincoln Ballard: p. 110; Bridgeman Images: pp. 137 (Richard Bebb Collection), 188 (Photo © Don Hunstein), 25, 34, 39, 68, 70, 111, 113, 181, 189, 190 (Lebrecht Music and Arts), 171 (Tully Potter), 40 (Sputnik); *The Etude*: p. 153 (December 1920), courtesy of Dr Pam Dennis of Gardner-Webb University at https://digitalcommons.gardner-webb.edu/etude; Getty Images: pp. 95, 175 (Bettmann), 161 (Fine Art Images/Heritage Images); Library of Congress, Washington, DC: pp. 8, 11 (Bain News Service, part of George Grantham Bain Collection), 149 (Genthe Photograph Collection); The Metropolitan Museum of Art, New York: p. 102 (Reisinger Fund, 1926); The Rachmaninoff Foundation/Sergei Rachmaninoff International Database, © 2014: p. 170; RGALI (Rossiiskii gosudarstvennyi arkhiv literatury i iskusstva): p. 120 (f. 2845, op. 1, ed.khr. 492); Shutterstock: p. 193 (Eric Schaal/The LIFE Picture Collection); *Vsemirnaia Illiustratsiia*: p. 48 (originally published St Petersburg, 12 September 1892, no. 1234, p. 209), reproduced with the permission of Bayerische Staatsbibliothek München (München, Bayerische Staatsbibliothek, Signatur 2 Per. 11 r-1892, 48); Wikimedia Commons (Public Domain): pp. 46, 92, 143.